AF386884

SHAKESPEARE'S MARGARET

ALSO BY CHARLES O'MALLEY

Toward a Just Pedagogy of Performance: Historiography, Narrative, and Equity in Dramatic Practice

ALSO BY SCOTT W. STERN

There Is a Deep Brooding in Arkansas: The Rape Trials That Sustained Jim Crow, and the People Who Fought It, from Thurgood Marshall to Maya Angelou

The Trials of Nina McCall: Sex, Surveillance, and the Decades-Long Government Plan to Imprison "Promiscuous" Women

SHAKESPEARE'S MARGARET

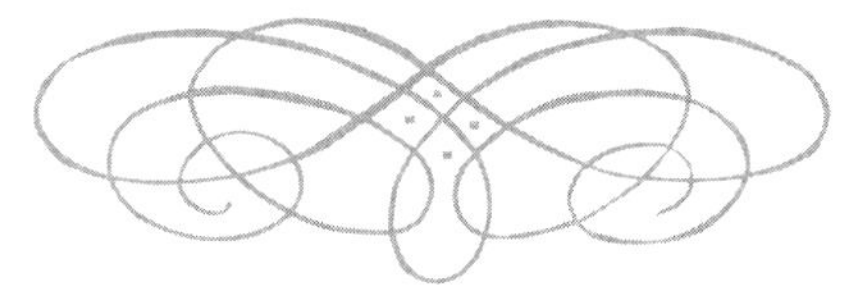

The Dramatic Life of a Warrior Queen

CHARLES O'MALLEY
AND SCOTT W. STERN

W. W. NORTON & COMPANY

Independent Publishers Since 1923

For information about permission to reproduce selections from this book,
write to Permissions, W. W. Norton & Company, Inc., 500 Fifth Avenue,
New York, NY 10110

For information about special discounts for bulk purchases, please contact
W. W. Norton Special Sales at specialsales@wwnorton.com or 800-233-4830

Manufacturing by Lakeside Book Company
Book design by Brooke Koven
Production manager: Julia Druskin

ISBN 978-1-324-07655-1

W. W. Norton & Company, Inc., 500 Fifth Avenue, New York, NY 10110
www.wwnorton.com

W. W. Norton & Company Ltd., 15 Carlisle Street, London W1D 3BS

Authorized EU representative: EAS, Mustamäe tee 50, 10621 Tallinn, Estonia

10 9 8 7 6 5 4 3 2 1

For Brendan and Nolan

CONTENTS

SHAKESPEARE'S MARGARET

Barbara Jefford as Queen Margaret in a 1957 production of the *Henry VI* plays at London's Old Vic.

Introduction

Slowly, miserably, the Queen of England entered a room in the Palace of Westminster, clutching a severed human head. It was late in the spring of 1450. Thousands of rebellious peasants were massing just south of London, preparing to invade the city and declare one of their own as king, but within the palace the queen was despondent. Her lover—the Duke of Suffolk, a military man, one of the closest advisers to her husband, King Henry VI—had just been murdered at sea by pirates. The queen could not stop weeping. "Here may his head lie on my throbbing breast," she lamented, holding the head to her, the king standing, appalled and annoyed, by her side. "But where's the body that I should embrace?" Even after another duke asked the royal couple how they planned to respond to the rebel leaders' demands, even after the king himself upbraided her, she could not look up from her lover's rotting visage—a "lovely face," she reflected, which "ruled like a wandering planet over me."[1]

What a line. What a scene. The bereft queen, the putrefying head, the scorned and cuckolded king of England—this tableau is so arresting that it begs a number of questions. Foremost among them, did this really happen?

In a very limited sense, yes. Queen Margaret, King Henry, the Duke of Suffolk—these were real people; Suffolk really did lose his life to marauders at sea; rebels really did gather at the city gates, not long after Suffolk's beheading.

In another sense, no, certainly not. There is no evidence Suffolk and Margaret were ever lovers, nor did his head make its way to London following his death.

Yet in still another sense—a literal sense—of course this scene happened, even if it did not happen until the late 1580s or early 1590s, more than a century after Margaret's death. By then, another queen—Elizabeth I—was on the throne of England, the righteous rebellion of the peasants had long faded into myth, and a young poet and playwright named William Shakespeare was attempting to make a name for himself by recasting his country's bloody history for fervent popular consumption. In one of his first plays—known now, though certainly not then, as *Henry VI, Part 2*—the twenty-something Will sent a teenage boy in a wig out onto a Shoreditch stage to depict the mourning Queen Margaret. Gripping tight to a prop head, the boy-queen wept for the eager audience. His emotion—her sadness—was abject. "My hope is gone," Margaret declared.[2]

Yet, as the audience already knew, whether from this play or from awed oral traditions, the queen was not one to wallow for long. The very next time Margaret spoke, the audience heard her spitting invective, proclaiming to her court, to all the world, and to the rapt London theatregoers that she would brook no retreat, that the crown—and her right to wear it—must be defended at all costs. Queen Margaret was vehement, violent, vital. She was nothing if not resilient. She would stay with many in the audience for years to come. And she would remain on England's stages—and those around the world—for centuries.

What follows is an unusual book. It is, for lack of a better word, a biography—but not the biography of a person. It is, instead, the biography of a *character*, one of the most complicated and compelling characters ever written, yet one that has, oddly, been consigned mostly to the dustbins of theatrical and popular history. The story of Queen Margaret, the person, has been told many times in the many centuries since her death—in French gossip, in Tudor disinformation, in academic treatises, in heavily romanticized volumes by ardent admirers. This is, rather, the story of Margaret, the character dreamed up by William Shakespeare, a playwright usually remembered for the many men he put onstage. Though many contemporary readers and playgoers have never heard of her, Margaret is the only character in Shakespeare's work whose entire life is depicted onstage. First seen as a girl and last as an old woman, Margaret speaks a full quarter more lines than any other female character in the Shakespearean canon (at 846 lines, she speaks more than Mark Antony or Lear and only a little less than the loquacious Othello, Richard III, and Hamlet).[3] In fact, Margaret appears as a central character in more plays than any other character in Shakespeare's body of work—four of them, *Henry VI, Parts 1, 2,* and *3,* and *Richard III.*[4] And she is one of the first women that Shakespeare ever wrote.[5]

In history, Margaret of Anjou (1430–1482) was queen of England during the Wars of the Roses. In his dramas, Shakespeare stitched together scraps of Margaret's biography to create one of the most complete arcs of character and stories of a soul in Western drama. Margaret is a child, a prisoner, a foreign princess betrothed to an enemy king when she first appears in the closing scenes of *Henry VI, Part 1.* In *Part 2,* Margaret sits on the English throne; she has a child, she has an affair, she celebrates her love then weeps over her beloved's detached head, and she wields power in a way that makes her loathed by both the Lancastrians (her followers) and the Yorkists (her foes). In *Part 3,* Margaret disclaims her husband, flees the victorious Yorks to exile in France, returns to England to lead the Lancastrian army to victory and to defeat, and, finally, watches her son die and, with him, her hopes for the final success of the Lancastrian cause. In *Richard III,* Margaret returns from exile, curses Richard and all Yorks, and reminds her audiences of the terrible price paid through decades of civil strife.

Margaret is the only character to appear in all four of these plays, which collectively form Shakespeare's "first tetralogy." (The "second tetralogy," written later in Shakespeare's career and consisting of *Richard II, Henry IV, Part 1, Henry IV, Part 2,* and *Henry V,* tells the stories of earlier English kings.) If the plays of the first tetralogy are read together as one unit—and there have been *generations* of fiery debate as to whether this is appropriate—Margaret is their connecting thread. She persists across all four installments, unlike those who share her stage: Joan of Arc is burned; the Duke of York is murdered; Henry VI succumbs in prison; and Richard III dies, horseless, at Bosworth Field. Both in history and in drama, Margaret is one of the only major players in the Wars of the Roses who survived them. While the second tetralogy (which centers on two kings named Henry) has for the past fifty years been known as the Henriad, the first tetralogy has no name. Due to Margaret's centrality, however, the scholar Phyllis Rackin has suggested it be called the Margaretsaga.[6]

Margaret is most remarkable, however, not for the ubiquity of her presence but for the ferocity of her character. In these plays, she commands armies, acts as regent without her husband's explicit permission, seeks revenge, strikes a rival, stabs a foe, and revels in the murders of the children of her enemies. Through Shakespeare's plays, she became one of the archetypal female villains of the age.[7] Margaret was, in other words, one of the first evil queens. It is a trope that has persisted across generations of popular culture, from the Queen of Hearts to Cersei Lannister.

At the same time, though, Shakespeare's Margaret is capable of genuinely touching moments of vulnerability, passion, and tenderness. To modern readers or viewers, it may seem unremarkable that a character in a play can embody both cruelty and compassion, but this dualism, this contradiction, was a genuine innovation in Elizabethan theatre. Just a decade or two before Shakespeare was writing, dramatic performance had been mostly the province of itinerant amateurs mouthing religious parables or didactic morality tales, and "characters" were often anthropomorphized concepts like "Pleasure" and "Folly" and "Vice." The creation of Margaret was at the forefront of a new era of experimentation, featuring newly complex roles. And while most of the memorable experiments in theatrical antiheroism were male characters—like Shakespeare's Richard III or Christopher Marlowe's Tamburlaine—Margaret is one of the first, if not the very first, female character to receive such a comprehensive, empathetic, and multidimensional imagining in English drama.

To create Margaret, Shakespeare—and a crew of collaborators, including Marlowe—departed from the historical figure, Margaret of Anjou, French princess and English queen, and instead drew from the society around him. Theirs was a world of constant surveillance, competing radicalisms, breathtaking inequalities, and even a kind of proto-feminist cult of personality that surrounded a few privileged women, most notably Queen Elizabeth. Members of this society witnessed witch trials and peasant uprisings, endured outbreaks of plague, saw independent young women ("masterless," in the parlance of the times) newly navigating life on their own, watched cross-dressing boys charm observers on and off the stage, and suffered the anxieties of a country at war even as the epic reign of its heirless Virgin Queen came to a close. This was the seething, bloody context for Margaret's emergence, and her words and her actions reflect this context as much as they do the actual, historical Margaret.

The great bulk of Shakespeare scholarship considers his later plays—plays like *Hamlet, Othello, Macbeth, Lear*—in part because we know so painfully little about his early years as a playwright.[8] In fact, at least three of the four plays to feature Margaret were written during the period that Shakespearean scholars call the Bard's "Lost Years"—lost, because essentially no records tell us what he was doing or even where he was. Yet it was precisely these early plays, written during the turbulent late 1580s and early 1590s—this great blank in the historical timeline—in which Shakespeare experimented with messy, angry female characters in ways he would not later in his career. Though many of his best-known female roles came later in his life—characters like Rosalind in *As You Like It*, Lady Macbeth in *Macbeth*, Cleopatra in *Antony and Cleopatra*, Ophelia and Gertrude in *Hamlet*, the daughters in *King Lear*—it was in this first decade that he investigated female rage, desire, displeasure, and capacity for revenge.[9]

In these early works, Shakespeare created female protagonists (and antagonists) who continuously subverted expectations of ladylike conduct—content not merely to manipulate the men around them but determined instead to engage in bodily violence themselves. They were undoubtedly shocking to sixteenth-century audiences—and they continue to astound even today. These are women like Tamora, Queen of the Goths in *Titus Andronicus*, Katherina in *The Taming of the Shrew*, the titular goddess in the narrative poem *Venus and Adonis*, and several women in the first tetralogy, Margaret foremost among them. These women—the "she-wolves," to borrow a term from the scholar David Mann—are among the most revealing artifacts of their era, this age of sexualized panic, repression, and experimentation, of Shakespeare's beginning and Elizabeth's end.[10]

Even before Shakespeare's death, the she-wolves began disappearing from his work, and in the following decades they likewise started to vanish from the English stage, as a fresh crop of dramatists and critics dismissed the Bard as old-fashioned and unrefined. A new generation of playwrights strove to update these old, provincial texts, so they chopped them up, condensed them, combined them, added music, and cut mercilessly. At the start of this age of adaptation, Margaret transformed—not only in her words and deeds but also in her representation, because, for the first time ever, female actors could portray her onstage. More than ever, she shocked audiences with her audacity.

Yet as the age of adaptation continued, Margaret's principal plays—the three parts of *Henry VI*—mostly faded from the Shakespearean repertoire, the victims of changing tastes. Her fourth, *Richard III*, remained a favorite of audiences and actors alike, but its most popular adaptation cut Margaret altogether to save space. Throughout the eighteenth and nineteenth centuries, therefore, the public largely encountered her not onstage but on the page, and a number of critics dismissed her as impressive yet ultimately unsympathetic. Others simply didn't know what to make of her. At age fifteen, roughly the same age Margaret had been when she left France to marry an enemy king, Jane Austen wrote in a piece of juvenilia that the historical queen was "a woman whose distresses & Misfortunes were so great as almost to make me who hate her, pity her."[11]

As Shakespearean performance spread, traveling the globe with the agents of empire and morphing from a pastime into something akin to civic religion, new generations of dramatists began "discovering" Margaret, restoring her text and reviving her centrality. First in nineteenth-century Germany, then in England, then around the world, the *Henry VI* plays began returning to the stage—and with them, so did Margaret. Multiple theatrical impresarios started staging the plays of the first tetralogy together and in chronological order, sometimes in nonstop "marathons," allowing audiences to encounter Margaret's entire life. As Shakespearean repertories developed in the twentieth century, she became a vehicle through which ambitious actors could explore their own range.

Since the sexual revolution, Margaret has experienced a genuine renaissance, with a handful of recent productions foregrounding her and depicting her as a liberated power player. Several even gave her whole new speeches, opening monologues, or the last word. Indeed, over the last half century, Margaret has become a favorite of actors as her role provides challenges unparalleled in the canon. Still, despite this esteem, she does not appear on twenty-first-century stages with much frequency. Actors and scholars love Margaret, but many audiences have never heard of her—or even of her plays. As the scholars John D. Cox and Eric Rasmussen have pointed out, "There is still, it appears, much to be said on behalf of Margaret."[12]

This book seeks to do just that, to recount the life, death, and afterlives of this remarkable character, from the historical figure who inspired her, to the origins of her dramatic life in the pubs and playhouses of Shoreditch, to her own lost years, to her breathtaking reemergence. The creation and transformation of Margaret over the centuries personifies changing attitudes toward, and stereotypes of, women in power. In life, Margaret bent but could never break patriarchal constraints, her ambitions circumscribed by ancient traditions, legal proscriptions, and sexist propaganda. In death, Margaret first became a fearsome termagant, a shrew who was defeated but never tamed, a she-wolf. More recently, the character of Margaret has faced the Nazis, decried American meddling in the Middle East, and been used to render commentary on figures ranging from Margaret Thatcher to Hillary Clinton. Some of the greatest actors in the world have played her, including Peggy Ashcroft, Helen Mirren, Jean Smart, and Sophie Okonedo.

And yet, readers should be wary of trying to locate in Margaret modern notions of heroism or justice, girlboss-ery or badass-ery. No queen can be a feminist. The maintenance of monarchy requires constant violence. The urge to lionize the most privileged women, while erasing the subjugation and exploitation of most other women, is an impulse that predated Shakespeare and one that continues to dominate art and media in our own time. Like her creator, Margaret is a case study in contradiction. Her centuries have allowed generations of talented actors to explore that dissonance, to lean into complexity, even to engage in a bit of transgression themselves.

· 1 ·

Daughter of Warfare, Princess of Peace

Her History

The first thing that Margaret of Anjou saw when she entered London was theatre. The year was 1445, and Margaret, a French teenager with little grasp of English, had just wed the King of England. Approaching this unfamiliar city from the south, the new queen's retinue made its way through Southwark toward London Bridge. There in Southwark—about a hundred yards from where a boy-actor in a wig would play her on the stage of the Rose Theatre a century and a half later—the queen's procession stopped to watch a performance. Two players, dressed as "Peace" and "Plenty," performed for the new bride. Following a display of pageantry that likely involved musicians, dancers, and other allegorical figures, the two addressed the French teenager directly, speaking in part on behalf of their characters, and in part for the entirety of war-weary England:

> Most Christian Princess, by influence of Grace,
> Daughter of Jerusalem, our pleasure
> And joy, welcome as ever princess was,
> With heart entire and whole affiance,
> Cause of wealth, joy, and abundance,
> Your city, your people, your subjects all,

With heart, with word, with deed at your entrance,
"Welcome, welcome, welcome" unto you call![1]

Margaret had just turned fifteen. Her uncle, King Charles VII of France, had only recently arranged her marriage to the young English king, Henry VI. Their two countries had been ensnared in a seemingly unending series of conflicts now called the Hundred Years' War, and marriage promised peace between these war-torn states. On her arrival in her new home, the teenager surely felt the weight of both countries' expectations on her shoulders. English folk of all classes gathered on London's streets and bridges, straining to catch a glimpse of this new queen as she made her way toward Westminster Abbey for her coronation.[2]

And England made its expectations known to Margaret through theatre. Stepping forward toward the queen, the personage of Peace spoke to her:

> So trusteth your people, with affiance
> Through your grace and your benignity,
> Twixt the realms two, England and France,
> Peace shall approach, rest and unite,
> Mars set aside, with all his cruelty,
> Which too long hath troubled the realms twain,
> Biding your comfort in this adversity,
> Most Christian princess, our lady sovereign.[3]

Even then, the people of England were working out ideas of nationhood, honor, hope, and identity through performance. As the young queen progressed into the capital city for the first time, watching a series of eight dramatic pageants staged just for her, she surely felt her importance in the story of England that was unfolding all around her. Yet she could never have guessed what lay in store for her contentious, volatile, and altogether unusual reign.

Margaret of Anjou and King Henry VI as depicted in the Talbot Shrewsbury Book (1444/5). This is the only known image of Margaret made during her lifetime.

Nestled among the lush, tree-studded hills of northeastern France, Château Keure once stood high and proud, overlooking the picturesque Moselle River. Today it is little more than stone ruins. But it was, for many years, a fine, fortified home, and it was in this château, in the small town of Pont-à-Mousson—almost two hundred miles from Paris, almost five hundred miles and more than a century from William Shakespeare's birth in Stratford-upon-Avon—that Margaret of Anjou was born on March 23, 1430.[4]

Margaret came into a world riven by warfare, drenched in bloodshed, torn asunder by jealousies petty and grand, as the Hundred

Years' War entered its hundred-and-third year. She was born in the Duchy of Lorraine, a small territory to the east of Paris, the control of which her mother was to inherit. At this time, Europe was fragmented, lacking in stable or coherent borders; it looked nothing like the neat nation-states we know today. France was ruled by a series of kings named Charles, but smaller constitutive fiefdoms like Lorraine, Anjou, and Provence (to name a few that played key roles in Margaret's early life) were ruled by their own kings or dukes, who in turn worked with the central regnant of France.[5] The Hundred Years' War, which was fought largely by France, England, and the now-forgotten Duchy of Burgundy, saw whole generations struggle and suffer and die, and, when it finally concluded in the mid-fifteenth century, had redrawn boundaries across Western Europe and solidified the very idea of the unified nation-state. It was this conflict—or, more accurately, this crushingly repetitive series of conflicts—that would form the context for Margaret's eventful life, her epic rise, her devastating fall, and her momentous afterlife.[6]

The Hundred Years' War began in the spring of 1337, when King Edward III of England decided that he was, by right of the royal blood of his grandfather, also the King of France. The French king understandably disagreed, and war raged in England and France for the next century. The constant warfare became a key part of English mythology; in the middle of his career, Shakespeare would memorialize the conflict in his Henriad, a tetralogy of plays depicting the events that led to the Wars of the Roses, the series of dynastic English wars of which Margaret herself was at the center.

Young Henry VI assumed the English throne as an infant in 1421, nine years before the birth of his future bride. His father, grandfather, and great-grandfather had all prosecuted the war begun by his great-great-grandfather, Edward III, but the untimely death of his father, the successful and popular Henry V, the remarkably favorable terms of a recent treaty, and then the surprise death of King Charles VI of France meant that even before he reached his first birthday, the infant Henry VI ruled both England and France.[7] As the boy-king grew slowly toward manhood, control of the two countries fell to a series of regents and governors who jockeyed with each other for pre-eminence and power. French dissatisfaction with England simmered, then boiled. A peasant girl from the French village of Domrémy named Jeanne claimed that angels and saints had visited her and commanded her to aid the French claimant, Charles VII, in battle against the occupying English so he could recapture France. Shakespeare later wrote about this girl: He called her Joan Pucelle; history called her Joan of Arc. It was as this female warrior was leading a legion of troops to liberate a besieged French town that another future warrior, Margaret of Anjou, came into the world.[8]

A few hundred miles from the battlefields, in a château on a hill in Lorraine, Margaret began to walk, to talk, to understand the violent society around her. It was an age when vassals controlled their lands from perches in fortified castles, and at Château Keure the young Margaret would have been surrounded by traveling knights and visiting lords, sleeping in the castle's main halls. The previous century had been hard on France—the Black Death swept through Europe in the 1340s and arrived in France in 1348—and war, economic depression, and illness all contributed to a massive population loss. By the time of Margaret's birth in 1430, however, the country was recovering. Though war and plague attacked every social class, Margaret's family, being nobility, was largely insulated from the worst effects of France's woes.

Her father was René of Anjou, who was, through his father, the first cousin once removed of the dearly departed French king, Charles VI, and second cousin of Charles VII, claimant to the French throne. In a quintessential example of the confusing jumble of royal bloodlines, Charles VII was also René's brother-in-law, as he had married René's older sister, Marie of Anjou. Margaret's mother, Isabella, was duchess in her own right of the territory of Lorraine. During their marriage, control of many other lands would fall into their laps. No doubt their daughter spent much of her childhood struggling to remember all their titles and chart the complicated web of royal relations.[9]

Margaret would not have had a difficult time finding powerful women in her family tree. Indeed, not only was she directly descended from recent kings of France, she could also trace her family back to Eleanor of Aquitaine: queen of France by her first marriage, queen of England by her second, and later a figure in Shakespeare's *King John*, about her son. Margaret was also related to Empress Matilda, the daughter of a king of England and wife of a Holy Roman Emperor. On the continent, queens like Eleanor and Matilda often ruled territories in the absence of their husbands. English queens rarely did.[10] In the fifteenth century, Britain knew little precedent for women leading countries or armies, and what Britons did know, they didn't like: In the early fourteenth century, the English *volk* had detested their queen, Isabella of France, whose Frenchness, femaleness, and supposed depravity intertwined in national myth to earn her the sobriquet "she-wolf of France," which Shakespeare would later apply to Margaret.[11]

Not only did Margaret descend from women who commanded armies, she had watched them do it. Margaret's earliest years were spent in Lorraine under the care of her mother, Isabella. René enjoyed a close association with his brother-in-law, the claimant Charles (the future Charles VII), and he soon found himself a prisoner of the Duchy of Burgundy, then at odds with the Kingdom of France. Thus, from the time she was one year old, Margaret lived without her imprisoned father. Isabella took power over René's family and his lands in his absence. Unfettered, she mustered a group of soldiers and fought (and failed) to free him.[12]

Throughout Margaret's childhood, her parents continued to accumulate lands—even though René remained behind bars. The captive René and the free Isabella soon held in their grasp claims to territories across Europe, and though they were rich in titles, they were low on funds. While still in captivity, René made Isabella his regent, and in mid-1435 she left Lorraine for Naples (the title that René had recently inherited, along with Jerusalem, Sicily, and Hungary), stopping first in Provence to see her husband's new territory there. Eventually, she arrived in Naples; she would stay to rule the city for the next three years, her small daughter still in France. When, not long after Isabella's departure, tensions between the French crown (to which René and Isabella were loyal) and the Burgundians eased, René was freed and he rejoined his wife.[13]

After her mother's departure for Naples, the five-year-old Margaret left Lorraine and was sent to live with her paternal grandmother, Yolande of Aragon, at her residence at the Château de Saumur on the banks of the Loire River in Anjou, a territory in what is now western France. René had grown up at the nearby Château d'Angers and the names Saumur and Yolande would have been familiar to the young Margaret, though it cannot be known if she had laid eyes on either the region or the relative prior to her 1435 move. Fifteenth-century Saumur, its turreted skyline, its drawbridge wide enough for horse-drawn carriages to enter the castle, its nobles draped in deep-blue silks, and its peasantry bent over working the surrounding fields were immortalized in the illuminated manuscript the *Très Riches Heures du Duc de Berry*, a vibrantly colored book that has shaped modern understanding of medieval French life. Despite centuries of use as a barracks, a prison, and a museum, the château looks nearly untouched today: Its square central building, its four crowning towers, its austere majesty overlooking surrounding vineyards on the banks of the Loire appear almost exactly like their depiction in the *Heures*. If the young Margaret arrived by boat, the edifice would have dominated the southern bank of the grand river.[14]

Upon her arrival in Anjou, Margaret no doubt discovered Yolande's legendary fierceness. The older woman had been widowed for nearly two decades when her granddaughter came to live with her, but she had lost none of her will to lead. As the regent of Anjou, Yolande had dispatched troops to fight the English invaders, those carrying the banner of Henry VI. She had worked steadfastly for the right of the claimant Charles (who happened to be married to her daughter Marie of Anjou) to rule her country as King Charles VII. Yet she also grew annoyed at this would-be king, dithering and doing little in semi-exile in Bourges. Hearing that Joan of Arc, a peasant girl with no military experience, just a mission from the angels, was leading the French army in the place of a king, Yolande decided she'd had enough of her son-in-law's inaction. Legend tells that Yolande, inspired by this young woman from the north, dressed herself in a suit of armor and confronted Charles in his palace, offering to lead France's troops in battle if he hadn't the courage to do it himself. Inspired—or perhaps intimidated—by the elderly woman in armor, Charles instructed Joan to lead her army to relieve the besieged Orléans. She succeeded, a hated siege finally ended, and for the final time in the Hundred Years' War, France had the edge.[15]

Just a few years later, as war waged on, this formidable dowager turned to a new mission: ensuring that her granddaughter acquired the trappings of an educated young noblewoman. Since Margaret was not firstborn but a later child of a later child, and as such, not a likely candidate to be a future queen, it is remarkable that Yolande gave the girl a complete education in manners, literature, finance, and history. Female children were not often sent to school in the medieval era, but it was not uncommon by the late Middle Ages for girls to receive some education at home, especially those who came from privilege. It is likely that, in addition to her training in manners, Margaret received reading lessons from Yolande (or her staff). Like her future husband, Margaret performed piety throughout her life; her prayer roll—a scroll that contained religious imagery and texts that she read in quiet contemplation—survives today.[16]

Throughout her unsettled childhood, Margaret met many leaders of Europe and their emissaries. In 1440, King Charles VII (who would later prove essential to Margaret's grasp on her own throne in England) visited his mother-in-law, Yolande, at Saumur, and in 1442 envoys of the future Holy Roman Emperor Frederick III came to stay. Knowing that her granddaughter was approaching marriageable age, Yolande sent for furs and fine fabrics from the merchants of Angers to dress Margaret, who was not yet a teenager, in outfits of silk, wool, and satin, white and trimmed with gold. Yolande had successfully married off her daughters and would have wanted the same for her granddaughter. Later chronicles claim (in terms slightly disconcerting when applied to a prepubescent girl) that the princess Margaret overflowed with charm, a paragon of intelligence, precocity, and canniness. She had fair skin and gold-strawberry hair

An artist's rendering of Queen Margaret for the 1846 book
Heroines of Shakespeare.

that she wore long, as was the fashion for young women and girls at the time. Though no reliable portraits of Margaret made during her life exist today, secondhand reports from diverse countries attest to her poise and good manners. It is possible, though unprovable, that Yolande had hoped to arrange a match between the emperor Frederick and Margaret. Just months later, in December of 1442, Yolande died at Saumur at the age of fifty-eight. Anjou lost its regent and Margaret lost the only parent figure she could remember. She was twelve years old.[17]

René and Isabella were in Provence when news of Yolande's death reached them. They returned to Anjou immediately; it might be nice to imagine that they ran to the side of their child, bereft of her guardian, but more pressing was the need to provide a ruler for Anjou. Yolande had served ably as regent in their absence, but they needed to show themselves in the Angevin court and assert their power. When they arrived at Saumur, Margaret's comportment reminded her parents—and those of their court—of stories of Yolande's beauty in her youth. On her death, Yolande left jewelry, tapestries, and precious mementos to Margaret, the queen Marie, and René. Adorned with these jewels, Margaret's grace and refinement were reportedly enough to make her suitors forget that she offered almost no dowry.[18]

As Margaret grew, René and Isabella no doubt wondered how they would come up with the funds to match their titles—and their ambitions for their daughter's future. During this time, René considered matches for Margaret from a stable of young noblemen. By February of 1444, preliminary discussions for a marriage between Margaret and the nephew of Philip of Burgundy were underway. Still upset with the Burgundian rulers for his treatment while their prisoner, René inserted into the agreement various hazardous clauses, and Charles VII was asked to intervene. Bureaucracy and bad blood stalled the negotiations, and the match was eventually abandoned, though not without good reason: Charles VII had learned of another offer for the hand of Princess Margaret of Anjou.[19]

Agnes Strickland, a Victorian biographer of English nobles, wrote in her twelve-volume *Lives of the Queens of England* (published between 1840 and 1848) that King Henry VI had heard of the beauty of a French princess named "Marguerite" and sent a messenger to see if these claims had a basis in truth. According to Strickland, the messenger brought back effusive reports of her charm, to Henry's delight. "Henry VI was then in his four-and-twentieth year," Strickland wrote, "good-looking, with a cultivated, refined mind, and excellent morals." René and Charles VII were delighted at the interest in the fourteen-year-old Margaret and began to make arrangements to solidify the match. "Neither money nor lands were required" for Margaret's dowry, wrote Strickland, with Margaret's charms enough "to outweigh all the riches in the world."[20]

Strickland's Romantic predilection to believe that funds played no part in the match is not entirely incorrect. It turned out that money and lands were not actually required for the coupling, or, at least, not on the scale traditionally associated with a transnational royal marriage; Margaret brought only 20,000 francs, a pitiful sum, and unfounded claims to the Mediterranean islands then called Majorca and Minorca for her dowry. More important than the money, though, the royal marriage portended the possibility of peace between the two countries—an invaluable offering after a century of bloodshed.[21]

William de la Pole, the Duke of Suffolk and trusted ally of the king, arrived in France in the spring of 1444 to arrange the marriage on behalf of King Henry, who would not set foot in France during the entire marriage process. Born in the tiny town of Cotton almost five decades earlier, Suffolk knew France well, having spent seventeen years in the country on various missions in the Hundred Years' War. He had become famous commanding the English troops at the brutal siege of Orléans, for which Margaret's people likely held a grudge. Nonetheless, this martial, middle-aged courtier believed in the power of diplomacy, and he hoped that a royal marriage could finally, finally end the fighting. In exchange for Margaret's hand, a two-year truce, and Margaret's near-imaginary dowry, Suffolk offered the French the disputed territory of Maine. In May, Margaret traveled with Isabella to Tours, to meet Suffolk and the English delegation. Suffolk interviewed her and, taken with her appearance, intelligence, and liveliness, finalized the contract between the two kingdoms, which was signed on May 22, 1444. Thus began one of the earliest and most important political alliances of Margaret's life: that between her and the Duke of Suffolk (and later with his wife, Alice de la Pole, Duchess of Suffolk). Though it is unlikely that the relationship became a sexual one, as Shakespeare would later speculate, the connection between Suffolk and Margaret would come to define the teenage girl, her marriage, and the fate of the House of Lancaster, of which she was now a part.[22]

Two days after the ink dried on the contract, Margaret and Henry were formally betrothed at an elaborate ceremony in Tours, with Suffolk standing in for the king, placing a gold ring on the bride's finger. Suffolk then sailed for London, where Henry made him a marquis for his successful efforts, and Margaret returned to her home in Anjou. There, Margaret waited with her family, possibly using the fallow months to learn English, a language she did not know, celebrating her final Christmas with her family before she left for the country of her erstwhile enemy. Margaret obviously had no say in her marriage, her location, or her actions. Whether she was excited to become a queen or disgusted to share the bed of a stranger, we will never know. What we do know, however, is that in early 1445, the fourteen-year-old Margaret of Anjou packed her belongings (or, more likely, servants packed for her) and left her family and her country with no guarantee that she would see either again.[23]

Her departure from the kingdom of her birth was a showpiece of medieval theatricality. First came Margaret's proxy marriage to Henry VI, with Suffolk (three times Margaret's age) again standing in for the absent king. French nobles from around the country poured into Nancy, the capital of Lorraine, to take part in the celebration; the French queen and king (and his mistress, Agnès Sorel), as well as Margaret's parents, were present. After the ceremony, Margaret prepared to leave Lorraine for good; chroniclers would later claim that she cried when parting from her parents and uncle, the king. All of France, it seemed, gathered to watch her depart: She was met by ceremony in public processions across France, in Nancy, Rouen, Paris, and St. Denis—a farewell tour of sorts.[24]

Margaret left France from the ancient port at Harfleur in April and had a difficult channel crossing. She had become ill around the time she set sail, possibly before, but her illness could not be allowed to affect the festivities too much. Her party landed in Hampshire, and she soon made the acquaintance of many figures who would become very important in her queenship. She met Henry's uncle and childhood regent, the Duke of Gloucester. Alice de la Pole, Suffolk's wife (and the granddaughter of Geoffrey Chaucer), who was to become one of her most trusted ladies, also welcomed her to England.[25] It was at this time too that she encountered Richard, Duke of York, who would prove to be a primary antagonist in her life. According to Shakespeare, Margaret would later be personally responsible for his death on a molehill at the Battle of Wakefield.[26]

Margaret of Anjou and Henry VI met shortly before their English wedding ceremony, which was held on April 22 or 23, 1445, at Titchfield Abbey, a small stone monastery on a hill overlooking the channel and, in the distance, the Isle of Wight.[27] The groom was twenty-three, the bride fifteen. Henry gave Margaret a ring featuring a ruby that had previously been the centerpiece of his coronation band, when he had been (symbolically) crowned King of France fourteen years previous. By all accounts, he was a handsome groom and she was a beautiful bride. Across England, observers eagerly anticipated Margaret's arrival, her wedding, and her entrance into London for her coronation. England had not had a queen since Catherine of Valois— Henry VI's mother—had been widowed over two decades before. Margaret wore white for her events, invoking the Virgin and motherhood. No doubt thousands of Englishmen and Englishwomen had the same idea on their minds: An heir was imminent. This promised a clear line of succession should anything happen to the king, greatly diminishing the possibility of a war of succession. Unfortunately for the English people, war would soon be upon them nonetheless.[28]

The citizens of London decorated their city extensively for Margaret's arrival. Given that so much of the population was illiterate, civic displays marking notable events were important, providing both entertainment and publicity. Londoners hung their streets with garlands and evergreen boughs and wore daisies—Margaret's emblem flower, for her French name, Marguerite, was a type of daisy—in their hats. The mayor of London issued mandates for repair to city buildings on Margaret's route, including the city gates, and the city council sought to stabilize the frames of houses on her path should people stand on their thatched roofs to catch a glimpse of the new queen. Perched atop a chariot, bedecked in jewels, Margaret arrived at London Bridge, where she was greeted by Peace and Plenty. She crossed the bridge and toured the city. At the conclusion of the procession, her litter reached Westminster Abbey, and Margaret of Anjou was crowned Queen of England.[29]

It was at this point, in a series of plays later named for her husband, that William Shakespeare would begin Margaret's story.

· 2 ·

"Of Witte and Wilinesse
She Lacked Nothyng"

Her Creation

The sound of annunciatory trumpets and hautboys rang out one afternoon. A crowd murmured excitedly within the playhouse. Those standing on the ground (who had paid one penny) and those seated on benches ringing the stage (they'd paid two) turned their attention to the stage. The blast of music was the first indication that the performance was starting.[1]

Seconds later, over a dozen actors flooded the stage and arranged themselves on the wooden planks to both demonstrate their characters' positions and to best situate themselves to make their faces seen and their voices heard by the hundreds—if not thousands—of eager spectators. There was little scenery and no lighting design (just the ambient sunlight) to indicate the scene's location. Costume, speech, and behavior were all the audience had to identify and locate the characters onstage. Only when the characters announced themselves or called each other by their names could the audience know who precisely appeared in the scene.

One actor dressed in the clothes of a nobleman moved to the center of the stage and addressed another, this one wearing a crown. He likely kneeled before the crowned man, and in his first words he called him "your high imperial majesty"—this was surely the King of England. This man then mentioned a "Princess Margaret," and at

23

this point he probably gestured to the woman—played by a boy in a dress—standing next to the king. The audience would soon learn that the character speaking was William de la Pole, the Duke of Suffolk, and he was one of the king's most trusted senior ministers. Suffolk had just brought this young woman back from France to marry his king, Henry VI—though perhaps the actors' body language signaled that the Duke and the Queen were to share an intimate attachment. Outside the playhouse it was the late 1580s or early 1590s, but onstage it was the spring of 1445, just a decade before the Wars of the Roses began. Though they might not have known each of the characters' loyalties, the members of the late sixteenth-century audience likely knew all about these wars that had led to the current reigning dynasty, the Tudors.

Slowly, the audience began to recognize other figures onstage. These characters had names from their country's recent past, some of whom they thought to be heroes, some villains. The king's uncle (the Duke of Gloucester) and his wife (Eleanor Cobham) stood beside the young king. Cardinal Beaufort, one of the most powerful figures in the church—he was also the young king's great-uncle—stood by as well. Richard, the Duke of York, who would one day lead his family and his army against King Henry, watched the proceedings, as did the Earl of Warwick, whom history would remember as Warwick the Kingmaker.

The drama began, as many of Shakespeare's plays would, in medias res, meaning the scene commenced in the middle of a conversation— and a story—already in progress. As exposition flowed from the mouths of the actors setting the scene and reminding those watching of the achievements of the Lancastrian dynasty and the overlong Hundred Years' War, the audience would have listened closely to pick up every detail included in this script, each aside a clever turn of phrase, each reference a keen insight, each joke a political jab.[2] The king kissed his new bride, calling her "beauteous." He said her appearance was a "world of earthly blessings to my soul." He wept with joy. The queen responded (with more composure):

> Great King of England, and my gracious lord,
> The mutual conference that my mind hath had—
> By day, by night; waking and in my dreams,
> In courtly company, or at my beads—
> With you, mine alder liefest sovereign,
> Makes me the bolder to salute my king
> With ruder terms, such as my wit affords
> And overjoy of heart doth minister.

A cheer went up among the assembled lords and ladies: "Long live Queen Margaret," they cried out, "England's happiness!"[3]

The audience assembled for this afternoon's debut, in the waning years of Elizabeth I's reign, might have chuckled at the irony in this salute to the country's former queen. The final battles of the Wars of the Roses had ended over a century prior, but long-lasting damage done by those wars had wholly reshaped their country. Margaret would live long, she would live longer than any of the other characters in this scene, but she would never be the happiness of the country.

The show this audience was there to watch, *Henry VI, Part 2*, is the first of the plays telling the story of the decades-long Wars of the Roses that has traditionally been credited to Shakespeare. (The "Part 2" was appended to the title years after Shakespeare's death; the play now labeled "Part 1" debuted later, as a prequel, and future editors wanted to make clear the chronological order of events.) The play chronicles the callow young king's struggles with powerful individuals in his court (his uncle Gloucester, aunt Eleanor, Cardinal Beaufort, the Duke of York) as well as those rising up from the populace to question his rule (the rebel leader Jack Cade). In this play (and throughout the *Henry VI* trilogy), the writers depicted the king as a weak man unable to make the difficult decisions required of a monarch—much less one ruling during a time of such instability.[4]

The opening scene provided the first indication that Shakespeare and his comrades would not adhere too closely to the historical record available to Elizabethan readers. The factual oversights are clear:

Eleanor Cobham, Duchess of Gloucester, was long gone by 1445 and never would have known Margaret; the royal couple did not meet in court but at their marriage ceremony at Titchfield on England's southern coast; young Margaret likely would not have had nearly enough fluency in English to speak in florid verse to her husband.

The opening scene also offered the first hint of this play's principal narrative innovation: It would place Margaret, a woman and England's queen, at the center of the action. It was a fitting intervention for a crowd ruled by yet another royal woman. As audiences would see, women—Margaret foremost among them—would remain at the heart of events in all the plays bearing the name of King Henry VI, even if such works were not built upon Margaret's biography and did not revolve around her. Sometimes these plays would lose sight of her (and other female characters) for a few scenes or an entire act, but they would always return to her, even (and especially) unhistorically.

Just weeks before this play debuted, a young man strode through the seedy, vibrant London suburb of Shoreditch. His name was William Shakespeare. This provincial youth had only recently arrived in the big city—or, more accurately, at its lively outskirts. And it was likely there, working alongside friends, that he began to create the character of Margaret.

To the young Shakespeare, this place must have seemed like the center of the world. Born in 1564, he had come of age in Stratford-upon-Avon, a leafy, provincial market town about a hundred miles from the country's capital. His father, John Shakespeare, was a farmer's son on the make; he had risen from ale-taster to high bailiff (essentially town mayor) in just six years. Will's mother, Mary, had come from a family of means, with ancestors who had fought in the Wars of the Roses. Young Will had thus grown up with access to literacy, to education, and even to theatre, which his father, as bailiff, had overseen. Yet sometime around Will's fifteenth birthday, for reasons still somewhat obscure, his father's reputation and finances began to crumble. Will apparently left school. He grew up fast; over the next five years, he would marry a local woman named Anne Hathaway, who would bear him three children. His life in the years immediately following this swift family formation is so mysterious that the period is known as his Lost Years. Almost all that scholars can say for sure is that at some point between 1585 and 1592, the young man, now in his twenties, likely left his wife and small children and found his way to London—and more specifically to Shoreditch—intent on joining the theatre.[5]

It's easy enough to imagine him walking through the neighborhood, on his way to a job as a lowly actor or lowlier stagehand, contemplating a play he wanted to write. Probably hungry—in a metaphorical as well as a literal sense—he must have stepped quickly, purposefully, but still he would have been struck by his surroundings, so un-Stratford-like in their chaos and variety. Shoreditch was a dense collection of tenements, cottages, shops, churches, and taverns, all arranged haphazardly in a misshapen nest of ancient streets and alleys. Passage through any of these was made difficult by the sheer profusion of people and speeding carts, of merchants hawking wares and porters shouldering loads, of beggars and pimps and prisoners crying out for bread from behind bars.[6] Shakespeare's walk would have taken him past brothels, past bull- and bear-baiting rings, past verdant park lands and the holiday homes set aside for wealthy urbanites.[7] Finally he would have reached his destination: the public theatres, their edifices rising gloriously above the other buildings nearby.[8] These were almost certainly the first freestanding playhouses the young man had ever seen.[9]

The oldest, and perhaps the most storied, was the Theatre (its name still a fairly novel term for playhouse).[10] Constructed of timber and festooned with ironwork on the grounds of a former Benedictine nunnery, the Theatre lay between the Shoreditch High Street to the east and open fields to the west.[11] Just close enough to London proper to make for an easy walk, and just far enough to be beyond the jurisdiction of the municipal authorities, the Theatre would be recognizable to modern playgoers as a "theatre"—with an elevated stage surrounded by raised seating, as well as a yard exposed to the elements for the "groundlings." Above the stage was an elaborately decorated canopy ("the heavens") and below was a trapdoor for storage and special effects ("hell").[12] The Theatre must have been quite a sight; contemporaries described it as "sumptuous" and "gorgeous."[13] It had been built, and was still owned, by James Burbage—a man with a helpful background in both acting and carpentry, though one who was famously cheap and combative. It is likely that Shakespeare had known some Burbage relations back in Stratford; it is also likely that the young man found lodging in one of the nearby tenements Burbage also owned.[14] No doubt Shakespeare encountered Burbage's son, Richard, who was a burgeoning actor just a few years Will's junior. One day, the short, sturdy actor would be among the first actors to portray Richard III.[15]

Next door—about a hundred yards to the south—was the Curtain. A round wooden structure with three galleries, the Curtain had come into the world shortly after the Theatre, and the two playhouses were closely associated—both by their owners and by their enemies. Indeed, at the time a young Shakespeare would have been walking by, the proprietors of the Curtain were pooling profits with their counterparts at the Theatre. If his stroll took him past this playhouse while a performance was happening, he would have spotted a flag fluttering above.[16] Hopefully he could not see the rats living in the thatches in the roof.[17]

If Shakespeare continued south, through the city and across the Thames, he would eventually have made his way to the third and newest public playhouse of the time, the Rose. Named either for a rose garden or (more likely) the brothel it had replaced (several others were still nearby), the Rose was a polygonal building made of wood and plaster on a brick foundation, possibly painted in such a way as to trick casual passersby into thinking it was made of marble. It was probably at this theatre that Shakespeare encountered yet another man who would play a major role in his life: Philip Henslowe, the playhouse's shrewd, self-made proprietor (and a notorious moneylender, pawnbroker, landlord, and pimp).[18]

It may well have been on some such journey through Shoreditch, quite possibly at the Theatre itself, that Shakespeare—then working as a hired hand or actor—came across a group of young men who would change his life.[19] They were a collection of playwrights called the "University Wits," and their names are still familiar even today to students of English theatre: Christopher Marlowe, Robert Greene, Thomas Kyd, John Lyly, Thomas Nashe, and George Peele, among others. Unlike Shakespeare, most of the Wits had won access to higher education (that is, to Oxford or Cambridge), yet the differences between the boy from Stratford and this glittering group of artists

A copy of a 1596 sketch of London's Swan Theatre made by Johannes de Witt, a Dutch tourist. This is one of the few surviving contemporary images of an Elizabethan stage.

can be overstated; almost all of their fathers had been craftsmen, with John Shakespeare at least as prosperous as the rest.[20]

The most brilliant and most memorable of the University Wits was Christopher Marlowe—indeed, it has become almost trite to note that, had Shakespeare never made it to Shoreditch, it would have been Marlowe to go down in history as the greatest Elizabethan playwright. At first glance, he and Shakespeare were of remarkably similar stock—the son of a shoemaker, Marlowe had been born in Canterbury just two months before Will—but their backgrounds had diverged when young "Kit" won a scholarship to Cambridge. There, he would meet two of the other Wits, Greene and Nashe. He would also develop his iconoclastic streak, begin writing poetry and plays, and, according to reports, dabble in atheism, espionage, and homosexuality. Upon arriving in London, Marlowe quickly developed a reputation as a partier and a brawler; he also achieved almost instantaneous success with his extravagant, tragic plays. He was thus already an established literary force when he was first introduced to the young man from Stratford. Yet each saw something in the other—some have speculated of a shared secret Catholicism or even the spark of attraction, but no doubt they also shared a love of poetry and an interest in history. Soon, the two would start borrowing from the work of the other and, most relevant to our purposes, working together on bold historical plays, full of characters like and unlike Margaret.[21]

Just a decade or two before, all of this would have been impossible. Bold historical plays did not exist. The primary forms of theatre were mystery and miracle plays (ritual retellings of biblical stories and the lives of saints) and morality plays (allegorical tales in which characters like Good Deeds, Pleasure, Folly, and Vice instructed audiences through parable and threat of damnation). Rarely were these terribly complex, at least according to modern literary standards.[22] University men like Marlowe or the other Wits would have had to content themselves with writing for "boy companies"—collections of boy-actors no older than teenagers, the main theatre troupes of the day.[23] Outside the boy companies, theatre had barely subsisted as a standalone activity; rather, it was often conflated with, and overshadowed by, clowning, dancing, tumbling, mime, and other forms of performance.[24] And while there were adult theatre companies in these years, the companies were not large—probably not even a dozen players, including the boys who played women and smaller roles—and they faced considerable resistance (even violence) from religious reformers opposed to the frivolity of theatre.[25]

Inarguably, the history of English-language theatre reached a turning point—one integral to the creation of Margaret—in the spring of 1583, when Queen Elizabeth, a theatre lover, and perhaps hoping that a royal performing troupe could help to unify a violently divided nation, agreed to become a patron for a new company, composed of the best players plucked from preexisting companies. Clad in iconic red livery, the Queen's Men focused its repertory on nationalistic history plays composed in verse, although its most popular offering was still clowning. It was larger, more professionalized, and more professionally secure than the other companies, and it quickly became the dominant (indeed, the monopolistic) theatrical force across much of the kingdom.[26] Shakespeare *may* have joined as a young actor, but if he did, it was just as the company's fortunes began to decline.[27]

The first upstart company intent on displacing the Queen's Men was the Lord Admiral's Men, which started appearing prominently in the records in the mid-1580s, led by a young actor, Edward Alleyn.[28] As brash and bluff as he was tall and handsome (a striking contrast to his shorter rival, Richard Burbage), Alleyn quickly developed a close working relationship with Christopher Marlowe, who joined the Lord Admiral's Men shortly after arriving in London and who would start to write grand, tragic parts for the actor. Their first offering was *Tamburlaine*, the tale of a legendary nomadic conqueror written in gorgeous, hyperbolic, daringly blank verse. Immediately upon its debut in 1587, *Tamburlaine* became a sensation among London audiences, elevating Alleyn and establishing the twenty-three-year-old Marlowe as the biggest literary celebrity in England. Soon, other young university men—soon-to-be Wits—were trying their own hands at epic historical plays, suffused with violence and written mostly without rhyme. It is possible, perhaps even likely, that young Will had arrived in London by this point and was similarly inspired. Certainly, his first plays—and their most memorable characters—reflect Marlowe's (and *Tamburlaine*'s) influence.[29]

Audience tastes were changing—the didactic morality tales were on their way out, secular offerings were in, and the chronicle histories (like those of Marlowe) started to dominate. Plays with large casts became popular. Boy companies began disappearing.[30] Not too long after *Tamburlaine* thrilled playgoers, Alleyn would decamp for an even newer, more audacious company: the Lord Strange's Men, which bore the colorful title of its colorful patron, Ferdinando Stanley. The Lord Strange's Men was the first of the companies to be based primarily in London, and it appears to have quickly catapulted itself to prominence and popularity. A number of scholars, equally fervent in their partisanship, argue that *this* was the young Shakespeare's company; after all, as many as six of the nine known Strange's players appeared in Shakespeare's first plays, including those with Margaret.[31]

At the time a young Will would have been taking his walk about town, London was emerging as the focal point and "home base" for playing companies. For decades, touring had been central to actors' identities.[32] Traveling in wagons to guard their costumes, instruments, and scripts from the elements, they journeyed hurriedly over all manner of roads, to towns that were liable to consider them blasphemers.[33] Yet the late 1580s was a period of transition. Theatregoing had become hugely popular in the metropolis— at least one in ten Londoners routinely took in plays—and it was among the cheapest forms of public entertainment or pleasure; only bearbaiting cost as little as watching a play from the yard.[34] The overwhelmingly illiterate populace thus sought out this exciting, new kind of performance, adding it to a diet of diversions that also included public executions.[35] Yet while the grislier forms of entertainment might instill in their viewers a sense of obedience, of consequences, theatre served a distinctly pedagogical role—it might, for instance, teach the audience about the main players in the Wars of the Roses.[36]

While in London, the companies performed six afternoons per week, with only Sundays and Lent providing a respite from the grind. Audiences demanded different plays every day and new plays every couple of weeks; particularly popular shows might return once a week, and spin-offs and sequels were increasingly in fashion. The clamor was such that the acting companies might even turn to an untested youth for a new script.[37]

Walking through Shoreditch, past packed playhouses, William Shakespeare took note.

Somewhere in Shoreditch, sometime in the late 1580s or the very early 1590s, Shakespeare and a group of other young men gathered to write a play that today is called *Henry VI, Part 2*. Picture, for a moment, these young men assuming their seats at some out-of-the-way tavern; it was, after all, common enough for playwrights or players to congregate at such venues, and gossip would later describe the young man from Stratford as a bit of a lush.[38] It would have been understandable for Shakespeare, apparently the least experienced among them, to feel nervous. He may also have felt excitement. This was to be one of his very first plays—quite possibly *the* first. From his and the others' spirited group discussion would, eventually, emerge a young queen named Margaret.[39]

Clustering around a rough-hewn table, the men considered the task in front of them. History plays, like Christopher Marlowe's, were in vogue. Shakespeare or a collaborator may have proposed a plot focused on King Henry VI, or a playing company may have pitched it to the men.[40] In any event, the men would have first settled on a story, hashing out the particularities of plot and character in order to fit the players at their disposal (and their perception of audience tastes). Then, they would have divvied up the work by act or by scene (quite possibly unequally). A "chief collaborator"—probably Shakespeare, in this case—might create an outline for the rest, and his fellow collaborators would quickly fill it in.[41]

The position of chief collaborator was an onerous one. An early draft of the play *Sir Thomas More* from the mid-1590s is, today, a wobbly collection of deteriorating vellum pages—and the only surviving document that shows Elizabethan playwrights writing together. (It may also contain the only remaining fragment of Shakespeare's own handwriting.) Most notably, this record reveals the existence of a playhouse scribe who strove to unite the disparate efforts of multiple playwrights, adding stage directions and regularizing the text as he saw fit. Such a figure was needed because the various contributors were often ignorant of what their fellows were doing; Shakespeare himself appears to have been unaware that another playwright had given one of his characters a brother.[42] This snippet, as well as a few surviving signatures, suggests that Shakespeare would have written his drafts—including his first pages of the future *Henry VI, Part 2*—in a competent "secretary hand," as opposed to the increasingly fashionable, beautifully slanting letters imported from Italy (that is, *italics*).[43]

After settling on his respective parts of the new play, Shakespeare would have then returned home to begin writing on his own. One of the young man's first steps was to crack open a trunk or chest, in which he kept a small collection of precious bound books.[44] Scholars have painstakingly tracked the texts he drew on in crafting his play, so it can be stated with certainty that he consulted a meaty historical chronicle by the sixteenth-century lawyer Edward Hall.[45] At the heart of Hall's chronicle was the glorious victory of the Tudors, national saviors who alone could reunite the warring nation.[46] Shakespeare also inarguably turned to a hefty tome by Raphael Holinshed, a Cambridge-educated antiquarian who plagiarized extensively from Hall and published his first monumental chronicle in 1577, with a splendidly illustrated (and politically scandalous) second edition following in 1587, just in time for the young playwright to devour.[47] Shakespeare consulted a handful of other chronicles as well, borrowing ideas and even phrases directly from them—though he did not hesitate to depart from the chronicles if it suited the characters he was creating.[48]

The chronicles were sources of astonishing richness, containing not just narrations of wars, plagues, and the lives of kings but also the weather, local color, and many strange, possibly apocryphal events.[49] They were not models of historical inquiry in a modern sense. Rather, the chroniclers understood themselves as part of a tradition of retelling; their obligation was to go no further than the "acceptable tradition."[50] Additionally, the chronicles themselves—along with all literary works concerning England's history—were heavily censored, scrupulously reflecting the official Tudor line.[51] This informed Shakespeare's writing, in ways large and small.

Leafing through these chronicles, the young man's eyes must have lingered on the startling depictions of King Henry's indomitable wife, Queen Margaret. She sought "to plucke the sworde of auethoritie" out of the hands of men, Hall wrote.[52] Indeed, she was much like "a man, full and flowying: of witte and wilinesse she lacked nothyng." Holinshed agreed: She was "a ladie of great wit, and no lesse courage."[53] She dominated her husband, she rallied armies, she refused to surrender. And though both men condemned her—she was "a manly woman," determined "to rule and not to be ruled," spat Hall—both had to acknowledge her savvy and strength.[54]

Such descriptions no doubt stuck with the young man. All around him were women who sought to rule. The first woman in Shakespeare's life, his mother, Mary, has attracted the speculation of centuries of biographers and scholars. At the time she was raising young Will, mothers could be both kind and cruel, alternately indulgent or violent, as circumstances demanded; it was they who might bare their offspring's skin for fathers to slap, but then comfort the crying child.[55] One biographer has speculated that Will received "emotional support" at home and was the "focus of Mary's very urgently watchful, intense love." Mary had "nourished" in him an "understanding of feeling."[56] Other biographers have speculated, based on nothing more than the character of Volumnia—the caustic mother in *Coriolanus*—that she was a terrifying, domineering figure.[57] One chronicler has suggested that the impressive number of daughters, and impressive voices of mothers, in Shakespeare's plays indicates that mother-daughter relationships had an "emotional hold" over him.[58] In truth, the plays themselves are too variable, too diverse in their characters, too inconsistent in their sexism and their celebration of female power, to reveal much of Mary Shakespeare.

As little Will grew older, he no doubt heard stories of Queen Mary Tudor, the woman who had sat atop the English throne until just before his birth. Mary was a famously inflexible monarch, a Catholic zealot; during her reign, the screams of martyrs assailed Stratford from all sides, as Protestant men, women, and even infants were burned alive.[59] Swiftly, she lost popularity, especially after her betrothal to a Spanish prince (a foreigner and a papist, her enemies hissed; he couldn't even speak English), and insurrection even reached London. The rebels were rebuffed, their leaders beheaded or hanged, but Mary grew weaker. Soon, she was dead.[60] Some have noted, though, her spirit resurrected in Shakespeare's depiction of Margaret, another aspiring queen regnant, in her cruelest moments.[61]

Yet one powerful woman stands above all the others, and, consciously or not, Shakespeare poured much of her into his new play. By the time he began writing, Queen Elizabeth I had ruled his homeland for three decades. Throughout her long reign, Elizabeth had to continuously contend with fears of, or simple hostility toward, a *woman* in power; the expatriate Cardinal of England even derogatorily accused Elizabeth of turning her country into a "cuntry." Such sentiments represented a threat to the stability of the Tudor dynasty, so the queen and her functionaries strove valiantly to stress a sense of *continuity* with the past.[62] The funding and licensing of works with powerful queens at their center could certainly be seen as part and parcel of this propagandistic project.[63]

Further, Elizabeth's rule itself had changed popular perceptions of female rulers. For years, Elizabeth had been leading the country in successful military forays against her former suitors. In fact, right around the time that Shakespeare sat down to write, she succeeded in quashing perhaps the gravest threat to her reign: her hated Catholic cousin, Mary Queen of Scots. Throughout the 1580s, the Queen's councilors had been obsessed with rumors that Mary was conspiring to assassinate Elizabeth. The pope—who had excommunicated Elizabeth more than a decade earlier—belatedly let it be known that he approved of such a plot. After Catholic agents fatally shot the Protestant Dutch prince, Parliament passed a law designed to ensure Mary's execution upon the slightest evidence of her participation in any such plot against her queenly cousin. In the summer of 1586, while out for a ride in the countryside, Mary was finally arrested. A court of noblemen hastily convicted her, and on February 8, 1587, she was sloppily beheaded while kneeling on a cushion. Elizabeth did her best to depict grief for the outside world, and perhaps it was genuine. No doubt young Will took note, for the parallel between Queen Elizabeth's role in the death of the pretender Mary and Queen Margaret's role in the deaths of her enemies is an analogue so obvious that it's slightly surprising it made it past the censors.[64]

At the same time, concerns continued to mount about the aging queen's husbandlessness and lack of an heir. Elizabeth's "irrevocable childlessness," writes the scholar Helen Hackett, meant that the queen's "body, and its fertility or otherwise, was a political and rhetorical battlefield."[65] This battle played out on the nation's stages; one could even see Marlowe's play *Edward II*—about a weak and decidedly gay king—as articulating the unease of a patriarchal nation ruled by a geriatric queen. Conversely, however, such a work might have validated Elizabeth's rule, by showing that a monarch's prowess does not depend on sex, that a "female king" is no doubt preferable to "an effeminate man."[66]

And, at this time, concerns about Elizabeth's childlessness had birthed a "cult of virginity" that sprang up across England, even drawing reluctant Catholics into the fold with explicit comparisons of the queen to the Virgin Mary. Just as Shakespeare was writing, then, Elizabeth was transforming into a symbol of nationhood itself, an uber-queen, supreme and autonomous and pure, unsullied by outside influence.[67] Such a symbol can likewise be seen reflected in numerous plays from this time. John Lyly—one of the University Wits and the country's most popular writer in the years just before Marlowe and Shakespeare emerged on the scene—had achieved prominence by writing a number of plays that almost invariably centered elite female characters, especially queens—even, repeatedly, virgin queens. Some scholars have, understandably, seen in this a sycophantic attempt to curry favor with Elizabeth, yet others have noted the radicalness of his depiction: powerful, defiant, even (almost) sexually liberated women. The sheer predominance of female characters within his oeuvre was unusual for the time, and it hints that Shakespeare was likely emulating Lyly—more established and a decade older, if a bit over-the-hill—as he began to craft Margaret.[68] Shakespeare may also have been imitating a younger Wit, Thomas Kyd, a tragedian (and Marlowe's onetime roommate) whose plays feature several "female revengers"—characters far less flattering of women with power.[69]

With his research complete (or complete enough), Shakespeare started writing. Yet, despite the perception of most theatre audiences today, he was not the only one doing so. In fact, especially early in his career, Shakespeare worked regularly with collaborators. At this time, anywhere from half to 80 percent of English plays were the product of collaboration.[70] It was not unusual for five writers to collaborate on one play.[71]

It is hard to dispute that several other playwrights contributed to *Henry VI, Part 2* in various ways—from lending their words to revising Shakespeare's, to say nothing of the words Will borrowed without others' direct involvement.[72] Imitation and even what today would be called plagiarism were unremarkable practices in an age without a conception of intellectual property.[73] Further, it was common for one playwright to be called in to alter the more or less completed work of another.[74] Playwrights at this time do not appear to have been precious about their work, in part because it was rarely printed and generally not meant to last, and in part because they produced so much of it—often writing or contributing to dozens, maybe even hundreds, of plays over the course of a career.[75] Many playwrights were freelancers, more concerned with getting paid than with creating art that might last for four centuries; some were even willing to sell the same play to more than one company.[76] (The companies, meanwhile, did not hesitate to occasionally buy and perform plays without their authors' consent or even awareness.)[77]

Yet Shakespeare also appears to have had direct collaborators for *Henry VI, Part 2.* In the last decade, several different scholars have identified the play's authors as William Shakespeare and Christopher Marlowe, with possibly another collaborator.[78] Earlier generations of scholars had proposed additional University Wits as collaborators; indeed, the theory dates back to the early eighteenth century.[79] More recent experts have sought to distinguish among the various collaborators based in part on some scenes that use "Oh" and some that use "O."[80] Many of these experts have also used increasingly sophisticated computer models to track potential collaborators by precisely delineating distinctive word preferences and grammatical tics.[81]

Marlowe's involvement seems likely. The *Henry VI* plays positively pulse with the presence of Tamburlaine—in their characters' bluster and boldness, in their rhetorical excesses, especially in direct allusions to Marlowe's conquering protagonist. Marlowe was the pioneer in endowing his characters with psychology, in dramatizing a compelling, appalling antihero, in turning his country's violent history into a nationalist epic.[82] And while some have dismissed the idea that an experienced dramatist like Marlowe would deign to work with a novice like Shakespeare, computational analyses have suggested Marlowe's active role.[83]

Nonetheless, Shakespeare was likely the driving force behind the creation of Margaret. Most of the computational analyses identify him as the author of most of her scenes, while to Marlowe apparently belongs the play's beginning and the memorable uprising of Jack Cade.[84] Further, the credit that Shakespeare would receive for this play from his contemporaries attests to his central role in its creation. Finally, the persistence of Margaret throughout plays for which he gets so much acclaim—including *Richard III*, which he almost certainly wrote alone—points to him as her originator or champion.

It probably took Shakespeare, Marlowe, and any of the other collaborators four to six weeks to write the play.[85] By modern standards, this is quite quick, and we can imagine young Will writing furiously, inspired by a vital vision of the old characters from his country's past. Shakespeare was, according to one of his contemporaries, a fast and fluid writer: "he never blotted out a line."[86] At a time when the demand for new plays was insatiable—and when writers were "plentiful as blackberries," in the words of one nineteenth-century scholar—Shakespeare's speed must have been much prized.[87] The going rate for a completed play in the 1590s was £5 to £7, possibly with a bonus to the playwright once it was performed; if a playwright could produce a handful of solo works in a year, he would make a solid living.[88] Nonetheless, playwrights were under constant time pressure, and many were so consistently indebted that they were "continually" at risk of arrest.[89]

Eventually, Shakespeare, Marlowe, and any other men involved in the undertaking would have met to unite their work. After a draft was complete, they would have handed over a copy to a company of actors for a "reading," so the players could see if it suited them and their needs.[90] It was rare, but not unheard of, for a company to reject a play as unsatisfactory.[91]

Yet even after a company accepted a play, its performance was far from assured. Before a new play could open in London, its authors or performers had to submit it to a royal officeholder, the master of the revels, for a scrupulous review. The master of the revels at this time was a well-connected man named Edmund Tilney. He had the power to censor virtually every play to be performed publicly across the realm.[92] Tilney could edit substantially, excising scenes that impugned the monarchy, invoked profanity, insulted powerful people, or otherwise offended his sensibilities. In the margin of one surviving manuscript, he scrawled, "Leave out the insurrection wholy." In another spot, he wrote simply, "Mend this."[93] The master of the revels could also arbitrarily change his mind, revoking authorization for a play he had previously blessed.[94] Tilney favored his friends and allies (including the Lord Strange's Men, as he was linked to the Stanleys by marriage).[95] To defy him risked not only landing an actor in prison; it could also mean the closure of every theatre in the city.[96]

It is clear that *Henry VI, Part 2* survived Tilney's scrutiny. And so, in some form, it was ready for performance. It was time for Margaret's debut.

· 3 ·

"Were I a Man"

Her Rise

In Shakespeare's history plays, people misbehave. Stabbings, conspiracies, war crimes, regicide, senseless cruelty—these are the norm, and modern audiences expect the blood and guts and curses and death. Yet four centuries ago, in the opening scene of the Elizabethan play we now call *Henry VI, Part 2*, Margaret behaved, well, well. She made a short, fawning declaration to her new husband, King Henry, thanked the assembled nobles for their kind wishes, and quickly left the stage. In the play's first moments, few in the audience could have guessed that this woman would become the show's most memorable character—and one who would occupy her principal creator's mind and three more of his plays in the years to come.

Instead, it would have looked like the play was going to be dominated by a different woman, one who questioned authority, disobeyed her king and queen, and conspired with a witch to bring demons from hell to earth to torment her enemies. Her name was Eleanor Cobham, and no more than a dozen minutes had elapsed when the teenage boy playing her erupted onto the stage. Decked out in the finery of a wealthy noblewoman, a long wig fluttering atop his head, this boy strode to center stage. Surely, he was nervous. He was probably just the second-most talented child performer in the troupe; the most skilled would have played Margaret. He was probably young, almost certainly prepubescent, and he likely had other roles to play that afternoon, once his turn as Eleanor concluded. And, for a brief moment onstage, he had to embody the play's most compelling antagonist, a complex character with dozens of lines. Soon enough, another teenage player would displace him as Margaret displaced Eleanor, seizing control of the court, the audience's attention, and the story's heart as the play's foremost female subject. Only then would it become clear to the viewers that Eleanor, appalling, intriguing Eleanor, had functioned more as a means of Margaret's development, a pointed contrast, an obstacle to be overcome on the upward climb of a young queen.[1]

But right now, swallowing any nerves, Eleanor ruled the stage. And the adult actor playing her husband, the Duke of Gloucester, cowered.

As any viewers well-versed in this history would have known, Eleanor was the second wife of the popular Duke of Gloucester (often called the "Good Duke Humphrey"), and as such, the aunt to the king.[2] On the Shoreditch stage, the duke and duchess both saw Henry as an unskilled leader and apparently perceived Margaret, this young, pretty new queen, as a threat to their station. But it was the duchess who first decided to do something about it. In lines laced with rage, Eleanor lamented her husband's weakness and suggested *she* take control of their destinies:

> Why droops my lord, like over-ripened corn
> Hanging the head at Ceres' plenteous load?
> Why doth the great Duke Humphrey knit his brows,
> As frowning at the favours of the world?
> Why are thine eyes fixed to the sullen earth,
> Gazing on that which seems to dim thy sight?
> What seest thou there? King Henry's diadem,
> Enchased with all the honours of the world?
> If so, gaze on, and grovel on thy face,
> Until thy head be circled with the same.
> Put forth thy hand, reach at the glorious gold.
> What, is't too short? I'll lengthen it with mine;
> And having both together heaved it up,

> We'll both together lift our heads to heaven,
> And never more abase our sight so low
> As to vouchsafe one glance unto the ground.[3]

The strength and certainty in Eleanor's harangue signaled many things to the play's audience: the importance of women in power in these history plays, the playwrights' understanding of the rigid structures of gender and the fortitude needed to resist them, and the many perplexing women that Shakespeare, more than his collaborators or contemporaries, would continue putting on London's stages.

It's obvious now, with the benefit of hindsight and familiarity with Shakespeare's subsequent plays, that Eleanor's eloquent protestation augurs future discontented wives in the Bard's work: Portia's melancholy complaint against her absent husband, Lady Macbeth's frustrations over her cautious one, and perhaps even the many misdeeds of Cymbeline's queen. Indeed, Eleanor's lamentations for her gender sound just like those of Lady Macbeth ("unsex me here"), which would ring out on London stages a decade later. Just a few moments after her speech concluded, Eleanor cried:

> Were I a man, a duke, and next of blood,
> I would remove these tedious stumbling blocks
> And smooth my way upon their headless necks.
> And, being a woman, I will not be slack
> To play my part in fortune's pageant.[4]

This afternoon, however, the play's audience could not have seen such similarities. Shakespeare was a largely unknown commodity at this time, and dramas with *plots* (as opposed to purely religious or didactic performances) were also relatively new to the English public. Characters like Eleanor were thrilling. Here was a depiction of English royals arguing in private, and more strikingly, of a woman excoriating her husband for his weaknesses—both foreshadowing Margaret's actions and raving speeches throughout the show. The connection surely struck members of the crowd later that afternoon, in the play's final act, when Margaret, running from the battlefield after bitter defeat, likewise berated her husband for his slowness in a manner nearly identical to Eleanor's:

> What are you made of? You'll nor fight nor fly.
> Now is it manhood, wisdom, and defence,
> To give the enemy way, and to secure us
> By what we can, which can no more but fly.[5]

Eleanor and Margaret's displeasure with their husbands for their unwillingness to defend what their wives believe to be their birthright showed the audience an image of England in the throes of disorder. Women were not supposed to make decisions on behalf of their husbands—especially not husbands given divine station by

An early twentieth-century illustration of Eleanor and Margaret's confrontation.

God.[6] There was something unnatural about both these women, the play implied. For Margaret, it was her foreignness.[7] For Eleanor, it was something more nefarious. Unconvinced that her husband was bold enough to do anything to seize the crown she believed to be his, Eleanor would hire a witch and a necromancer to summon a demon from hell to predict the future, all before the end of the first act of the play.[8]

It was, in fact, Margaret who broke the last straw and directly motivated Eleanor's turn to the dark arts. When, just minutes after Eleanor's speech, the young queen attempted to participate at court, the Duke of Gloucester dismissed her, remarking, "These are no women's matters." Irate at this treatment, Margaret dropped her fan, instructing Eleanor, her inferior in court, to pick it up. As Eleanor stooped to do so, Margaret struck her. Many in the audience must have gasped at the confrontation. Physical violence was hardly queenly behavior. Eleanor swore vengeance: "She shall not strike Dame Eleanor unrevenged," the duchess thundered to the king.[9] The conflict was the first sign that Margaret, and not Eleanor, would be the play's principal female role.

One scene later, in a terrifying tableau, Eleanor summoned her demon. Another young player, this one no doubt painted or costumed in hellacious colors, appeared onstage. The demon—named Asnath, an anagram of the early modern *Sathan*—turned to the throng and made three prophecies—divinations that, like the ones Shakespeare later wrote into *Macbeth*, would mislead those seeking answers in their ambiguous wording.

In short order, Eleanor was found out, arrested, put on trial, found guilty, and driven to exile and near-madness (like Lady Macbeth, she would walk alone in a flowing dress holding a candle, speaking largely to herself). In the last of the lines her teenage avatar had to memorize, Eleanor lamented her tragic state, though she regretted not her actions, only that—in her eyes—Margaret (as well as the Duke of Suffolk, another rival) still had so much influence over the king.

Turning away from her viewers, the boy playing Eleanor left the stage quietly, not to be seen or heard from again that afternoon.

A rash act of sorcery, and its legal consequences, thus removed the most formidable obstacle from Margaret's path—to power at court and to center stage.

The fact that witchcraft heralded Margaret's rise and Eleanor's fall reflects the profound anxieties that the occult—and the women that many believed were its principal practitioners—was generating across Elizabethan England. In fact, a likely candidate for the first acting troupe to stage this play, the Lord Strange's Men, was sponsored by a man whose own mother had recently been accused of witchcraft and was ultimately disgraced and banished from court.[10] In history, Eleanor Cobham had indeed consulted astrologers (who predicted a grievous illness for the king) and maybe even sought to obtain potions. Soon, an ecclesiastical court (stacked with her husband's enemies) would sentence her to public humiliation, divorce, and life imprisonment.[11] The historical Eleanor may have been driven to some manner of necromancy by her ambition—the daughter of a humble knight, she had risen to be just one childless sovereign away from the throne—but in the play's telling it is her envy of another woman, Margaret, that leads her to sorcery and ruin.[12] Clearly, the situation captivated the group of playwrights; while the Tudor chronicles of Hall and Holinshed had devoted little space to Eleanor's travails, Shakespeare and his comrades lavished attention on the doomed duchess.[13]

Young Will was beginning to write just as widespread witch-hunting was sweeping the English countryside as never before. Hundreds of individuals—mostly women—were accused of all manner of dark arts and then tortured, tried, and gruesomely executed, with such cases increasing precipitously in the 1580s.[14] As English society reeled from these profoundly unsettling episodes, witches would appear routinely as characters onstage—including, repeatedly, in Shakespeare's plays.[15] According to the scholar Deborah Willis, some of these characters were obviously demonic, "witches in a legally culpable manner." Others, however, were "associated with witchlike powers." These women, she posits, might rightly be labeled "the 'real' witches in these plays." Though Eleanor was guilty of witchcraft, Margaret was the true threat to the prevailing order.[16]

Eleanor's presence onstage that afternoon was brief and merely the second- or third-most important storyline at this point in the narrative. Why, then, did the play's writers choose to include her? For this truly was a *choice* of the playwrights: Eleanor never actually knew Margaret. Margaret arrived in England in 1445, and Eleanor's trial and banishment occurred in 1441.[17] The reason is clear: They included her contrary to the narrative copied from the chronicle sources and placed her in the beginning of this sequence of plays as a foil to Margaret. They included her to introduce the crowd at the playhouse to women's vengeance and capacity for drastic action. In Eleanor's brief interlude on the boards, the play's authors constructed, in miniature, a warning for those like Margaret: Resist too strongly the expectations of your position and your sex and you will find yourself alone and in peril. As the audience would see, that is just what the dramatists, and history, had planned for Margaret.[18]

In the scenes immediately following Eleanor's banishment, the boy-actor playing Margaret moved to center stage, literally and figuratively. His gown was probably even more sumptuous than Eleanor's, and—unlike the boy playing the duchess—he wore a crown. Calling out Margaret's lines in a voice unchanged by puberty, the boy-actor strove to take this character—one from history, and one who had not previously dominated the play—and turn her into one who dominates *everyone*.

His task was a considerable one. The boy playing Margaret first had to draw a sharp contrast with Eleanor, her erstwhile foil. Both women were dissatisfied with their tentative husbands, but while Eleanor sought salvation in sorcery, Margaret would grasp for power by entering into an affair with a man, the Duke of Suffolk. The boy-actor had to believably depict their adulterous relationship, which forms the metaphorical and narrative center of *Henry VI, Part 2*. He had to gaze at, embrace, declare love for an adult man—and convince the audience he was doing so *as* an adult woman. He had to master

Margaret's emotional dialogue, for out of the entanglement between the queen and the Duke of Suffolk would soon emerge some of the play's most touching prose. Finally, he had to make the audience *like* Margaret, feel pity or passion or some sympathy for her. To do so, he had to play a part that was, in its time, singular: While Eleanor and other female characters from Shakespeare's early plays are consumed and eventually ruined by their fury, Margaret's hardest edges are softened by her capacity for love. Her affair is a tragic one, but in it her creators allow her a nuance virtually unprecedented among the Shakespearean villainesses.

Watching this play, watching this woman, Elizabethan audiences first saw Margaret and Suffolk orchestrate a murder. At her urging—"This Gloucester should be quickly rid the world," she tells allies at court—Suffolk would soon hire assassins to dispatch the duke in his bed.[19] It would have been an especially thrilling plot twist for those who knew their history. In reality, the circumstances around Gloucester's death in 1447 were murky. It is possible that Suffolk was involved, but unlikely that Margaret, not even sixteen years old when her husband's uncle died, played a part. However, the play's writers went far beyond the chronicles on which they depended to insist that the homicide was the work of this nefarious couple.[20]

Those watching from the ground—in the cheap, exposed standing area—were the closest to the action. If the first performance of *Henry VI, Part 2* took place at the Theatre in Shoreditch, as some have guessed, the stage itself protruded into the middle of the yard, with grasslike plants sprouting up from the elevated platform.[21] The performance apparently demanded a large stage, as well as a trapdoor (Asnath had to come from somewhere).[22] Staring across this broad expanse, surely the viewers relished this violent, and unexpected, crescendo: the death of the good duke. "What have we done?" cried one of the murderers, running across the stage, away from the scene of the crime. "Didst ever hear a man so penitent?"[23]

Tensions continued to mount. In both the play and in history, danger stalked Suffolk. He quickly consolidated his influence over King Henry, which earned him resentment from enemies within the government. In fact and in fiction, the King's consigliere was suddenly on the brink of banishment, or worse.[24]

It was at this pivotal moment, with Suffolk staring down death or dishonor, that the actor depicting this war-hardened courtier declared his forbidden love for Margaret. "If I depart from thee, I cannot live," he cried, in a voice no doubt aching with passion. "O, let me stay, befall what may befall!"[25]

This pronouncement rang out through the playhouse. It was an ardent declaration but an *earned* one, for it built on groundwork laid throughout the first two acts: audiences had learned that Suffolk was the one who brought the French princess to the English throne (though whether the play construes that action as a rescue or a kidnapping—or both—is debatable) and introduced her to her adopted country. For her part, in the minutes leading up to the lovefest, Margaret constantly commended Suffolk for being the vision of a man that she believed her husband was not, a fact she made clear the first time she appeared onstage without her husband: "I tell thee, Pole," she said to Suffolk, using his family name rather than his title, in a display of familiarity,

> when in the city Tours
> Thou rann'st a-tilt in honour of my love
> And stol'st away the ladies' hearts of France,
> I thought King Henry had resembled thee
> In courage, courtship and proportion.[26]

Yet it was not until act 3, scene 2, the centermost (and longest) scene of the play—and the scene that Shakespeare would often come to reserve for expansive monologues and linchpin revelations in his plays—that the two characters would reveal the extent of their relationship. It was in this scene that Margaret and Suffolk announced their love in front of their audience.

Left alone for only the second time in the play, with the threat of an imminent banishment for Suffolk, the two actors decried their piteous circumstances and declared their passionate ardor, confirming a sexual and romantic relationship. Margaret's anguish for her lover was as severe as her adoration of him:

> O let me entreat thee cease. Give me thy hand,
> That I may dew it with my mournful tears;
> Nor let the rain of heaven wet this place
> To wash away my woeful monuments.
> O, could this kiss be printed in thy hand,
> That thou mightst think upon these by the seal,
> Through whom a thousand sighs are breathed for thee!
> So get thee gone, that I may know my grief;
> 'Tis but surmised whiles thou art standing by,
> As one that surfeits thinking on a want.
> I will repeal thee or, be well assured,
> Adventure to be banishèd myself.
> And banishèd I am, if but from thee.
> Go, speak not to me; even now be gone!
> O, go not yet. Even thus two friends condemned
> Embrace, and kiss, and take ten thousand leaves,
> Loather a hundred times to part than die.
> Yet now farewell; and farewell life with thee.[27]

It was a speech full of intimate touches, the gentleness of which is nearly unmatched in the Shakespearean history plays. In it, Margaret spoke of the most fragile of objects: a hand dewed with "mournful tears," a kiss "printed in thy hand," and "a thousand sighs breathed," sound like turns of phrase more suited to the sonnets than to a war play.[28]

Audiences surely drank in this display of vulnerability, an openness surpassing that which Margaret or any other character in the play had yet shown. This scene was "Shakespeare's first essay in tragic, destructive love," the poet and critic Gwyn Williams later wrote, following the convention of attributing the play to Shakespeare alone, "and there is something grand in this shameless affection between two passionate, ruthless, and physically splendid lovers." The lovers would soon part ways in an oddly pat rhyming couplet ("SUFFOLK: Even as a split-ted barque, so sunder we— / This way I fall to death. QUEEN: This way for me.") and never speak again.[29] If Shakespeare did indeed compose these lines, this was quite possibly the first real love scene he wrote.[30]

It was in this amorous passage that Margaret's complexity and her humanity were on fullest display. She may have just engineered the exile of one enemy and the death of another, but she was capable of sensitivity, of softness, of love. While such dynamism is unremarkable in modern theatrical characters, it was notable in the late sixteenth century—especially in a female character.

An eighteenth-century illustration of Margaret
and Suffolk.

Observing Margaret, this assured and alluring and appalling teenage boy, some in the crowd may have reflected upon another play from nearly this precise moment, one in which Shakespeare (and possibly some collaborators, probably George Peele, perhaps Thomas Middleton) likewise explored adulterous love in a strong female lead—and one whose differences from *Henry VI, Part 2* make plain Margaret's distinctiveness.[31] *Titus Andronicus* was a Roman epic, inarguably the goriest of the plays attributed to Shakespeare, and though the exact chronology is unclear, it likely debuted on a London stage around the same time as *Henry VI*. In *Titus*, audiences saw the play's chief antagonist, Tamora, Queen of the Goths, another wig-wearing prepubescent lad, arrive in Rome a prisoner, marry the useless emperor, cuckold her husband through an affair with her lover Aaron, and fight for the rights of her sons, Goth princes, over the expected inheritors to power in her new home. Surely some viewers realized that, like Margaret, Tamora experiences great personal loss over the course of her time onstage: In *Titus*'s first scene her son Alarbus is killed in front of her, and in the final scene she is served a meat pie at a royal banquet only to learn after swallowing that her sons Chiron and Demetrius have been murdered and baked into that very dish. Others may have startled upon registering that, like Margaret, Tamora is called a tiger by her enemies, an epithet frequently used by Yorkists to refer to Margaret. Ultimately, though, canny watchers probably recognized that, unlike Margaret, Tamora is indisputably her play's villain: She is evil in character and functions as the story's antagonist.[32]

The two women's similarities—and thus Shakespeare's fixation, one that is apparent across two plays credited to him with *different* collaborators—would have been clearest in the scenes depicting the extramarital affairs. Both women have a love scene in the middle of their plays. In *Titus*, much like in *Henry*, Tamora and Aaron find themselves alone onstage, and Tamora speaks to her beloved in a tone and with an intimacy that momentarily echoes Margaret's declaration of love:

> My lovely Aaron, wherefore look'st thou sad
> When everything doth make a gleeful boast?
> The birds chant melody on every bush,
> The snakes lies rollèd in the cheerful sun,
> The green leaves quiver with the cooling wind
> And make a chequered shadow on the ground.
> Under their sweet shade, Aaron, let us sit.[33]

Tamora and Aaron—a "Moor" (to use the play's term) who experiences profound prejudice for his race from the Goths and the Romans throughout the play—transgress social norms very obviously in their story, and they are duly punished for their sins. There is no ambiguity to their evil; in this scene, Aaron identifies his actions as "a very excellent piece of villainy" just three lines before Tamora's speech.[34] For both these women, their adultery helped the actors and playwright to demonstrate their character: Tamora is a selfish usurper, and Margaret is an isolated foreigner torn between love and duty. Tamora's actor performed a love scene full of innuendo that ended in her commissioning the sexual assault of Titus's daughter, Lavinia. Margaret's, by contrast, embodied a woman who loves, fears, frets, and has not yet understood her own capacity for vengeance.[35]

As for Margaret and Suffolk, the play took flight from Hall and Holinshed's suggestions of a closeness between the queen and a duke nearly three times her age and imagined an ardent romance between peers.[36] There survives no evidence that the duke was ever more than an elder adviser figure to Margaret.[37] Still, Suffolk's genuine unpopularity in the late 1440s would have reflected poorly on the historical Margaret too; they were both blamed for England's loss of land to France in the barter for peace.[38] From deep within the archive have surfaced hints of the queen's reputation at this time; the constable of Gloucester Castle apparently remarked that he'd be pleased to see her drowned, and a man from Canterbury declared that she should not be queen at all, since she had borne no heir.[39]

Such accusations pulsed through the rest of *Henry VI, Part 2*, as the hardworking boy-actor developed Margaret's character beyond the importuning, lovestruck naïf into something more powerful and more nefarious. These later scenes were the true test of endurance for a teenager who had only begun acting a few years earlier. Assuming he passed this test, his evolving depiction of Margaret would have gradually cohered into an argument that the queen—despite her capacity for tenderness—erred in allowing her ambition to overtake her prudence, leading to disorder, war, and even an uprising of her own subjects. In this play (but not in its sources), it was Margaret who conspired in the downfall of Gloucester, champion of the common people, making rebellion more likely.[40]

In history, the years following Gloucester's death were indeed hard ones for Margaret—and undoubtedly hardened her as a ruler. After a trial in early 1450, the Duke of Suffolk received his sentence: banishment. On his way to Calais, an English municipality on the continent, his ship was intercepted (by pirates, the play stated very explicitly, though the identity of the historical culprits is disputed), and he was beheaded.[41] According to one report, his naked body was left on the beach at Dover and his head was set atop a pike. After festering in the sun for some days, his remains found their way to his wife, Alice, who oversaw his funeral and a Christian burial. Margaret and Henry were said to have mourned the loss of their adviser and friend while many others in the country celebrated his demise. However, by the summer of 1450, Margaret and Henry had larger issues to deal with.[42]

Decades of economic stress, military loss in foreign wars, bickering by court nobles, and no charismatic monarch to calm the country's tense nerves led to a situation finally untenable for the precarious kingdom.[43] "So broad and so deep was the failure of the government," the historian John Watts has written, "that the authority of king and lords momentarily, but entirely, collapsed."[44] The crisis had many fronts: the unignorable, imminent loss of the Hundred Years' War in France; Suffolk's fall from grace and death, which signaled to the entire country that Henry had no power over his nobles; and most immediately, violent domestic disturbances, not least of which was the rebellion led by the peasant upstart, Jack Cade. Even further complicating matters were the ever-rising ambitions of Richard, Duke of

York, who had begun to locate strategically placed nobles sympathetic to his brewing claim to the English crown. Soon enough, York would break away in open rebellion, seeking to seize the throne for himself and his sons—a development that would consume the remainder of *Henry VI, Part 2* (and much of *Part 3*).[45]

During this period, the historical Margaret was not yet involved in national affairs. In the late 1440s, she associated with the noble families of England and occasionally dedicated her attention and money to causes across the country. In 1448, she lent her name to education, and Queens' College, Cambridge, was named for her. (Henry had given his royal patronage to the founding of Eton and King's College, Cambridge, in 1440 and 1441, respectively.)[46]

A century and a half later, in a bustling Shoreditch playhouse, actors crowded the stage in the scenes following Suffolk's death. A fractious army of peasant upstarts, commanded by Jack Cade—one of the most charismatic and idiosyncratic characters in the history plays—surged into view. Their goal, they announced, was to overthrow King Henry VI. It was a rebellion drawn directly from history, and it dominated the play's fourth act, the only act in which the rebels appeared. Their scenes—exciting, confusing, memorable for the line, "The first thing we do, let's kill all the lawyers"—reflected the rage of discontented laborers who, in Shakespeare's time and in this play, rose up against high food prices and the enclosure of the commons by a small elite, marching on London and all across the countryside, demanding radical change with dramatic force.[47]

But suddenly, jarringly, the rebels exited and the play took a break from the action. Just as the playwrights had fabricated the love scene between Margaret and the duke, here they invented a sublime scene of mourning for the queen, too. As the king and one of his dukes discussed Cade's uprising, Margaret, who had not appeared onstage since she bade farewell to Suffolk, reentered carrying a fake human head, perhaps gory, perhaps realistic, almost certainly unexpected. (Years later, this entrance would lead to one of the play's strangest stage directions: "Enter with King with a Supplication, and the

Queene with Suffolkes head.") Turning to the audience, she spoke in sad asides even as the men in the room ignored her grief (a dynamic that would recur in *Richard III*):

> Oft have I heard that grief softens the mind,
> And makes it fearful and degenerate;
> Think, therefore, on revenge, and cease to weep.
> But who can cease to weep and look on this?[48]

Yet again, astute viewers may have flashed on Shakespeare's contemporaneous—and remarkably bloody—tragedy, *Titus Andronicus*. Gallows irony, familiar to audiences of *Titus*, swiftly became the scene's dominant tone. No sooner had Margaret lamented her lover's severed head than Henry and one of his nobles (Lord Saye), who could not (or did not) hear the queen's speeches, had a head-related exchange:

> KING: Lord Saye, Jack Cade hath sworn to have
> your head.
> SAYE: Ay, but I hope your highness shall have his.[49]

The extremity of this situation must have been unsettling for all: a queen weeps over the head of her lover as the cuckolded king, discussing heads, cannot notice her. It's the same form of tonal whiplash with which *Titus* overflows. In that play, violence immediately follows flirtation, jokes follow dismemberment, and the audience is always kept aware of agonizing ironies that the characters do not yet understand. The dramatic irony in *Titus*—when the audience sees a trauma lines or scenes before the characters realize it—is constant. *Titus Andronicus* is a tragedy that has taken a lot of advice from comedy; *Henry VI, Part 2* is a history that samples from the comic and the tragic for dramatic effect.

As the scene continued, Henry finally noticed his wife. He asked her if she would mourn so for him, should he meet a similar fate. "No, my love," she replied, "I should not mourn but die for thee."[50]

An early twentieth-century illustration of Suffolk's headless body on the beach.

This strange, brilliant scene leaves so much unclear. Questions must have raced through the minds of the young actors playing Margaret and Henry. Does anyone but Margaret see that there is a severed head onstage? No one else mentions it. Does anyone but Henry know that Margaret is onstage? No one else acknowledges her. Does Henry hear Margaret's words? His lines do not acknowl-edge her speech. Is Margaret's declaration to her husband sincere or sarcastic? The playwrights leave it up to the actors. Does Henry know that Margaret has had a love affair with Suffolk? His lines do not provide us with any indication that he has figured this out. Margaret exists in this scene—her only appearance in act four— almost as an afterthought, or at least, as a *different* thought. She does not engage with the threat of Cade's rebellion. Rather, she shows the human cost of war, the splintering of Henry's court (and by extension the Lancastrian dynasty), and the play's emphasis on duality. In this play, scenes can serve two purposes and queens can love two men.[51]

By the time this play debuted, the surviving Suffolk family had been stripped of its title, and, further, the direct de la Pole line had come to an end. The playwrights thus could have followed the chronicles and made Suffolk the play's central villain. That they did not—the play's Suffolk is misguided and besotted and mutinous, but not evil—may gesture at the influence of some living Suffolk relations who were jockeying for power (or even the throne after Elizabeth's death) just as Shakespeare and his collaborators were creating the character. Indeed, at least one scholar has argued that this influence could have led Shakespeare to give Suffolk a truly touching eulogy (as Margaret is cradling his head) and to make Margaret, not Suffolk, the instigator of their murderous machinations.[52]

With the performance inching toward its close, the audience starting to grow restless, it was clear to all that Margaret was a threat to her country's patriarchal order (she had, after all, cuckolded her royal husband and set in motion the assassination of a duke). The other character explicitly threatening the orderly rule of England's kings was the rebel Jack Cade.[53] Yet he lacked Margaret's staying power. In life and in the play, Cade's rebellion failed. Not long after his army of thousands entered the city of London and Cade, sword in hand, declared himself lord mayor, the city's residents turned against the rebels. Cade's forces lost a vital battle atop London Bridge and Cade himself was fatally wounded while fleeing. Shakespeare—or Marlowe, as some have asserted that the up-from-nothing antihero smacks of his influence—depicted all of this with a fair degree of loyalty to the historical facts.[54] But whereas the chronicles made clear that Cade was articulate, sober, and notably literate, Shakespeare/Marlowe made him pugnacious, ignorant, and sloppy.[55] Whereas the chronicles had taken the rebels' motives and ideologies somewhat seriously, Shakespeare/Marlowe presented them as promising little more than anarchic merriment—"exhort all the world to be cowards," Cade declared from the stage floor, vanquished by a prop sword.[56] It was probably for this reason that the master of the revels let an act full of rebellion onto the stage in the first place.[57]

On this note, the play proceeded to its final act.

Late in the afternoon in that sixteenth-century playhouse, as the sun started to set over the River Thames, the Wars of the Roses began. Two rival factions met on that Elizabethan stage, each likely coming from a separate door on either side of the tiring house (the small room upstage in which actors awaited their entrances). The two sides—the Lancastrians (Henry and Margaret's dynasty) and the Yorkists (led by the breakaway Duke of York)—were now known to the audience, as the play was nearing its end. Over the past couple of hours—as Margaret had fought for dominance at court, had loved and lost and mourned—the audience had also watched York conspire to replace the weakened Henry on the throne, gather nobles to his side, and even instigate Cade's uprising. Now, at last, these two narrative threads converged in a fight for the crown. Margaret led her husband's forces and York his own.

Facing off across the stage, the two started to taunt each other, Margaret insulting York's children and he disparaging her foreignness:

> QUEEN: Call hither Clifford; bid him come amain,
> To say if that the bastard boys of York
> Shall be the surety for their traitor father.

> YORK: O blood-besotted Neapolitan,
> Outcast of Naples, England's bloody scourge!
> The sons of York, thy betters in their birth,
> Shall be their father's bail, and bane to those
> That for my surety will refuse the boys.[58]

With this, York gestured to his sons, Edward and Richard, who here entered the play, and the tetralogy, in this crucial final act. In a battle unfolding across the act's three scenes, Shakespeare and his collaborators began to draw their characters and to set expectations for their future development. (One Lancastrian ally calls Richard—known to history as Richard III—a "[h]eap of wrath, foul indigested lump, / As crooked in thy manners as thy shape!," the first in a long series of insults directed at Richard's disability over the succeeding plays.[59]) In reality, however, Richard—who was just two years old at the time—was not present at this battle, now known as the First Battle of St. Albans, the first major conflict of the Wars of the Roses. Neither was Margaret, although the playwrights have her onstage as well, close as ever to the action. Typical for dramas of the time, this play condensed numerous historical events into a few quick scenes. Less typical for dramas of this time, this condensation served to emphasize the centrality of a woman, Margaret, to the armed struggle.[60]

Many in the audience—though, of course, not nearly all—knew their country's recent history. For these privileged playgoers, the experience of seeing Margaret, Henry, and York pacing, arguing, and reciting on that Shoreditch stage must have been considerably enriched by the thrill of recognizing all that was altered or cut. They could have realized, for instance, that the play omitted entirely much of the discontent that led the Yorkists to split from King Henry's rule. Crucially, the play elided the respectful relationship that Margaret and the Duke of York had enjoyed in the years leading up to the Yorkists' split from King Henry, a dynamic that might have complicated the Manichean struggle the play sets forth between Margaret and the duke. They could also have recognized that the play skipped over the sudden mental break that Henry suffered in 1453, shortly after Cade's rebellion but before the First Battle of St. Albans. At the time, Margaret was pregnant with her son, the future Prince Edward, and the king did not recover in time to recognize his heir when Margaret presented the baby to him. A precise diagnosis of

Henry's illness has evaded history. Those close to the king described his condition as "a rash and sudden terror," that his "wirt and his reson [were] withdrawen," that he had "no natural sense nor reasoning power."[61]

Indeed, astute audience members may have paused to contemplate the absence not only of Henry's incapacitation but also of Margaret's political response. In January of 1454, her husband still indisposed and her son just months old, Margaret proposed a regency to Parliament: Until her husband regained his ability to do so, she would lead the country. Though there was little precedent for a queen's rule in England, this sort of arrangement was common on the continent. After all, Margaret had watched her mother and grandmother rule dukedoms in the absence of their husband and son, respectively.

Uneasy with the idea of a (foreign) woman ruling the country, Parliament appointed the Duke of York as "protector and defender of the realm and church" in April. This much the playwrights reproduced in *Henry VI, Part 2*, but they depended on their audience to recall (or intuit) much of the context. Orphaned at a young age, York had been raised by a series of regents, just as Henry had; unlike the king, however, York had distinguished himself as a knight in the Hundred Years' War. Fabulously wealthy and unquestionably powerful, he was also the king's closest male relative (other than Henry's infant son), and therefore he had some claim to the throne. No Elizabethan playgoer—and, indeed, no modern historian—could know with certainty how Margaret reacted to the news of York's appointment, but there can be no doubt that the ruling powers passing her by alarmed and upset her.[62]

Just months later, in late 1454, Henry experienced a sudden recovery. As he resumed kingly duties, an overjoyed Margaret by his side, York left London for the north, bringing with him the Earl of Warwick, one of his closest allies. By this point, York had all but decided to seize the throne from Henry, and as he assembled an army in the hinterlands, Margaret and the Lancastrians' closest allies began to build one of their own.[63] The following year, the two sides—Henry's

Lancastrians and the duke's Yorkists—clashed at the First Battle of St. Albans. Although the participants were few and the dead fewer than sixty, the battle shocked both sides of the conflict into realizing that civil war had arrived in England.[64]

News of St. Albans threw the country into disarray. York was forced from his position as lord protector, rulers in Scotland and France started contemplating military action against the weakened and distracted regime, and Margaret began to travel the country with her infant son to rally support for the Lancastrian cause. Skirmishes—some bloodless, some brutal—erupted across the country. In the wake of this disruption, Margaret took charge of the monarchy. Her first task was to consolidate the king's supporters. She began with the nobles she knew she could trust: the kin of those killed at St. Albans and those who had feuded publicly with the Duke of York. By the next year, it was undeniable to all that Margaret ruled in court.[65]

More than a century later, with an aging Elizabeth on the throne, the *Henry VI* plays created by William Shakespeare and his collaborators would overlook much of the early history of the Wars of the Roses, condensing the chronology of the fighting, foregrounding and accelerating the development of Margaret as a martial leader of men. By the conclusion of *Henry VI, Part 2*, Queen Margaret had become the true head of the Lancastrian faction. Following the defeat of her forces at St. Albans, she ordered her husband to flee ("Away my lord, you are slow, for shame, away!"), calling him weak and denigrating his "manhood" for good measure.[66] Here, Shakespeare or a collaborator may have been drawing on older sources. While the chronicles depicted Henry with a restraint reflecting nationalism and censorship, chroniclers from Henry's own time labeled the king ignorant, gullible, stupid, and (in the words of Pope Pius II) "more timorous than a woman."[67]

The light faded behind the stage and the groundlings departed the performance amid anxiety about a female ruler, enthusiasm for a female ruler, and propaganda promoting a female ruler. The character of Margaret is inseparable from this swirling, ambient disquiet. By play's end, Shakespeare's Margaret embodies the feverish discourse—both the danger of an ambitious woman and the potential of a fierce female leader to triumph over cunning foes. Her seizure of power leaves the play's ending unresolved; no one knew—in Margaret's time or in Shakespeare's—what to do with such a woman.[68]

· 4 ·

"Tiger's Heart Wrapped in a Woman's Hide"

Her Rule

Surely, from the very moment that Margaret came into view, during the first performance of the play we now call *Henry VI, Part 3*, everyone in the playhouse could feel something shift in the atmosphere. She was the first female character to walk onto the stage that afternoon, her face alight with rage. Immediately, it was clear to all that she was in charge.

"Here comes the Queen, whose looks bewray her anger," a powerful Lancastrian confided in the audience. "I'll steal away."

Margaret's husband, King Henry, tried to do the same, but his wife stopped him short. "Nay, go not from me," Margaret declared, "I will follow thee."

"Be patient, gentle Queen," Henry begged, "and I will stay."[1]

This placating sentence was enough to ignite her fury. "Who can be patient in such extremes?" Margaret exploded. She called the king a "wretched man," accusing him of disinheriting his son, the young Prince Edward. Henry beseeched his wife and his child for forgiveness. The Duke of York and the Earl of Warwick had "enforced" him to surrender the throne, he insisted.

"Enforced thee?" Margaret bellowed. "Art thou king, and wilt be forced? / I shame to hear thee speak. Ah, timorous wretch, / Thou hast undone thyself, thy son, and me, / And giv'n unto the house of York such head / As thou shalt reign but by their sufferance."[2]

Henry VI, Part 3 had barely begun, and already so much was clear to the men, women, and children in the audience that day in the late 1580s or early 1590s. No doubt many, perhaps most, recalled the end of *Henry VI, Part 2*, with the insurgent Yorkists victorious, the ruling Lancastrians defeated and fleeing. This play, the sequel, had picked up immediately where *Part 2* left off, with the king, queen, and Lancastrian forces in full retreat, the triumphant Yorkists in hot pursuit. The forces converged, and a confrontation ensued in the halls of Parliament. York demanded that Henry step aside, that he allow York's descendants to assume the crown forevermore. After a few token protests, Henry agreed. It was because of this concession that Margaret berated her husband. If the Lancastrian dynasty were to be saved, the audience could tell, it was only because this fiery woman was there to stand in York's way.[3]

This audience, Shakespeare's original audience, played a significant role in shaping the character that Margaret became.[4] Notably, women packed the playhouse.[5] The old norm that female playgoers would attend only if escorted by a man had been changing fast, and foreigners began commenting on the freedom with which women circulated in playhouses (although some wealthier women may have disguised themselves with masks).[6] These female audience members, as much as their male counterparts, enjoyed and exercised outsized influence over the transgressive female characters they were there to see.

The crowd that day had shown up early and then played cards or snacked on fruit and sweetmeats while waiting for the show to begin.[7] They had arrived in the afternoon, since public plays in Shakespeare's day had to start soon enough in the day to capture optimal sunlight.[8] Wealthier patrons might have arrived by boat, by coach, or even carried in a roofed chair.[9] Some probably hadn't even known what they were there to see.[10]

Playhouses such as this one were far from luxurious. The odors of perfume, onions, and garlic competed with the distinctive smell of tobacco, a recent arrival from the New World.[11] (The Rose theatre apparently smelled so bad that Juliet's famous line, "that which we call a rose / By any other name would smell as sweet," may have been a joke at its expense.)[12] Several thousand spectators squeezed in to gawk at the drama.[13] There they remained—except, perhaps, for individuals who needed to duck out to urinate into a bucket.[14] Fighting, soliciting, and pickpocketing were not uncommon, although crime was probably not as rife as critics of the theatre claimed.[15] Moralists declared that sex workers circulated through playhouses in great numbers—centuries later, scholars would argue that this proximity is reflected in the profusion of prostitution in Shakespeare's plays.[16]

Exterior light flooded the theatre, as did precipitation. London was, as today, often dreary and soaked with rain, but there is little evidence that this disrupted the onstage activity, even though the groundlings were naked to the elements.[17] Thus, unlike in modern theatres, Elizabethan audiences did not sit in the darkness. Their visibility to one another led many to embrace their roles as active participants in the drama.[18]

And participate they did. They shouted. They hissed. They cheered. They clapped. They wept. Some audience members even interrupted the proceedings with loud criticisms.[19] One angry preacher denounced "wild youths of both sexes" using "lively gesture and voices" to disrupt the plays and arouse the crowd.[20] Vendors hawking drink (water, wine, or ale) and food (including apples, pears, oranges, and nuts, all of which could also be thrown in displeasure) circulated freely.[21] Audience members might even leave after a lead actor "died" (which is probably a reason that tragedies often save the big bloodbaths for the end).[22] On the whole, Elizabethan audiences were far less inhibited than audiences today.[23]

These audiences were astonishingly diverse in terms of background, class, and gender. Men, women, and children attended, rich and poor alike, although the rich could afford to pay for chairs, cushions, private boxes, or even apparently seats on the stage itself.[24] Many wore their very best clothing, including colorful hats with ostentatious plumage.[25] The outspokenness and variety of such audiences meant that dramatists like Shakespeare simply could not ignore audience tastes or reactions.[26] It is incomplete, therefore, to characterize Shakespeare's plays as pure male fantasy, for they had to please substantial numbers of female playgoers as well.[27]

Shakespeare, along with any collaborators, undeniably wrote Margaret with his audience in mind.[28] The *Henry VI* plays were enormously popular among London playgoers. The battle scenes in particular were probably a draw, as was the plays' unabashed jingoism.[29]

But the character of Margaret was, no doubt, a crowd-pleaser as well. The scholar David Mann has argued that the men in Elizabethan audiences may have felt "a certain dark attraction" in seeing Margaret onstage.[30] He speculates that Margaret and other female characters like her "must have been popular with women too, offering a tangle of contradictory feelings," not least of which, we add, might also have been attraction.[31] Other scholars have postulated that female viewers may well have enjoyed witnessing powerful female characters transgress the bounds of gender for all to see.[32]

Watching this terrifying woman disparage her ineffectual husband, in other words, was something of a thrill for her viewers—a thrill the play's authors deliberately sought when creating the character for a cosmopolitan audience in the first place. Many Elizabethan Londoners—inhabitants of a violently patriarchal society—must have reacted with a dissonant mixture of astonishment and delight when a woman called her husband (the King of England, no less) a "trembling lamb" and a "foul disgrace."[33]

"Had I been there, which am a silly woman," Margaret declared before her rapt audience, "the soldiers should have tossed me on their pikes / Before I would have granted to that act," decrying Henry's surrender of his throne to York. "But thou preferr'st thy life before thine honour," she spat. According to the chronicles on which Shakespeare relied, Henry never actually capitulated, but the alternative history served to craft a bolder and more radical Margaret.[34]

Margaret avowed that she'd had enough. "I here divorce myself," she told the king, "Both from thy table, Henry, and thy bed."[35] This too appeared nowhere in the Tudor chronicles but completed the image of a Margaret who would not allow her lord and husband to hinder her any longer.[36]

The northern lords, Margaret announced, who had forsworn Henry's colors would surely follow hers. "Come, son, let's away," she told Prince Edward. "Our army is ready—come, we'll after them."[37]

"Stay, gentle Margaret, and hear me speak," Henry begged.

"Thou hast spoke too much already," Margaret retorted. "Get thee gone."

A moment later, the queen and the prince left the stage. They had a war to win.[38]

Discreetly watching not just the actors but also the audience, young William Shakespeare no doubt took note of any reactions—positive or negative, appalled or titillated or both—to Queen Margaret. At the time, initial performances could be treated as "rehearsals," and it was common for Elizabethan playwrights to gauge audience reaction to see how they might alter the text for future performances. In fact, audience members may have been charged twice as much to attend such a trial performance.[39]

Shakespeare would not have been alone in scrutinizing his early audiences. In writing the sequel to his popular *Henry VI, Part 2*, Shakespeare apparently worked again with Christopher Marlowe, as well as possibly some others.[40] Undeniably, *Part 3* bears the mark of Marlowe's style.[41] Yet, as with *Part 2*, the fact that Shakespeare would receive the lion's share of the credit for *Part 3* from his peers suggests that he was its principal progenitor or "chief collaborator" or simply pushiest playwright—meaning he likely did the most work in shaping Margaret. The probable period of creation for this play was, after all, a hectic time for Marlowe; the second part of his celebrated play *Tamburlaine* had debuted to great acclaim, and he was likely hard at work on the script that would become his *Doctor Faustus.*

Following a trial run of the Margaret of *Part 3*, Shakespeare may well have told the actor to alter some aspect of her depiction—or even to use new lines for her character. Any such changes, while anticipated, would no doubt have annoyed the overworked players. They were, like all Elizabethan actors, very busy.[42] As soon as the company committed to a new play, players would receive a copy of a script and immediately chop it up, pasting together their own part (or parts) into a scroll and adorning this with any needed cues or stage directions.[43] (A rare surviving scroll from about 1591 is seventeen feet long.)[44] The actors had just a few weeks to memorize their lengthy scrolls full of lines to prepare for the play's debut. Extended rehearsals were a luxury that evolved in the nineteenth century; in Shakespeare's time, each actor prepared alone. Any eleventh-hour line changes would only have added to the actors' burden.[45]

They were an eclectic bunch. Some of the earliest performers to put on the *Henry VI* plays included the Elizabethan thespians John Holland, John Sincler, Gabriel Spencer, and Humphrey Jeffes.[46] The details of their lives are few and far between: Holland and Sincler may have been Lord Strange's Men and appear to have worked repeatedly with young Shakespeare.[47] Unkind references from Shakespeare's texts further suggest that Sincler may have been a memorably scrawny—even ugly—man, although one used to jokes about his appearance.[48] Spencer would be killed by the celebrated playwright Ben Jonson in a duel a few years later.[49]

Some have speculated that Shakespeare himself might have shown up to supervise whatever informal rehearsals these men undertook; he was, after all, firmly ensconced within the community of actors.[50] Indeed, there are hints that Shakespeare was on hand for the run-through of *Henry VI, Part 3* in particular; for instance, a stage direction appears to have been added noting that an arrow had wounded Clifford in the neck, something reflected in the Tudor chronicles but not in the play's text.[51] It is tempting to imagine the nervous young playwright running back and forth, eager to ensure that his early work would be performed perfectly.

All this labor paid off. The text of *Henry VI, Part 3* that survives today is stuffed full of story, action, character, pathos, and philosophy. The play skips from country to country, the narrative envelops over a decade of historical action, and the tides of war turn repeatedly against its heroes—though who those heroes *are* changes, too.[52] The play cuts major historical events for time, but it also spends time in invented scenes that show the immense pain and stress that the common soldier feels as a pawn in the disputes of the unfeeling few who try to run the war-racked country of England. The play (at least in its modern edited versions) has twenty-six scenes, at least sixty-seven roles, and five battles.[53] The longest soliloquy in any of the plays attributed to Shakespeare, a seventy-one-line Goliath of a speech spoken by Richard, the Duke of Gloucester—later known as Richard III—sits at the center of this work; it is the jewel in the drama's crown of rhetorical richness. It is "a remarkable play," remark the scholars John D. Cox and Eric Rasmussen, one that displays "a confidence and sureness that very few earlier plays can rival."[54]

The result, *Henry VI, Part 3*, is a rollicking good time. The play created a critical vision of England both as it existed during the turbulent civil wars of the 1400s and the more placid, though still unstable, late Elizabethan era of the 1500s.[55] Into these five acts, the authors squeezed events that occurred over a span of fifteen years, creating a narrative that feels swift and necessary, as if all these disparate events occurred over one bloody summer.[56] And throughout, Margaret reigns over both her husband and her kingdom.

Mere minutes into the performance that afternoon, Margaret's capacity for cruelty erupted onstage in startling fashion. Suddenly, she was at her most martial and least sympathetic—and, tellingly, it was at this moment that the play's characters most forcefully impugned her femaleness.[57] Such declamations—that she is a monster, a prostitute, an unhuman—are especially intriguing because they mirror, with shocking accuracy, the accusations that moralists were lobbing at the young men and boys playing women on Elizabethan stages. Women such as Margaret. In other words, the play indicted Margaret's womanhood on account of her mannish violence—an indictment that doubled as a critique, albeit an implicit one, of those who would assail the propriety of gender exploration onstage, of boys in dresses and wigs.

Margaret's speeches of rage and rupture, insulting King Henry and claiming command for herself, were just the beginning. She next strode onto the stage flush with victory, her vast army (twenty thousand men, or so a breathless messenger informed the audience) seizing York's castle.[58] A defeated York stumbled to the fore, cursing the Lancastrian queen:

> The army of the Queen hath got the field.
> My uncles both are slain in rescuing me;
> And all my followers to the eager foe
> Turn back, and fly like ships before the wind,
> Or lambs pursued by hunger-starvèd wolves.[59]

Animal imagery overflowed from this scene into the entire play; thirty-seven species appear in metaphor across the tetralogy.[60] No doubt many in the audience noted that characters on either side of the civil war called their followers lambs and their attackers wolves and lions; York likened himself to the phoenix, Clifford compared the warriors to doves and falcons.

As the men portraying York and Clifford delivered these memorable lines, they would have positioned themselves in symmetrical arrangements. The acting style of the day involved bold gestures and meaningful poses.[61] Players generally did not strive for realism or ignore the audience (as many modern actors do). They stood and pronounced their insults directly to their viewers. Indeed, actors were liable to change the lines from one performance to the next, improvising as they saw fit, less committed to rendering realized "characters" than to completing a symbolically significant tableau.[62]

Just as *Part 3* debuted, however, a new generation of actors was beginning to experiment with a new style, more focused on inhabiting their characters *as characters*—as realized individuals—than on simply orating their lines and gesturing emphatically.[63] It is intriguing to consider the possibility that the men playing York and Clifford—and perhaps even the young man playing Margaret—may have been doing more than just saying their lines.[64]

Rushing into view after her victory in battle, Margaret cornered the actor depicting the defeated York with the help of her two most loyal lords: Clifford and the Earl of Northumberland. The three taunted York for his loss, calling him names: coward, traitor, proud Plantagenet.

Margaret then ordered her lords to bind him: "Brave warriors, Clifford and Northumberland, / Come make him stand upon this molehill here, / That wrought at mountains with outstretchèd arms, / Yet parted but the shadow of his hand." With this relentless rebel, her husband's tormentor, now bound to die at her hand, Margaret—and the talented boy-actor embodying her—could show her mettle. She continued:

> What—was it you that would be England's king?
> Was't you that revelled in our Parliament,
> And made a preachment of your high descent?
> Where are your mess of sons to back you now?
> The wanton Edward and the lusty George?
> And where's that valiant crookback prodigy,
> Dickie, your boy, that with his grumbling voice
> Was wont to cheer his dad in mutinies?
> Or with the rest where is your darling Rutland?[65]

And here, Margaret produced a prop, one simple to make but horrifying in implication: a cloth soaked in the blood of York's son Rutland, killed in the previous scene.[66] Brandishing the rag, she declared:

> Look, York, I stained this napkin with the blood
> That valiant Clifford, with his rapier's point,
> Made issue from the bosom of the boy.
> And if thine eyes can water for his death,
> I give thee this to dry thy cheeks withal.[67]

Tormented by the news of his son's death, York could not yet form words. And so the queen decided to mock him further. She placed a crown made of paper on his sweaty, bloody brow and then continued, with relish:

> York cannot speak unless he wear a crown.
> A crown for York, and, lords, bow low to him.
> Hold you his hands, whilst I do set it on.
> Ay, marry, sir, now looks he like a king;
> Ay, this is he that took King Henry's chair,

Barbara Jefford as Queen Margaret placing the paper crown on York's head, in a 1957 production of the *Henry VI* plays at London's Old Vic.

> And this is he was his adopted heir.
> But how is it that great Plantagenet
> Is crowned so soon, and broke his solemn oath?
> As I bethink me, you should not be king
> Till our King Henry had shook hands with death.[68]

Margaret mocked York on all conceivable fronts: for the death of his son, his defeat in battle, the failure of his rebellion and his ambition, and his loss of the crown.[69]

The queen finished her speech, one of the most spectacular and revolting pieces of oratory found in the many Shakespearean histories of England, thus: "Off with the crown, and with the crown his head; / And, whilst we breathe, take time to do him dead."[70]

But before the Lancastrians' blades could pierce his skin, the duke lifted his head, still wearing the paper crown, to spit back venom at the queen, in a speech even longer than hers. He began his rebuttal invoking the unnaturalness of her kind, a woman doing a man's worst bidding, using the foulest imagery he could imagine—predators, prostitutes, foreigners—to decry her personhood:

> She-wolf of France, but worse than wolves of France,
> Whose tongue more poisons than the adder's tooth—
> How ill-beseeming is it in thy sex
> To triumph like an Amazonian trull,
> Upon their woes whom Fortune captivates!

For several minutes more, the queen, Clifford, and Northumberland allowed the duke to rail on, uninterrupted, insulting every aspect of Margaret's person that he knew. Deep into his speech, he unveiled his major accusation; that she could not be woman, or perhaps not even human:

> Thou art as opposite to every good
> As the antipodes are unto us,
> Or as the south to the septentrion.

O tiger's heart wrapped in a woman's hide!
How couldst thou drain the lifeblood of the child
To bid the father wipe his eyes withal,
And yet be seen to bear a woman's face?
Women are soft, mild, pitiful, and flexible—
Thou stern, obdurate, flinty, rough, remorseless.
Bidd'st thou me rage? Why, now thou hast thy wish.
Wouldst have me weep? Why, now thou hast thy will.[71]

Within moments, the Duke of York was dead. Clifford, eager to continue to avenge the death of his father, stabbed him twice, and Margaret stabbed him once, a reprisal, she said pointedly, for her "gentle-hearted King."[72] A sponge or animal bladder concealed in York's armpit may have thrilled the audience with a bright spurt of blood.[73] The queen ordered his corpse decapitated and his head placed upon the battlements of the city of York, so all who opposed the powers of England could see the bloody fate awaiting them.

By the time the boy playing Margaret exited the stage, just moments after murdering York and concluding the play's bear of an opening act, he must have been exhausted. Yet he may have had to leave quickly, darting out of sight to change costumes before reentering as someone else entirely.[74] For economic reasons, the plays of Shakespeare and his contemporaries depended heavily on the practice of "doubling"—a single actor portraying multiple roles—and most of the boys playing female parts would thus have doubled in several other minor roles.[75] To trust a boy burdened with other parts to also convincingly portray Margaret was a true vote of confidence from Shakespeare and his collaborators in one specific actor. Indeed, the creation of memorable female roles—such as Margaret—may gesture to the availability of a remarkably capable boy-actor, one with the ability to depict complex (and older) women.[76] Will was unusual among his contemporaries for the relative abundance of thorny, demanding female parts in the early plays that his contemporaries would attribute to him; Christopher Marlowe, for instance, did not do likewise in his solo works.[77]

That Margaret herself was portrayed by a young man in drag

inescapably shaped how the play's first viewers perceived her character. Alien though it may be to modern audiences, the person who soliloquized so powerfully, struck Eleanor, stabbed York, and cradled Suffolk's head was a boy who had been informally apprenticed to an adult actor when he was between ten and thirteen. Like other boys who played female parts in Elizabethan plays, he lived in the adult actor's home for a term designed to last approximately seven years.[78] The adult actor, and not the boy, received payment for his acting, though this was not abnormal in apprenticeships, and there are several recorded instances in which boy-actors developed close and lasting friendships with their "masters."[79] (By contrast, some of the boys who acted for boy companies appear to have been kidnapped and forced into the trade.)[80] The boy-actor playing Margaret was probably cast based on his skill, as well as how well he suited the "womanly" ideal, which at the time was rather "slim-hipped and flat-chested."[81]

His identity (along with that of nearly all boy-actors from this time) was not recorded. (At least one academic has asserted that Shakespeare himself may have played Margaret, though this seems quite unlikely.)[82] Even his age is a mystery, as scholars have long disagreed fiercely about how old the boy actors were—that is, were they teenagers, young men, or even full-fledged male adults?[83] On balance, it seems most likely that they generally spanned a boy's teenage years, with some perhaps performing female roles into their early twenties.[84] Intriguingly, it appears that the onset of puberty was somewhat later in the sixteenth century than it is today, so boys' voices may not have changed until they were well into their teenage years.[85] Records reveal, nonetheless, that one Elizabethan performance around the year 1600 had to be delayed because "the queen was shaving."[86] Due to the demanding nature of Margaret's part, her actor may have been on the older end.

The boy playing Margaret surely dressed with particular extravagance.[87] Wealthy women—such as she—wore corsets, stays, gowns, petticoats, girdles, and aprons made of the finest material, often all at once, and boy apprentices apparently could borrow these from the ladies of the homes where they boarded.[88] Her actor probably wore a long-haired wig, atop which would have perched a high, pointy crown.[89] In battle scenes, he may have worn men's armor.[90] The playing company for which her actor worked would have had an ample closet of costumes to choose from, with fine, colorful garments of cloth, taffeta, satin, velvet, and lace (some of it the discarded attire of nobles).[91] Margaret, along with her fellow actors, may have dressed anachronistically in clothing from her own era, rather than in period pieces.[92] The adult actors may have dyed their beards to match their costumes. Londoners probably had a good eye for garments, knowing how to distinguish between "gentleman's gray" and "beggar's gray," for instance. This was a time of significant interest in the symbolic weight of certain colors, so the audience would have known that servants wore blue or tawny, the powerful wore scarlet, and "Catherine-pear-coloured beards" signaled wickedness.[93]

Yet despite the skill and gaudy costuming of the boy playing Margaret, some in the audience (and certainly many outside the playhouse) considered her to be positively satanic—a parasite, pervert, or criminal—but for reasons having little to do with her actions.[94] Rather, they objected—loudly, angrily, and at great length—to the fact that plays at this time featured boys in dresses and wigs depicting women.

Historically speaking, "boy-actresses" (as many scholars call these performers) were novel. For centuries, women had appeared on provincial English stages without controversy.[95] By the late sixteenth century, however, their presence was firmly verboten, making England unusual among European countries in its prohibition of female actors.[96] Outside of the theatre, men wearing women's clothing was, generally speaking, unacceptable.[97] Indeed, in the wider world, a man donning a dress was considered tantamount to his embracing deviant sexuality, and sodomy was a crime. Interestingly, though, sodomy was rarely prosecuted—and even when it was, its practitioners were generally dealt with lightly. Women who had sex outside of marriage, by contrast, were dealt with far more harshly.[98]

Nevertheless, many in England *loathed* the boy-actors. Religious reformers, violently opposed to the theatre in general, reserved particular ire for boy-actors—calling them "Man-women monsters," labeling them avatars of homosexuality, and decrying "witty, comely youths" seduced into acting "those womanish, whorish parts which Pagans would even blush to personate." Other Elizabethans, however, revered boy-actors for their skill in portraying women, or for their appealing lack of masculinity.[99] And, for aspiring actors, there was apparently no shame in this work. Edward Alleyn and Richard Burbage—the two most famous actors of the day, both paragons of masculinity—likely began their careers as boys playing women.[100] Even Shakespeare himself may have appeared in a female role as a youth in Stratford.[101]

How did the fact that Margaret was played by a boy inform the audience's reception of her character? It is hard not to imagine that some in Shakespeare's audiences were thrilled or amused or outraged or even titillated to see gender-play onstage, but several scholars have asserted that Elizabethan spectators simply accepted this convention and *saw* female characters when they gazed at the boys in wigs.[102] Indeed, so familiar was this practice that one Englishman expressed surprise upon observing that Italian actresses "were quite as good at playing women as English boys were."[103] Some scholars have argued that the boy-actress demonstrated the instability of the boundaries separating one gender from another at this time.[104] Others, by contrast, have asserted that the boy-actress ritually enacted, even reinforced, female exclusion.[105]

Margaret presents a puzzle, for she is a boy pretending to be a woman who, in the eyes of many, was acting much like a man. According to one critic, Margaret (along with other women from the first tetralogy) can "be considered as male impersonators who unsex themselves in order to ape the violence and cruelty of men: though they participate in history, they do not participate in history *as women*."[106] Another scholar argues that when York curses Margaret, she is in his eyes "a sort of monster; neither woman nor man, she is a composite." Her disordered gender performance mirrors the disorder of her country—a disorder that is, in large part, her fault.[107]

In our own time, sighs still another commentator, "the subject of the boy-actress" has become "one of the most hotly debated topics" in

Shakespeare studies. Our perception of him/her inevitably reflects the biases and assumptions of our own cultural moment and milieu.[108] In other words, when we squint too hard at the boy portraying Margaret, we end up seeing ourselves.[109]

Fair enough. Yet when Elizabethan audiences watched Margaret murdering a foe—and being duly insulted, unsexed, by that same foe—they were watching a cross-dressing boy performing at the peak of his controversial trade. They were witnessing the absurdity of that insult, the ludicrousness of any insistence that gender norms are rigid and unyielding and not to be transgressed. Clearly, a boy can play a queen. And, clearly, that queen can lead an army.

For the historical Margaret, the battlefield victory and the killing of York were thrilling developments, even though (contrary to her depiction on the Shakespearean stage) she was not actually present for the fighting. After the duke's death, she wasted little time in marching her troops south to London, allowing her swelling ranks to pillage and terrorize the countryside they passed through from Yorkshire down to Hertfordshire. There, her immense army again crushed a Yorkist contingent, this one led by the Earl of Warwick.[110] Margaret reunited with King Henry, who had been kept Warwick's prisoner since the previous fall. In contrast to the play's portrait of a militant divorcée, she was apparently pleased at the reunion.[111] After the battle, mentioned only briefly in *Henry VI, Part 3*, Margaret and the Lancastrians had ample reason to celebrate. The Duke of York had been humiliated and eliminated. The king was free.

Yet half of the divided country saw Henry as illegitimate. And York's son and heir, Edward, was still on the march. Edward had won a great victory just days before the defeat of his ally, Warwick, and—as if God were blessing the Yorkist cause—a striking meteorological anomaly had made it appear as if three suns graced the sky, an image Edward thereafter adopted as his emblem. Within days, he had retaken London. Holding the capital and the crown, he assumed the throne as King Edward IV.[112]

England now had two kings. And each commanded an army.

· 5 ·

"You Fight in Justice"

Her Fall

Three men advanced on Margaret, surrounding her. She had just killed their father, the Duke of York, in a sickening, savage spectacle. The sons, one of them stooped and smeared with makeup, one of them wearing a crown, wanted revenge.

It was a scene with no basis in history. Flanked by soldiers, York's three surviving sons—Edward, Richard, and George—encountered Margaret and Henry in York, the city bearing the usurpers' family name. Insults, some of the play's most vivid, flew fast. To Margaret's dismay (but not to her surprise), Henry could not insult the now-fatherless York sons. But she could. Over the hot minutes that followed, the gawky boy playing this ruthless queen got to show a crowd of spectators just how Margaret felt about these men who would be king. Slyly, subversively, her role evoked Queen Elizabeth I, the current ruler of England, a woman who brooked no male challengers. Yet the subversion did not stop there, for then the men surrounding Margaret—two of whom would indeed be king—got to return the favor.

"Go rate thy minions, proud insulting boy!" Margaret spat at Edward, before turning her attention to Warwick, one of York's most loyal ministers.[1] "Why, how now, long-tongued Warwick, dare you speak?" she admonished him. "When you and I met at Saint Albans last, / Your legs did you better service than your hands."[2] When in turn Richard insulted her son, Margaret derided his physical form: "But thou art neither like thy sire nor dam," she began, deploying the play's oft-repeated animal imagery, "But like a foul misshapen stigmatic, / Marked by the destinies to be avoided, / As venom toads or lizards' dreadful stings."[3]

The brothers wasted no time in returning her insults. Richard invoked her father's empty titles and her husband's sham kinghood—"Iron of Naples hid with English gilt"—and Edward called her a "shameless callet" (strumpet) and a beggar, saying that for all her sins, at least Helen of Troy had been pretty, "fairer far than thou."[4]

In history, King Edward IV of the House of York was a formidable foe. Though he was just eighteen years old when he claimed the throne, he was six feet four, muscular and charming, too. A fifteenth-century writer who met the young monarch described him as "one of the handsomest men of his age" and noted that he "gave himself up wholly to pleasures, and took no delight in anything but ladies, dancing, entertainment, and the chase." That, and leading his followers to victory in battle.[5] By contrast, Margaret's standing suffered with the circulation of Yorkist propaganda painting her as an interloping foreigner.[6] Her army had also gained a reputation for plunder, and upon their arrival at the capital, they found London's gates barred by the citizenry, who feared their barbarity. Frustrated, the queen turned her troops to the north. All suffered from a lack of rest and sustenance, a sorry state of affairs that became clear when, on Palm Sunday, on a windswept and snowy day, they again met the Yorkists in battle.[7]

The play depicted this battle, the Battle of Towton, perhaps the biggest and bloodiest domestic clash in English history. Trumpets sounded, flags waved.[8] Tens of thousands of Yorkist troops took on tens of thousands of Lancastrians, their blood reddening the swirling snow.[9] A crowd of actors in armor and helmets dove at one another, their onstage savagery mirroring the violence of the world beyond.

Outside the playhouse, London of the late 1580s and early 1590s was a notably bloody place.[10] Duels at its outskirts were commonplace, and even the well-heeled and the bohemians took part, with young playwrights and scholars knifing their peers and teachers.[11] One of this play's apparent authors, Christopher Marlowe, found himself in the lower dungeon of Newgate prison in 1589 after an altercation near the Theatre left his assailant with a sword stuck six inches into his chest.[12] It is no coincidence that such interpersonal violence suffused *Henry VI, Part 3*, one of the most sadistic of the Shakespearean plays of struggle and strife—embodied above all in Margaret, queen of the carnage.

Most prominently, Margaret's martial presentation in the battle scenes mirrored Queen Elizabeth—who, in rallying English troops against invaders, appeared in armor and spoke some of the most famous wartime oratory in her island's history. This provides critical context to explain the truculent general that Margaret, by this point in *Henry VI, Part 3*, had become. Elizabeth's most famous military conflict began in the spring of 1588, when more than a hundred heavily armed Spanish ships set sail from the hilly Portuguese coast, conveying tens of thousands of soldiers and sailors across the channel to invade England. The English fleet was outnumbered, outgunned, and, by all appearances, outmatched. Yet bad weather delayed the Spanish Armada, and further storms and unfavorable winds aided the swifter, smaller English ships. Late that summer and into the fall, the English definitively repulsed the Armada, and only about half of the troops returned, devastated and mourning their lost comrades, to Spain.

The Armada led to an explosion of works onstage about war, as well as a proliferation of elaborate swordplay and general hostility toward the Catholic monarchy in English theatres—all true of *Henry VI, Part 3*.[13] A number of strikingly xenophobic plays—like this one— ruled the stage in the years after the Armada.[14] And people all across England were beginning to speak of what Queen Elizabeth's trusted alchemist called an "incomparable British Empire."[15]

Yet the English sailors themselves were ill, dispirited, anxious about a Spanish return, and waiting to get paid; everyone else was enduring an extended war of attrition.[16] England's less-remembered "Counter Armada"—its attempted naval invasion of Spain in 1589—failed, further draining public enthusiasm. Around the same time, English attention turned to France, where Elizabeth sent multiple waves of troops to try to help the Protestant King Henri remain on the throne in the face of ferocious opposition from Catholic nobles. Yet the fighting was hard in France. Despite some victories, Henri proved unable to take Paris, and Elizabeth had to withdraw the English troops not long thereafter. (A few years later, much to Elizabeth's chagrin, Henri renounced Protestantism, converted to Catholicism, and in so doing safeguarded his crown.) The loss of English influence in France, due to an ineffectual king named Henri, was as much the backdrop for the *Henry VI* plays as the more famous Armada.[17] Many have noted that, while Shakespeare's history plays are undeniably nationalistic, they are also rather grim.[18]

Still, from this historical moment emerged the image of a militant female monarch leading her nation's army—an image surely recognizable to every member of the original audience for *Henry VI, Part 3*. In August of 1588, Queen Elizabeth arrived on horseback at the port town of Tilbury, reportedly wearing a full set of male armor, ready to rouse her troops to defend English waters against the coming invasion.[19] Turning to the soldiers, Elizabeth proclaimed, "I know I have the body but of a weak and feeble woman; but I have the heart and stomach of a king."[20] This echoes with remarkable similarity the precise words Shakespeare famously yoked to Margaret in *Part 3*: "tiger's heart wrapped in a woman's hide."[21] (The line probably did come from Shakespeare, rather than a collaborator, as it was later parodied to mock him.) It also echoes the words the Tudor chronicler Edward Hall used to describe Margaret: "This woman excelled all other, as well in beautie and favor, as in wit and pollicie, and was of stomack and corage, more like to a man, then a woman."[22] Finally, it echoes a medieval king's description of Margaret's grandmother, Yolande: "a heart of a man in the body of a woman."[23]

In the play and in history, the Yorkists crushed their foes so completely at Towton that many thought the conflict between the two houses finished. The battle devastated both Margaret and Henry. In the play, though, the defeat weighed far more heavily on the king than on the battle-ready queen. The fighting had been nonstop, the tension palpable, but then came a break from all of the action. The actor playing King Henry—one of the production's finest performers, if not its star player—found himself alone on the stage, lamenting that ever he was born to see this fight. Perhaps more than any other scene in the trilogy bearing Henry's name, this tableau would demonstrate that he was a good person—possibly even a good king—though not a leader appropriate for wartime.

There followed a long, sad soliloquy that stretched on for many minutes, and then two soldiers joined Henry onstage, each bearing a large, unsettling prop: the body of a man he had killed in the fray. The first was a son who has killed his father, the second a father who has slain his son. At no other time in the entire cycle of *Henry VI* plays would the toll that war takes on the commoner be clearer than in this scene. Edward may fight for his father and Margaret for her son, but crowns mean nothing to these two men, forced to kill their kin. After their long speeches, the three men, each thinking himself alone, spoke in poetic similes:

KING HENRY
> Woe above woe! Grief more than common grief!
> O that my death would stay these ruthful deeds!
> O pity, pity, gentle heaven, pity! [. . .]

FIRST SOLDIER
> How will my mother for a father's death
> Take on with me, and ne'er be satisfied!

SECOND SOLDIER
> How will my wife for slaughter of my son
> Shed seas of tears, and ne'er be satisfied!

KING HENRY
> How will the country for these woeful chances
> Misthink the King, and not be satisfied!

FIRST SOLDIER

Was ever son so rued a father's death?

SECOND SOLDIER

Was ever father so bemoaned his son?

KING HENRY

Was ever king so grieved for subjects' woe?
Much is your sorrow, mine ten times so much.[24]

Such attention to the bloody wages of civil strife furnished a critique, implicit yet devastating, of warfare. The rivalries of those with power—like Margaret, like Elizabeth—invariably destroy the lives of those without. By the play's end, Margaret herself would bear the grief of a parent who has lost her child.

In history, Margaret fled England following her army's defeat at Towton—first to Scotland, and then to France, where she would remain in exile for most of the next nine years. The Yorks solidified their hold on England, France welcomed a new king, Louis XI, and a displaced Margaret waited. Yet Shakespeare and his collaborators included none of this in the play. After the Battle of Towton (March 1461), Margaret would not appear again on the Shoreditch stage for almost a full act, finally reemerging in a scene set (very loosely) in 1470.

Margaret's 1460s could have provided fodder for a story of adventure to rival those of Pericles, Prospero, Viola, or Antony. During her years in the wilderness, she plotted land invasions of England, went undercover, faced robbers, lived in poverty, operated a court-in-exile, and manipulated the leaders of numerous European countries to support a claim that had little real chance of prevailing. Hardly had she landed on Brittany's shores in 1462 than Margaret entered into secret negotiations with her cousin, Louis XI of France. That summer, with an infusion of French troops, she led a small flotilla back toward

England, determined to strike fear into the heart of Edward IV.[25] The "invasion" was a complete failure, as far stronger Yorkist armies and a devastating storm decimated Margaret's paltry forces; she barely made it ashore in a fishing boat. Margaret fled once again to Scotland, but this time she was swiftly sent packing by its queen.[26] She gathered her few remaining belongings, her son, Prince Edward, and a few nobles still loyal to her and her cause and departed Edinburgh, leaving Henry behind for good.[27]

Though these events did not make it into the play, they informed the character who would return at the close of *Henry VI, Part 3* and then again in *Richard III*. Shakespeare and his collaborators had read deeply; they knew their history well. Most fundamentally, the plays accurately captured the historical figure's indefatigable militancy, a dedication to her own power (and that of her son) unmatched by her pious husband. Penniless and threadbare upon her arrival on the Flemish coast, Margaret sent pleas for help to Philip, the Duke of Burgundy. A chronicler in Philip's court lamented Margaret's penury: "It was a thing piteous to see, truly, this high princess so cast down and laid low in such danger, dying of hunger and hardship."[28] Accompanied by her son and three ladies, she dressed as a peasant and rode to meet the duke herself, driving a horse-pulled wagon all the way to his court, reportedly fleeing a gang of highwaymen along the way.[29] Yet her efforts were for naught; the meeting with the duke was a bust. Defeated, Margaret returned to her father's care and took up residence for the winter at one of his estates in the small walled monastery town of Saint-Mihiel, just over a day's journey from her birthplace at Pont-à-Mousson. She intended to remain in Saint-Mihiel just for the winter. She stayed for seven years.[30] Hundreds of miles from France, meanwhile, Yorkist forces again captured Henry and took him to the Tower of London, where he would remain for years.[31]

Yet all was not lost. Promising whispers made their way to Saint-Mihiel—that King Edward's court was fracturing, that Edward himself had impulsively married a noblewoman of minor birth and major beauty, that the French king (whose niece Edward had been supposed to marry) was seriously offended. In October of 1468, at long last, King Louis promised his support to the English queen—Margaret, that is.[32]

And it was from this geopolitical and romantic mess that Shakespeare picked up the plot of his plays. After years of Margaret's life spent offstage, she reemerged as a central figure in the third scene of the third act of *Henry VI, Part 3*.

The scene began with a flourish—an instrumental fanfare—as the actor playing the French king Louis XI, anglicized by the play as Lewis (and pronounced onstage as "loose"), entered in a procession. The boy-actor playing Margaret followed him, and as Lewis took his seat on his prop throne, the queen-in-exile stood in front of him. Flags or banners probably clarified for the audience that the action had left the island of Britain, the only time this play would depart from English soil.

Standing onstage, in the court of her cousin, Margaret would experience her last hopeful moments—which, tellingly, would be the product of her own persuasive arts and the tactical errors of others, rather than the military incursions she was so fond of leading. War, in this play, was a brutal affair, and its costs—on Margaret as on her subjects—far outweighed its rewards. Unlike her subjects, however, Margaret bore significant responsibility for the war; it was a product of her character's awesome ambition, as all could see.

It is possible that the young actor playing Margaret knew his history, knew about Margaret's decade in exile. But the play—and thus, its audience—did not focus on her travails. Smoothing over much history—forgotten battles, letters, alliances—Shakespeare and his collaborators brought forth the Earl of Warwick—one of Edward's most trusted nobles and Margaret's most detested adversaries—to arrange a treaty between England and France: He had come to propose a marriage between King Edward and Lady Bona, a French royal. Such a match tying France to the Yorkist rulers of England would spell certain doom for Margaret and Henry.

Yet just moments later another figure interrupted the meeting:

A messenger rushed onstage to inform all assembled that King Edward had impulsively married Elizabeth Woodville, a famously alluring Lancastrian widow of shockingly middling birth. Humiliated and furious with his king for this betrayal—the Woodvilles were historic enemies of Warwick's family, the Nevilles—Warwick disavowed Edward and the Yorkist cause:

> I here renounce him and return to Henry.
> My noble Queen, let former grudges pass,
> And henceforth I am thy true servitor.
> I will revenge his wrong to Lady Bona
> And replant Henry in his former state.[33]

Indeed, everyone present was furious with Edward. Everyone, that is, but Margaret, who, by sheer luck (and Edward's spontaneity), had

An early twentieth-century illustration of Margaret pleading her case in the French court.

gained some powerful allies. "Tell him [Edward] my mourning weeds are laid aside," she declared. "And I am ready to put armour on."[34]

As the scene drew to its close, Warwick promised the hand of his daughter, Anne Neville, to Margaret's son, Prince Edward, and Lewis promised France's support for an invasion of Yorkist England. Suddenly, providentially, Margaret was ready, with a new general by her side and the backing of England's greatest foe, to retake the throne—for her husband, for herself. It was a marvelous scene for the character, the actor, and the play. Margaret had again become the figurehead of the Lancastrian cause.[35]

In both history and drama, Margaret certainly did not trust this former Yorkist, but her top priority was to preserve the birthright of her son. If the turncoat Warwick could be the one to topple the House of York, she had no choice but to work with him.[36] And so Warwick set sail, under cover of storm, for England. He landed in Devon and made for London, taking the capital quickly. He marched to the Tower of London, located an aged, starved, ragged Henry, freed him from captivity, and reinstalled him on the throne.[37]

Word of Henry's restoration—known to history as the Readeption—spread quickly to the continent, thrilling King Louis, Queen Margaret, and Prince Edward. Louis ordered great celebrations in Paris, a city where—forty years before, in a completely different geopolitical moment—Henry VI had once been crowned King of France. Now, the French king oversaw efforts to assist the Lancastrian English in their furious fight against the usurping Yorkists.[38] The ceremonies in her honor that Margaret witnessed in Paris no doubt reminded her of the weeks of celebration that had preceded her previous journey from France to England, the one just before her marriage to Henry. But this time, she knew, she would have to be cautious. The life of her son, the sole Lancastrian heir, was of ultimate importance to her cause. She could not move him until she knew, for certain, that he would be safe. If Prince Edward were to die, the Lancastrian line would immediately cease, and all that she had fought for would vanish in an instant.

Through the winter, as 1470 gave way to 1471, Margaret remained in France, waiting for the perfect moment to reemerge victoriously on the soil of her adopted country. A barely seventeen-year-old Prince Edward married Warwick's daughter, Anne Neville, then only fourteen (the same age Margaret had been at her proxy wedding), at the stupendously ornate Cathédrale Saint-Maurice in Angers, where Margaret's grandmother Yolande and mother, Isabella, were buried, and where, in some years, her father, René, and eventually Margaret herself, would also be laid to rest.

As Margaret waited, Edward IV of the House of York, with the assistance of his Burgundian allies, assembled an army to retake the English capital. As winter passed into spring, the Yorkist forces seized London, and, on a fog-clouded morning three days later, Edward met Warwick and his Lancastrian army in combat in the Battle of Barnet. Edward and the Yorkists won the battle decisively, and many Lancastrian nobles, including Warwick himself, died on the field.[39]

The second half of *Henry VI, Part 3* depicted much of this back-and-forth—along with many imagined conversations between Warwick and the York brothers—exemplifying the novel approach of this play. Replete with violence, kidnappings, and murders, it would nonetheless return, inescapably, to the human toll that wars take. Indeed, as the performance inched toward a close, Margaret, perhaps being punished by a male playwright for her overweening ambition, would suffer so exquisitely that she would wish to die—a mercy that, throughout the remainder of the play and the tetralogy, her creator repeatedly would refuse to bestow.

Margaret's last stand—at the Battle of Tewkesbury—was a grand but baleful one. Just moments after Edward told his men that he spied "a black suspicious threatening cloud"—Margaret's approaching forces—the queen herself strode onstage, followed by her son, the Duke of Somerset, and the Earl of Oxford (the only Lancastrian nobles left standing at this point in the play), along with whatever soldiers bearing the Lancastrian shield could be summoned from the cast to appear beside them.[40]

Audiences in this Elizabethan theatre, about 120 years removed from the events at Tewkesbury—a small Gloucestershire town about 120 miles northwest of London—might not have known the details of the upcoming battle, but if they remembered the shape of the Wars of the Roses, they knew well this battle's outcome.

The boy-actor playing Margaret walked to the front of the stage, the boy-actor playing her son, Edward, affectionately called Ned, in her/his wake. All eyes turned to the queen. Margaret's speech must have reminded those present of Elizabeth's famous words at Tilbury, when that queen too had to electrify the masses in defense of the motherland.[41]

MARGARET
> Great lords, wise men ne'er sit and wail their loss,
> But cheerly seek how to redress their harms.
> What though the mast be now blown overboard,
> The cable broke, the holding-anchor lost,
> And half our sailors swallowed in the flood?
> Yet lives our pilot still. Is't meet that he
> Should leave the helm and, like a fearful lad,
> With tearful eyes add water to the sea,
> And give more strength to that which hath too much,
> Whiles, in his moan, the ship splits on the rock
> Which industry and courage might have saved?
> Ah, what a shame; ah, what a fault were this.
> Say Warwick was our anchor—what of that?
> And Montague our top-mast—what of him?
> Our slaughtered friends the tackles—what of these?
> Why, is not Oxford here another anchor?
> And Somerset another goodly mast?
> The friends of France our shrouds and tacklings?
> And, though unskilful, why not Ned and I
> For once allowed the skilful pilot's charge?

> We will not from the helm to sit and weep,
> But keep our course, though the rough wind say no,
> From shelves and rocks that threaten us with wreck.
> As good to chide the waves as speak them fair.
> And what is Edward but ruthless sea?
> What Clarence but a quicksand of deceit?
> And Richard but a raggèd fatal rock?
> All these the enemies to our poor barque.
> Say you can swim—alas, 'tis but awhile;
> Tread on the sand—why, there you quickly sink;
> Bestride the rock—the tide will wash you off,
> Or else you famish. That's a threefold death.
> This speak I, lords, to let you understand,
> If case some one of you would fly from us,
> That there's no hoped-for mercy with the brothers York
> More than with ruthless waves, with sands, and rocks.
> Why, courage then—what cannot be avoided
> 'Twere childish weakness to lament or fear.[42]

This battlefield speech, Margaret's ultimate entreaty, did not contain the same inspiring exhortations that Shakespeare would later give her father-in-law in his appeals to violent nationalism in *Henry V*: There was no command to travel "once more unto the breach," no offer that "he today who sheds his blood with me / Shall be my brother."[43] Her speech did not mention England or St. George. Hers was a declaration of purpose—that purpose being, as it had been for over a decade, to retake her throne and ensure her son's inheritance. The speech was meditative, mournful even, a playwright's omen of impending doom.

Historically, Margaret, her son, Prince Edward, and her followers landed on the English coast the very day that the Lancastrian forces killed her fair-weather ally, Warwick, and crushed his forces. She had hoped that she might land as queen, bearing with her the heir to the throne. Had she arrived earlier, she and her troops might have been able to assist Warwick in battle and bring defeat upon the House of

York once and for all. Instead, she was met with devastation and the need to, once more, rally the followers who remained to her.[44]

Margaret and her troops moved west, hoping to find assistance from the armies of Jasper Tudor, King Henry's half brother, and Jasper's nephew, Henry Tudor, in Wales.[45] Such hopes were dashed when, after weeks of marching her army day and night across the English countryside (at one point pressing her soldiers to trudge fifty-seven miles in about forty-eight hours), the Lancastrian and Yorkist armies met at Tewkesbury on the morning of May 4, 1471. Margaret spent the night before the battle at Gupshill Manor (a house that still stands today and operates as a pub), and in the morning, she assembled her armies next to the River Avon, the very waterway that, a century later, a young Shakespeare would come to know in his hometown of Stratford.[46]

According to the chronicles, in the moments before the Battle of Tewkesbury began, Margaret mounted her horse and rode up and down the line of Lancastrian troops. She commanded as many as six thousand men, and she called to all who could hear her voice, urging the men to fight bravely for their country and for King Henry. Not if, but *when* they won the battle, they would see great rewards. After her cry to arms, she had a private conversation with her son, the hope of the Lancastrian cause, preparing to fight in his first battle. Historians do not know what she said.[47] But Shakespeare (and several computational analyses suggest the author of this scene was indeed Shakespeare) gave her a striking piece of oratory, a speech of defiance in the face of mounting doom.[48]

In a remarkable (and unhistorical) moment following Margaret's battlefield speech, King Edward IV entered the stage and the two shared a few lines of reflection before they met in battle. It was a moment akin to a split screen in a modern film, both leaders standing onstage and speaking to their armies independently. The author did not make it clear if the characters saw each other or were in separate locations—that he left to the actors. Margaret, with flint in her eye and fire in her gut, then turned to her troops once more, this time asking for blood:

> Lords, knights, and gentlemen—what I should say
> My tears gainsay; for every word I speak
> Ye see I drink the water of my eye.
> Therefore, no more but this: Henry, your sovereign
> Is prisoner to the foe, his state usurped,
> His realm a slaughter-house, his subjects slain,
> His statutes cancelled, and his treasure spent—
> And yonder is the wolf that makes this spoil.
> You fight in justice; then, in God's name, lords,
> Be valiant, and give signal to the fight.[49]

In text published years after Shakespeare's death, the scene would end with an evocative stage direction: "Alarum, retreat, excursions. Exeunt."[50]

In real life, Margaret did not fight at Tewkesbury. She waited nearby, and when news of the worst arrived—her armies had lost, and more importantly, her only child was killed—she hid, with a few of her ladies, including her daughter-in-law, Anne Neville, who had lost a father and a husband in quick succession. Yorkist troops found them a few days later and seized them as prisoners.[51]

Elizabethan audiences would witness the loss and capture as a pietà—a scene in which Margaret cradled her son after he was stabbed by Edward and Richard—but this almost certainly did not happen.[52] Shakespeare's queen then begged for death from the three York brothers—but did not receive it. "Murder is thy alms-deed," she cried. "Petitioners for blood thou ne'er put'st back." Instead, King Edward ordered her sent away, and she left him with a curse: "So come to you and yours as to this Prince!"[53]

With that, Margaret was carried away, not to be seen again in the trilogy of plays bearing her husband's name. It was a strikingly disempowering end for this strong woman—defeated, she could not even compel the men opposing her to take her life.[54]

In the play's final moments, King Edward's wife, Elizabeth, appeared on the stage with her newborn son (a prop, most likely). This image of traditional femininity (albeit represented by a boy in a wig) made for a subtle contrast with Elizabeth's martial predecessor, Margaret.[55] At the very end, then, in its symbolism, the play implicitly condemned Margaret's model of leadership, of motherhood, even though so much of the play had exulted in her subversions and boldness.

The audience filed out, back into the cold, bracing air and the hot, teeming crowds, horrified or satisfied (or both) by the performance that had just concluded. Most likely, few lamented that they had not gotten to witness the events in Margaret's life after Tewkesbury (though Shakespeare would soon imagine a vengeful, mournful

A nineteenth-century painting of Queen Margaret
cradling her son at Tewkesbury.

An early twentieth-century illustration of Richard of Gloucester (the future Richard III) killing Henry VI.

return for her in *Richard III*). In history, just weeks after crushing Margaret, Edward IV reentered London as the undisputed king of England, a title he would keep for the rest of his life. With Prince Edward dead and his parents in captivity, the Lancastrian bloodline had been severed. King Edward triumphantly advertised his prisoner Margaret as one of the brightest baubles of Yorkist victory. It was almost exactly ten years since the bloody Battle of Towton, which had cemented Edward's first claim to the throne and sent Margaret and Henry fleeing.[56]

One spring night in 1471, days after the defeat of the Lancastrian dynasty at the Battle of Tewkesbury, King Edward's troops took Margaret to the Tower, where she was to be imprisoned until the king and his advisers could figure out what to do with her. That very night, Henry died—murdered, the play proposed, by Richard, the future king of England. Only half a millennium later would forensic evidence—dried blood on an ancient, cracked skull—emerge that supported the playwright's theory of regicide.[57]

It is likely, though it cannot be proven, that Henry and Margaret were kept in nearby or even in adjacent cells for that final, fatal evening.

It is unlikely, though this too cannot be proven, that either knew the other was there, just feet away, weeping for the world that might have been.[58]

$$\cdot\ 6\ \cdot$$

"As Lightning from the Sky"

Her Return

The play that we now call *Henry VI, Part 1* opened to a packed house on the afternoon of Friday, March 3, 1592.[1] Excitement surely pulsed through the crowd. The audience members—artisans and laborers, butchers and cobblers, lords and ladies—had traipsed over Rose Alley from the west, or walked across Maiden Lane from the south, or even cut through a hedgerow from the east to get there.[2] If the year's drought were not yet so severe that it restricted boat crossings, they may have arrived by ferry, crossing the Thames from the north. Roughly a thousand of them crowded the galleries of the Rose Theatre, with still hundreds more on the ground.[3] All were there to see the prequel to two recent—and clearly beloved—plays.

For the actors, and especially for the man funding the whole enterprise, a lot was riding on this new production. Philip Henslowe, the Rose's cunning proprietor, had secured the presence of that night's company of actors, the Lord Strange's Men, just months before. The company was on the rise—they had just performed before the queen an unprecedented number of times over the Christmas season, and London's dashing star actor, Edward Alleyn, had recently joined their ranks.[4] In anticipation of the Lord Strange's Men performing at his theatre, Henslowe had shelled out more than £100 to renovate the Rose in the first days of 1592.[5] With an outbreak of plague compelling the closure of the city's theatres, a fleet of workmen constructed a new roof (a "heavens") for the Rose, to shield the stage from the elements (even as the groundlings remained exposed). They also added new balusters, new brick walls, a new dressing room, an actual ship's mast (from which to fly the flag bearing the emblem of the rose), and lots of fresh, exuberantly colorful paint.[6] Above all, the renovation expanded the Rose's capacity—a sign of Henslowe's confidence, and his ambition.[7]

For Henslowe, then, it was vital that the Lord Strange's Men recoup his outlay. Alleyn, too, needed his company's performances to make a mark; he may have been risking stability and status in moving to the Lord Strange's Men.[8]

Things had not been going terribly well. The Rose had reopened for business on February 19, a Saturday afternoon, with Strange's Men trying their hands at *Friar Bacon and Friar Bungay* before a half-filled house. So eager was Henslowe to recover his investment that he had the actors put on another play the next day, even though playing on Sunday was technically illegal. Yet that performance, too, was far from a hit. A week later, Strange's Men found more success putting on Christopher Marlowe's much-loved *Jew of Malta*, with Alleyn a horrifying sight in the miserly title role of Barabas (a character familiar to Elizabethans for his role in Christ's passion). But all of this was prologue for the real attraction—a new play by young Will Shakespeare (and probably several others, too) to open on Friday, March 3.[9]

At last, actors emerged onstage, entering through multiple openings in the surrounding walls.[10] They strode over wooden planks, resting atop a "floor" of compacted earth.[11] Painted cloths likely hung from the support posts.[12] The galleries were high, the acoustics a marvel—even a whisper could bounce from wall to wall.[13]

The play opened, as would many of Shakespeare's plays—*Richard III*, *Titus Andronicus*, and *Hamlet*—with a funeral, that of King Henry V (father of Henry VI). "Hung be the heavens with black," called out one actor, his words full of portent. "Yield day to night."[14]

For the next few hours, the Lord Strange's Men thrilled the

audience with sensational action, exhilarating combat scenes, and even explosions. Pyrotechnics lit up the groundlings' faces.[15] The actors strode back and forth across a part of the stage that thrust directly out into the ground, where audience members stood.[16] Alleyn probably played Sir John Talbot, a gallant English soldier—and one of the play's central figures.[17]

When all was said and done, Henslowe—who claimed half of the pennies eagerly forked over at the door—recorded earnings of more than £3 for "harey the vj," as he scrawled in his diary (apparently indicating "VI" with "vj" in this age of variable spelling). This was a *very* good night. Over the next nine months, in fact, Strange's Men would put on "harey the vj" at least seventeen more times, yielding a handsome £33 and change for Henslowe.[18]

The new play was a smash.[19] It would generate a buzz of interest in (and resentment toward) young Shakespeare, whose principal role in writing the play is again evident in the credit he would receive for it from his contemporaries—though, like the other *Henry VI* plays, *Part 1* too was almost certainly the product of collaboration. Soon, the buzz surrounding Shakespeare grew into a rumble that grew into a roar that has never really abated. The play would ensure profits and accolades for Henslowe and the Lord Strange's Men. And it would mark the return—albeit a brief one—of one of Will's most enigmatic characters: Margaret of Anjou.

Set over two decades, *Henry VI, Part 1* establishes the social and geopolitical conflicts that simmered and overflowed in *Part 2, Part 3,* and later *Richard III.* Whether *Henry VI, Part 1* works today as a standalone drama—scholars disagree, and contemporary directors seem to think it does not—the play inarguably contains several elements that, in performance, would have delighted the audience at the Rose. This one play boasts numerous scenes of conflict, court intrigue, scheming foreign leaders, lengthy eloquent speeches, a divine and pugnacious female warrior, a supernatural conjuration scene replete with demons crawling over the stage, and a full utilization of the Rose's many elevations, with actors traversing multiple levels on backstage staircases and onstage ladders. The play assembles the events of twenty-two turbulent years of two countries' history into two hours' frenetic traffic of the Rose's stage.

That spring afternoon in 1592, the audience saw two warriors leading opposing armies: Lord Talbot commanded English forces working to save their territories in France, and Joan Puzel (known to history as Joan of Arc) led French troops to drive out the English invaders and regain the land lost to the dead British king Henry V. Viewers must have sensed the dissatisfaction that festered in an England beset by war, a disquiet epitomized in the moment that the long-ruling House of Plantagenet split into the House of Lancaster and the House of York.[20] Shakespeare created a scene to depict this split—set in the garden of Temple Hall in London—in which Henry's followers, the Lancastrians, affix a red rose to their garments while the Yorkists identify themselves with a white one. In this scene, the playwright established a visual iconography that demonstrated to any confused groundling watching the performance who fights for which side. This unambiguous symbolism—the red Lancaster and the white York—would forever dominate subsequent public imaginings of the civil wars and lay the groundwork for the nineteenth-century retroactive retitling of the conflict as the Wars of the Roses.[21]

The image of red and white roses is one of the few lasting influences of this oddly erratic play. So inconsistent is the surviving text (one character is variably referred to as a bishop and as a cardinal) that few today doubt it was the product of collaboration.[22] Many have concluded that act 1 was written separately—probably by Thomas Nashe, a satirist, pamphleteer, and playwright. The involvement of Christopher Marlowe in writing the play's later acts is supported by modern computer studies. Shakespeare's precise role has been the subject of fervent debate for centuries. Some suggest that Shakespeare was not even one of the play's original coauthors, but rather that the play we know today as *Henry VI, Part 1* is the product of his later revisions. Others disagree. Remarkably, though, few scholars quibble with Shakespeare's primary authorship of the Temple Garden scene (an event he invented out of whole cloth, without basis in the Tudor chronicles).[23]

Margaret appears—a princess and a prisoner—in only one scene of *Henry VI, Part 1*. So passing is her presence, in fact, that some have argued that the play that debuted in 1592 could have been performed without Margaret entirely—that her brief cameo was the product of Shakespeare's later revision.[24] Yet it is undeniable that Margaret's presence pulses through the play—in Henry (her future husband), in the Duke of Suffolk (her future lover), and most prominently in the figure of another young Frenchwoman, the peasant girl from Domrémy, Joan of Arc.

For any audience members who had arrived at the Rose expecting to see a play focused on the familiar character of Henry VI, they must have experienced a flash of shock at discovering that Joan was the show's central figure. If Joan Puzel, as she would call herself in the play, was not its protagonist (the play obviously aligns itself ideologically with the English forces), she was certainly its antihero.[25] In history, Joan called herself "la pucelle," French for maid or virgin, and the play deploys the near-homonymous "puzel," meaning whore.[26] The character of Joan was almost certainly written after the Margaret of *Part 2* and *Part 3*, and the influence must have been clear to all: Like Margaret, Joan would emasculate the men who doubt her, spar with the Duke of York, and fight for her country.[27]

Joan first appeared onstage just minutes into *Part 1*, claiming to have been heralded a savior by heaven and goading any man present to test her mettle. "My courage try by combat, if thou dar'st," she sang out. "And thou shalt find that I exceed my sex."[28]

Like Margaret, this warrior represented a double evil: She was a woman and she was foreign.[29] Played by yet another boy wearing a blond wig, Joan represented an ultimate horror for the patriarchal order.[30] She was a woman and yet she was stronger than all the men who surround her; she was foreign and yet she served her country better than any man.[31]

In these two characters, foreignness, femaleness, and Catholicism (and all the fears of it during Elizabeth's reign) merged to create figures who threatened the contemporary English order.[32] Throughout *Part 1*, Joan relied heavily on prayer, and she repeatedly invoked the Virgin Mary. Yet, in her downfall, she strayed; in her moment of need, she called demons to the stage to assist her—much like her predecessor on the Shakespearean stage, Eleanor Cobham.[33] "Appear, and aid me in this enterprise!" the bewigged boy-actor cried.[34] In the eyes of the more zealous Protestants of Elizabeth's England, the line separating Catholic practice and witchcraft was unclear—and frightening.[35]

Though both women led their armies to success in the chronicle plays, Joan one-upped Margaret on martial terms, repeatedly engaging in combat onstage. Though Joan was more physically aggressive than Margaret, the women shared in their oratorical gifts. Joan's speech before the Duke of Burgundy, asking for his support against the English, repeatedly invoked her womanhood and recalled Margaret's speech to her troops at Tewkesbury. "Look on thy country, look on fertile France," she declared, her armor flashing. "And see the cities and the towns defaced / By wasting ruin of the cruel foe."[36] In part due to the rhetorical power of this speechifying, many modern scholars believe Marlowe, not Shakespeare, wrote the bulk of the scenes involving Joan. This has some support in the computer models that analyze texts for distinctive word choices—although it's also true that early critics may have shied away from attributing Joan's more vulgar and risqué passages to their beloved Bard.[37] Ultimately, it matters little; Margaret and Joan echo one another regardless of who wrote which scenes.

In the Tudor chronicles on which the play was based, neither Joan nor even Talbot figured prominently. The play was virtually a battle of the sexes—Joan versus Talbot—in which both ultimately perished. So radically did the play's authors recast history that Joan was even present at Talbot's death—though Talbot actually died almost a quarter century after Joan was burned at the stake.[38] Why do this? One obvious answer is that Shakespeare, or Marlowe, or even the audience, was still working through the anxiety of living in a patriarchal world with an aging, childless "virgin" queen in power.[39] Joan, a general, pronounced herself a virgin, but the play revealed her promiscuity. Similar, conspiratorial rumors flew concerning the sex life of Queen Elizabeth.[40]

As she did in history, Joan left the play suddenly; she was abruptly captured and sentenced to death by the English. Richard, Duke of York, called Joan "the ugly witch" and "fell banning hag," names that evoked the misogynist taunts that Yorkists would throw at Margaret in *Part 3* and *Richard III.* She was hastily swept offstage mere moments before Margaret made her first entrance.[41] The two women, whose paths never crossed in reality (indeed, Margaret had just passed her first birthday when Joan died), passed a symbolic torch—one French interloper replaced another.[42]

The afternoon at the playhouse was winding down when the boy-actor playing Margaret finally made his entrance—an entrée for an ambitious young player to interpret ambiguous text according to his own whims, and, if he wished, to add tenderness to a violent play, to inject nuance into a misogynistic work, to broaden the characterization of a now-familiar, memorable queen.

A story that had, until then, depicted revolution, bloodshed, and gender transgression pivoted, awkwardly and immediately, into romantic comedy.[43] Margaret, a young man playing a young woman, entered the stage on the arm of the Duke of Suffolk, a senior courtier to King Henry. Clearly besotted, Suffolk proclaimed "thou art my prisoner" but then followed up this declaration with his purplest prose:

> O fairest beauty, do not fear nor fly,
> For I will touch thee but with reverent hands,
> And lay them gently on thy tender side.
> I kiss these fingers for eternal peace.[44]

Suffolk had the power over his "prisoner" in this scene, yet he could not act; he was far too taken with the princess to exercise any authority.

Margaret, ever canny, recognized that he lacked such competency in her presence: "He talks at random; sure the man is mad," she murmured to herself, or really, to her audience.[45]

Was this Margaret a naïve child, the very "gentle princess" that Suffolk believed her to be? Or was she something more? Did the tiger's heart beat in the chest of a warrior biding her time, ready to seize control? The play, likely purposefully, did not give an answer. Shakespeare, as he often did, left this for the actor to decide.

The two characters bantered and bickered, largely in asides, for most of their time together. No doubt many were charmed. Suffolk reminded himself of his mission—and that he was married—and Margaret teased him for his kindly incompetence. The two make an odd pair: an established military leader, speaking only to himself, and a young foreign woman, a prisoner in name only, each pleased with the other and leading themselves toward love. Much like first-time viewers of *Romeo and Juliet* (a play premiering around the same time), those seeing this scene might not have expected this gentle flirtation to end the grisly way it does. But any playgoer at the Rose who had seen the earlier *Henry VI* plays knew that this love affair, beginning with banter and bashfulness, would lead to a tormented liaison and gruesome decapitation—lending this exchange a subtle poignancy.

And yet, in this scene, love blossomed quickly and Suffolk could not help himself.[46] The flirtatious wordplay and verbal jests today summon to mind similar passages in Shakespeare's comedies, notably *Love's Labour's Lost* and *Much Ado About Nothing*.[47] Suffolk's "She's beautiful, and therefore to be wooed; / She is a woman, therefore to be won" recalls comparable remarks from characters like *Much Ado*'s Benedick or *The Taming of the Shrew*'s Petruchio.[48] In this single episode, one surrounded by political chicanery and scenes of battle, Shakespeare the charmer came out.

Margaret's motivation in the scene was then, and is now, unclear, as is her awareness of her situation. Does she think she has a choice in her marriage to the king? Does she fear Suffolk, or does she immediately figure out how to manipulate him? How sincere is she, really? To answer these questions, the actor in the role must decide if this wry young woman is the same savage queen found in *Part 2* and *Part 3*. Margaret's speech in this play is limited—she recites only thirty-three lines. From text alone, it is difficult to discern how much she knows, of what she is capable, or what she wants. It's up to the actor.

After its strong debut on March 3, 1592, the new play was unquestionably a hit.[49] Just four days later, the Lord Strange's Men staged it again. Additional performances followed every week or two for the next four months—this, in a time when audiences usually demanded novelty.[50] In all, at least ten thousand spectators crowded in

An early twentieth-century illustration of Suffolk wooing Margaret.

for *Henry VI, Part 1*.[51] So rapturous may have been the reception, and so consistent may have been the demand, that the other two *Henry VI* plays may well have been playing that spring as well, in different theatres across London.

Edward Alleyn's star turn as Talbot was probably one of the new show's principal draws. The handsome leading man was the most famous actor in the country. One account claims his Talbot moved audiences to tears—a striking reaction at a time when the emotion usually attributed to audiences was laughter.[52] Such an audience probably included Lord Strange himself, not just because his Men were up onstage but because he was closely associated with direct descendants of Talbot.[53]

The audience also included a strange, smart, strident man named Thomas Nashe. Three years Shakespeare's junior, but with a Cambridge degree, Nashe had moved to London around the same time as the boy from Stratford and quickly established himself as one of the more biting of the University Wits. Today, precious little of his writing survives. Extant works include just one of his plays, a long-unpublished erotic poem known indelicately as "Nashe's Dildo," and, most relevant here, a satirical pamphlet published in London in August 1592, titled *Pierce Pennilesse: His Supplication to the Divell*. The pamphlet is the plea of a man named Pierce, directed at the devil. To stare long enough at its crumbling pages is to glimpse hints about the popularity of *Henry VI, Part 1*.[54]

Much of *Pierce Pennilesse* was devoted to defending theatre against "shallow-braind censurers"—arguing, for instance, that history plays were an effective antidote to "these degenerate effeminate dayes of ours." As an example, Nashe invoked "brave Talbot (the terror of the French)," who (Nashe imagined) would have been thrilled to learn that he had returned to life a century and a half after his death to move audiences. Nashe had to be referring to the Talbot of *Henry VI, Part 1*—it is the only surviving play from this time to feature the character, and the descriptor "terror of the French" appeared in both Hall's chronicle and the text of the play itself.[55]

Some have suggested that Nashe's enthusiasm stemmed in part

from his own role as a collaborator.[56] Intriguingly, Nashe dedicated *Pierce Pennilesse* to Lord Strange, who had bankrolled the production.[57] Yet it is worth noting that Talbot featured in scenes that are not usually attributed to Nashe.[58] Far more likely, then, that its reference to Talbot simply signaled the character's—and the play's—popularity. After all, Nashe could count on his readers getting his reference.

Just a month after the publication of *Pierce Pennilesse*, another pamphlet entered the Stationers' Register, this one written by another of the University Wits, Robert Greene. A good-looking man with a red beard and mane, Greene had worked hard to distance himself from his humble roots, obtaining degrees from both Cambridge and Oxford—before sacrificing a life of refined prosperity to his addiction to London's underworld.[59] In short order, Greene apparently frittered away his wife's dowry, abandoned her and their young child, and descended so deeply into debt that he was forced to shield himself from arrest by paying a bodyguard known as Cutting Ball.[60] Pompous and prolific, Greene spent his days pumping out plays, poems, novels, and other works at a feverish pace, desperate to remain liquid enough to slake a seemingly insatiable thirst for drink.[61] (So unquenchable were his appetites, in fact, that some have speculated he was the model for Shakespeare's character of Falstaff.[62]) Late that summer of 1592, Greene dined with his friend and fellow Wit Thomas Nashe, gorging himself on pickled herring and Rhenish wine.[63] The hearty meal broke whatever was left of Greene's fragile health. Sick, destitute, and teeming with lice, he avoided the streets only by finding shelter in the home of a poor shoemaker. He dwindled for weeks, finally succumbing before even reaching his mid-thirties.[64]

Greene's wretched death triggered a swell of voyeuristic interest, and accounts of his last days soon hit London bookstalls. These were followed, shortly thereafter, by a pair of pamphlets allegedly containing Greene's final words.[65] The first was a pamphlet titled *Greene's Groats-worth of Witte*, much of it a barely disguised autobiographical sketch (the protagonist a young man named "Roberto," rather than Robert). A haphazard jumble of Greene's near-illegible final scrawlings, *Groats-worth* eventually turned to discussing the playhouse itself. While Nashe had defended theatre, Greene attacked it, especially actors—especially one actor in particular: "Yes trust them not: for there is an vpstart Crow, beautified with our feathers, that with his *Tygers hart wrapt in a Players hyde*, supposes he is as well able to bombast out a blanke verse as the best of you: and being an absolute *Johannes fac totum*, is in his owne conceit the onely Shake-scene in a countrey."[66]

Since the early eighteenth century, readers have concluded that Greene was clearly alluding to Shakespeare—not only in the pointed pun, "Shake-scene," but also in the italicized "*Tygers hart wrapt in a Players hyde*," which obviously recalls York's description of Margaret as having a "tiger's heart wrapped in a woman's hide."[67] Many believe that Greene was accusing Shakespeare of plagiarism—an "upstart" who was not to be trusted, who had "beautified" himself with "our feathers," who presumptuously "supposes" he can write as well as his more educated, bohemian betters.[68]

The fact that, in disparaging his fellow playwright, Greene invoked a description of Margaret is highly significant. This was no throwaway line from *Henry VI, Part 3*, but rather a powerful, pivotal accusation in one of the play's most memorable scenes.[69] Greene was also expressly comparing Shakespeare to Margaret, a male playwright to a female monster, with Shakespeare's presumption as an artist cast as equivalent to Margaret's transgression as a woman.[70] Both Margaret and Will have forgotten their proper place. There is an irony to this analogy, for Shakespeare is being likened to the depiction of Margaret at her cruelest.[71] It is especially ironic to consider that Greene himself—at best, an inconsistent playwright—was at his strongest when writing female characters. In fact, Greene's play *Friar Bacon and Friar Bungay*, which had returned to the stage just two weeks before *Henry VI, Part 1*, featured a memorable female character named Margaret.[72]

Some have suggested that *Groats-worth* was a forgery—that someone other than Greene, perhaps even Nashe, wrote the "Shake-scene" passage in *Groats-worth*. Indeed, a few weeks later, a wholly different set of Greene's "last words," *The Repentance of Robert Greene*, hit the bookstalls. The latter is a much less bitter document; it is hard to imagine both are genuine.[73] Yet whether Greene himself was truly the (sole) author of *Groats-worth*, the passage itself is evidence that Shakespeare, and Margaret, were memorable, even famous, and linked. After all, Greene not only recalled the scene but knew his readers would too.[74]

In the days and weeks after *Groats-worth* appeared, its charges echoed through London's literary society. Several playwrights objected to Greene's characterizations, leading the man who had edited the pamphlet to hastily issue an apology. In a revised version of *Pierce Penilesse* released around this time, Nashe vehemently denied the rumors that he was also the author of *Groats-worth*.[75]

After Greene's attack, it appears Will largely stopped working with others—an inflection point in the young man's career. "Shakespeare, atypically for a professional playwright in this period, apparently did not write another collaborative play for more than a decade," the scholar Gary Taylor noted, as "the upstart crow set out to demonstrate to the world that he did not need anyone else's feathers."[76]

Yet even as the young playwright set off on his own, he would remain fixated on the character of Margaret.

Between mid-February and mid-June of 1592, the Lord Strange's Men put on more than a hundred performances at the Rose, laboring six days a week over eighteen weeks (with Good Friday a rare day off).[77] This kind of sustained residency in one playhouse was a novelty and an innovation.[78] Indeed, it may well have been the first time a company had ever played a "season" in London, focusing so squarely on the city rather than merely visiting it as part of a tour.[79]

This remarkable run ended with a bang that June. The trouble started after debt collectors violently arrested a servant and threw him in Marshalsea, a widely loathed prison in Southwark—often the place to which debtors were dragged. That afternoon, a group of apprentices gathered at the Rose and then marched together to Marshalsea to demand the servant's release. A rowdy crowd of war veterans and other men—no doubt angered by a recent rise in taxes and unemployment, as well as the summer heat—joined them. A standoff ensued at the prison, with each side armed. Hearing of the commotion around 8 p.m., the lord mayor hastened to the scene and read a proclamation to the "great multitudes of people," as he later recorded. Although his quick arrival stopped the crowd from storming the prison, tensions simmered across London in the days that followed. The lord mayor determined that the crowd had "assembled . . . at a play." The theatre itself, he wrote, "giveth opportunitie of committing these & such lyke disorders." Seeking to head off another popular uprising, the Privy Council increased patrols and commanded a stop to all plays until the Feast of St. Michael, more than three months away (in late September).[80]

The feverish anger pulsing through London refused to break. It was a blisteringly hot, dry summer, and many native Englishmen were blaming immigrants for their economic woes. Then, in August, the plague returned to London. Much of public life—schools, dances, public meetings—shut down immediately. The courts closed except to hear the most serious cases. Queen Elizabeth forbade anyone but a few councilors and servants from coming within two miles of her retinue.[81]

As winter approached and the city grew colder, caseloads increased—and thousands perished.[82] Graveyards overflowed with recent victims.[83] Plagues were cacophonous tragedies—in some places, bells tolled with each reported illness and rang for an hour or longer with each funeral, often resulting in an almost continuous din.[84]

Orders from on high demanded that the houses of those infected be shuttered for more than a month, with the sick and their entire families subject to strictest quarantine. The clothes and bedding of plague victims were burnt, and people desperately experimented with roots, onions, amulets, spices, and objects dipped in vinegar to ward off disease. The remains of the dead piled up in graveyards and on the carts of body bearers. Watchmen patrolled the streets to enforce plague closures (and provide the quarantined "inmates" with food), generating fear, resentment, and terrifying rumors. Draconian punishment was threatened for anyone who so much as criticized the plague rules.[85]

The plague was devastating for London's burgeoning theatrical scene. The Privy Council—already itching to prohibit plays—extended the shutdown of theatres for months, destroying some companies and scattering others to the hinterlands.[86] Desperate for money, the Lord Strange's Men promptly hit the road, touring the country that summer and fall, likely taking *Henry VI, Part 1* with them.[87] It was a whirlwind trip—with stops in Cambridge, Rye, Canterbury, Bristol, Shrewsbury, Chester, York, Ipswich, Bath, and Oxford.[88]

The life of a touring company was not easy—the bumping of the wagon on rough roads, the physical strain of setting up and tearing down the stage, the possibility of a rude or violent welcome.[89] Further, the constant travel probably prevented the players from adding new plays to their repertory. Yet this might mean that the Lord Strange's Men carried Margaret to many more audiences than they otherwise would have. Thus, during the plague-stricken year of 1592, men, women, and children all across England might have briefly encountered the princess of Anjou.

Her principal creator probably filled the months of plague with writing.[90] Shakespeare may have stayed in London to create new works, grateful for the silence and solitude. He may have returned home to Stratford, which appears to have avoided the plague.[91] Some biographers have even speculated that he left England entirely, pointing to a heap of travel imagery in his works from the time.[92] Wherever he was, it would prove to be an uncommonly productive time for the young playwright.

The plague ebbed enough for the Lord Strange's Men to return to the Rose at the end of December 1592, reviving *Henry VI, Part 1*, as well as many of their other plays from earlier in the year.[93] Among the company's new works was *The Massacre at Paris*, written by Christopher Marlowe, who was enmeshed in ever-mounting legal difficulties. It survives as a short, ungainly play, clearly dependent on other popular works of the time, borrowing from other Marlowe plays and from *Henry VI, Part 2* and *Part 3*.[94]

Still, the return of the Lord Strange's Men was well received, and *The Massacre at Paris* made out very well at the box office. The plague-stricken populace, riding out a freezing winter, was starved for entertainment. The company was invited to perform at court three times after Christmas. Yet the comeback was not to last long. The persistence of the plague had shuttered the theatres once more by early February 1593.[95] Beggars packed the streets of London; some observers warned that the vagrants wished to abolish private property.[96] Parliament assembled, intent on quashing dissent on the home front.[97] The Lord Strange's Men hit the road again.[98] Weeks stretched into months. Some may have believed the theatres would never reopen.[99]

When the playhouses closed, Shakespeare turned to poetry. His first poem, *Venus and Adonis*, hit bookstalls in 1593 and his second, *The Rape of Lucrece*, was printed the following year.[100] The wildly successful publications swelled the popular esteem for Shakespeare—to the point that before the late 1590s, he was largely thought of as a poet, not a playwright.[101] In the female protagonists of these poems, Lucrece and especially Venus—and in another stage heroine that he created at this time, Katherina of *The Taming of the Shrew*—the young writer tested his audience's limits for challenging female characters. All of these women are of a type with Margaret, though only she has four plays and hundreds of lines in which a playwright can most thoroughly probe female contradiction. It was a theme that Shakespeare most richly explored through these characters at the beginning of his career—and one far less present as he became a more seasoned playwright. In the poetry, Shakespeare also tested the limits of the dramatic form: What was possible in verse on the page that was not possible on the stage? Was certain behavior, especially in complex women, easier to portray when the creator need not depend on the fickle skills of a teenage boy?

In Shakespeare's early dramas, he looked to England's recent past, but in these poems he looked to the Roman poet Ovid (although, as always, Shakespeare departed substantially from his source).[102] Both poems endow their female protagonists with an interiority not usually seen in drama, as Shakespeare renders their thoughts as well as their speech and actions in his nondramatic verse. In *The Rape of Lucrece*, Shakespeare tells the story of a woman who, like Margaret, navigates treacherous and tragic territory in a man's world—and who, like Margaret, endures terrible hardships inflicted by men.

Venus and Adonis, the richer poem, is filled with florid imagery and allusion. It tells the story of Venus, the Roman goddess of love, who, in mortal form, becomes enamored of the human Adonis, a beautiful youth who spurns her affections and looks for intimacy elsewhere. Margaret's presence in the poem is clear. Shakespeare almost certainly wrote *Venus and Adonis* after his *Henry VI* plays, and probably just around the time that he was planning, or even composing, Margaret's return from exile in *Richard III*. In the poem, Shakespeare grants his goddess an astonishing inner life, as the narrator delves into the consciousness of the heroine. Venus's passions recall Margaret's tender words for Suffolk, and her forthrightness echoes Margaret's assertiveness toward her enemies and her allies. Like Margaret, Venus is messy and contradictory, prickly and imperfect, in ways that some of Shakespeare's later heroines—like Viola or Desdemona— would not be.

Even *Henry VI, Part 1*'s conflict between the Red and the White repeats throughout the poem, with red representing passion and white illustrating innocence:

> O, what a sight it was, wistly to view
> How she came stealing to the wayward boy,
> To note the fighting conflict of her hue,
> How white and red each other did destroy!
>> But now her cheek was pale; and by and by
>> It flashed forth fire, as lightning from the sky.[103]

The division between the Houses of Lancaster and York, as well as the fire of Queen Margaret, were never far from Shakespeare's mind, it seems, even while his playhouse remained closed.[104]

Katherina, the uncontrollable paramour assigned to the misogynist Petruchio in *The Taming of the Shrew*, almost certainly written in the early 1590s, also bears comparison to Margaret.[105] Like Margaret, Katherina was a woman who did not want to play by men's rules, who did not understand the conventions of womanhood to apply to her. Unlike Margaret, who, in the plays, accepted marriage and motherhood, Katherina rejected the confines of married life. Both women, in their plays, were handed from a father to a husband. Both women bristled at their roles, and both, in the end, were punished for their transgressions (especially Katherina, the titular "shrew," who was violently "tamed").

The scholar David Mann has identified this character type—the powerful, angry, loquacious, and morally complex female protagonist—as the "she-wolf," a term he borrows from the Duke of York's epithet for Margaret in *Part 3*. She-wolves came to the London stage in the late 1580s and represented "the male fear of women at its most extreme," Mann writes. "She is beautiful and womanly in appearance but lacks the gentler qualities usually associated with her sex [in drama] and instead tends to acts of gratuitous and excessive evil."[106] The she-wolf bucks expectation and offers "gratuitous escapist pleasure" to her audience.[107] Both Margaret and Katherina give their audience the chance to see brilliant women transgressing, but of course, they both face eventual punishment for their rebellion. Margaret is the paradigmatic she-wolf.

Just as Will was writing, England was racked by a persistent concern about young women bucking the convention of marriage and living and working independently—or "masterless," to use a term from the time. "Women scolding and brawling with their neighbours, defying or even beating their husbands, seem to be distinctly more common than in the periods before or afterwards," the historian David Underdown has noted. Accusations of witchcraft were one result. Another was the explosion of unfaithful, untamed, unruly women in literature, as mostly male writers worked through their anxieties about the patriarchy in crisis.[108] The she-wolf archetype was so pervasive that versions appeared in the works of many other playwrights of the age, including George Chapman, Thomas Heywood, and William Rowley. There are even indications that the writer George Peele revised his play *Edward I* to slake the public hunger for "terrible queens" that followed in Margaret's wake.[109]

The she-wolf roles of Shakespeare's early career—Margaret, Joan, Tamora, Eleanor, and Katherina—required boy-actors of incredible ability. In an epic poem such as *Venus and Adonis*, however, Shakespeare could explore the she-wolf, both her behavior and her interiority— without concern for the limitations of the child performer.[110] Joan's player needed to be skilled in stage combat as well as oratory, Tamora's to play scenes of passion and of brutality, Katherina's to inhabit a character arc moving from liberated to subjugated, but Margaret's player had the greatest task of all. Her actor had to depict her anger, demonstrate her vulnerability, learn her long texts, and, depending on which plays he appeared in, portray her at all ages. In his Venus, Shakespeare could further explore the conflicts that a woman in power—here a goddess, in his plays, a queen or a warrior—felt moving through her world as, fundamentally, an inferior.

For his part, young Will was done feeling inferior—assuming, as some have, that he felt acutely his lack of an Oxford or Cambridge degree.[111] He had proven himself as a writer. Yet he remained in need of money. In later years, Shakespeare would return to poetry, but after *Venus* and *Lucrece* he would focus his attention largely on the playhouse; the poetry just wasn't lucrative enough.[112] Soon, Shakespeare would revive Margaret for the stage one last time. This time, in an undisputed masterpiece.

• 7 •

"Dead Life, Blind Sight,
Poor Mortal Living Ghost"

Her Death

R ichard of Gloucester stepped onstage. Alone. Coated in exaggerated makeup, radiating an erotic charge and a memorable
swagger, he walked with a hunched back and a pronounced
limp.[1] It was the debut of a new play by William Shakespeare, *Richard
III*, and it's possible that—from this very first moment—discerning
audience members could tell this was something different. Richard,
the titular villain, is the only lead character in Shakespeare's work
to speak his play's prologue.[2] Imperiously surveying his audience,
Richard declared to the groundlings crowding the stage, the nobles
reclining in the gallery, and to all of England:

> Now is the winter of our discontent
> Made glorious summer by this son of York;
> And all the clouds that loured upon our house
> In the deep bosom of the ocean buried.
> Now are our brows bound with victorious wreaths,
> Our bruisèd arms hung up for monuments,
> Our stern alarums changed to merry meetings,
> Our dreadful marches to delightful measures.[3]

Bolstered by such an opening, *Richard III* brought Shakespeare to a new level of his career.[4] The play was long, dramaturgically complex, ostentatiously loquacious—and, notably, a solo-authored work. The titular role was bawdy and vicious enough to appeal to a crowd coming from a nearby bearbaiting, but clever and involved enough to tempt nearly every leading actor for the next four centuries. There remains something untouchable about this crazed king, this ruthless Machiavel.[5] He is—in Shakespeare's oeuvre and in the Western canon—unique.[6]

Yet despite the presence of such an exceptional male lead, *Richard III* is also notable for its four central female characters, who together speak almost a quarter of the play's 3,718 lines.[7] On Shakespeare's stage, the voices of these four women—Cecily, the Duchess of York, Anne, Elizabeth, and the deposed queen Margaret—articulated the play's clearest critique of England's leadership and its past. England knew no long-ruling queens regnant until Elizabeth; the medieval period saw only kings command power. As the country looked ahead toward the conclusion of the (very popular) queen's reign, Shakespeare created multiple women—on various sides of a century-old armed conflict—to question the administration of power in England.[8] Most notably, he returned Margaret to the stage for the final time—a homecoming with no support at all in the historical record, yet one that allowed her to voice a sharp critique of the wars of kings.

This bold new play debuted sometime in the early 1590s, possibly featuring a troupe of actors led by Richard Burbage, one of the stars of the Elizabethan stage.[9] It was Burbage's first major partnership with Shakespeare, commencing an extraordinarily fruitful collaboration between the two men that would last for decades.[10] The setting for this effort was a newly Yorkist England. At its start, King Edward IV sat on the throne, the Lancastrian stain on the English flag all but washed clean. The House of York had finally vanquished the House of Lancaster, which would never again seat a monarch on the throne of England. The corpse of King Henry (dead at the hand of Richard, scheming younger brother of King Edward) rotted in the

Tower, his son Prince Edward of Westminster dead on the battlefield at Tewkesbury, and his queen, the wicked French Margaret, banished.

Over the next three or so hours—*Richard III* was Shakespeare's longest play to date, and it would remain so until *Hamlet* came along half a decade later—the Elizabethan audience would laugh with and at the wicked and waggish royal, cry alongside a chorus of grieving mothers, and watch as Henry VII, the first monarch of the Tudor dynasty, dealt the final blow of the Wars of the Roses by defeating Richard at the Battle of Bosworth Field. The Tudors still reigned over England when *Richard III* premiered—Elizabeth's grand-father, Henry VII, was the king who ousted Richard III from the throne—so the play told of the origin of the country's current ruling house. Shakespeare shrewdly presented this final chapter of the York-Lancaster battle as "solved" by the triumph of the Tudor dynasty (represented in its founder, King Henry VII) over the forces of evil and mayhem (represented in Richard).[11]

Yet *Richard III* also debuted at a time of instability and mounting unrest. The aging, unmarried Tudor queen still had not identified an heir. Fear of the generations of violence that had marked England's past was palpable through this play.[12] No doubt the original audience felt an uneasiness watching this wickedly brilliant monarch wreak havoc on their nation. Civil war could soon return should warring factions contest Elizabeth's throne.[13] In fact, violence already stalked the streets of London. In the spring of 1593, roving gangs of unemployed men sought out immigrants to abuse and handed out angry broadsheets to passersby. Shakespeare's friend and collaborator Christopher Marlowe lost his life when a dispute resulted in a knife to the skull. Summer once again reared its fiery head, even hotter and drier than the last. The rich fled town; the poor remained—and died of plague or exposure. Sickness exacted a mounting toll that hot summer, with plague's death rates reaching more than a thousand a week.[14] Now writing on his own, Shakespeare metabolized the ambient anxieties, the seething discontent, the murder of his friend. The debts to the latter are clear: Shakespeare drew on Marlowe's work as he was creating the play's central role, borrowing the Machiavellian villain, the vivid antihero, from plays such as *Tamburlaine*.[15] Shakespeare echoed Marlowe's muscular verbosity and may even have taken imagery directly from Marlowe in writing new lines for a familiar character he returned to the stage, for the final time, in *Richard III*: Margaret of Anjou.[16]

The young playwright had little choice but to dream outside his sources.[17] The chronicle histories that Shakespeare consulted for his dramas often skimmed the stories of women. Shakespeare dedicated the play's central scenes to four female characters, and to do this, he needed to imagine their experiences, going far beyond the historical accounts written at their expense.[18] He adopted some of the biases intrinsic to the Tudor chronicles, but he also took time to find the humanity inside each of these four women. For Anne Neville, the widow of Margaret's son and later Richard III's queen, he wrote a sharp tongue and fierce love for her nephews. For Elizabeth Woodville, herself also a Lancastrian widow who later married a Yorkist king (Edward IV), he wrote a pivotal role and speeches of passion. For Cecily Neville, Duchess of York (and Richard's mother), he wrote heartfelt passages as she mourns three of her sons and excoriates the one who survived.

And for Margaret, a defeated queen vanquished to France, he wrote a return, a curse, and the last laugh.

⚜

She stepped onstage. A gasp, or a rustle, may have stirred the audience. The queen's arrival was a genuine shock, unhistorical and therefore unexpected, utterly reorienting the power dynamics onstage.[19] The actor playing Margaret may well have been covered in makeup meant to make her look ugly—and old. After all, Richard would insult her appearance repeatedly, calling her a "foul wrinkled witch" and a "withered hag."[20]

Richard III, like all of Shakespeare's early history plays, featured a cast of dozens and a plot of mind-numbing complexity; today, a York-Lancaster family tree often accompanies a cast list in theatrical programs. From the play's first moments, various royals, wives, nobles, and soldiers battled for both power and the audience's attention. By the time Margaret entered the play in its third scene, Richard's designs in pursuit of the crown—to marry Lady Anne and dispose of his brothers (and nephews)—had become clear. As Richard argued with Elizabeth, the wife of Edward IV and, thus, Margaret's replacement as queen of England, Margaret crept onto the stage unseen.

The young man depicting the old woman turned to the audience. What followed was one of Shakespeare's earliest (and most prolonged) uses of the aside: a passage spoken to the audience, while feigning to be out of earshot of the other characters onstage. For almost fifty lines, Margaret spoke only under her breath, hiding herself from the royals she was disparaging, aligning herself with the audience. Viewers thus watched the Yorkist infighting from her perspective. They would see the other characters through her eyes, but they would never truly see her through the eyes of others.[21] Finally, after listening to her throne's usurpers bicker for long enough, she stepped out of the shadows to confront them, immediately reminding them—and her audience—of not only her anger and fierce sense of wrong but of her rhetorical skill. She grabbed her stage and did not let it go, even to Richard, the play's primary windbag. She exhorted:

> Hear me, you wrangling pirates, that fall out
> In sharing that which you have pilled from me.
> Which of you trembles not that looks on me?
> If not that I am queen, you bow like subjects;
> Yet that by you deposed, you quake like rebels.[22]

The last time Margaret saw Richard—at the climax of *Henry VI, Part 3*—he had tried to kill her, only to be stopped by his brother King Edward. "Why should she live," Richard then asked, "to fill the world with words?"[23] It was a prophetic moment, for here she stood, filling the world with her words.[24]

With no power or followers, looking like a "withered hag" to

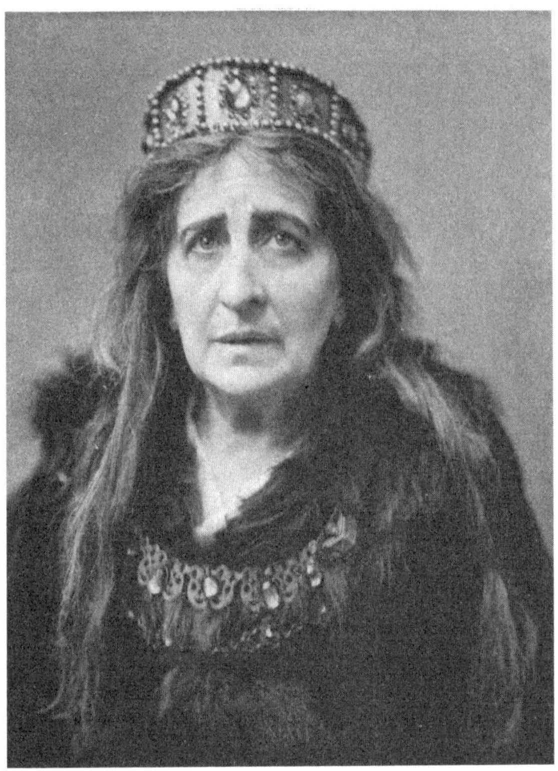

Geneviève Ward as Queen Margaret, a role she played
opposite both Henry Irving and Frank Benson as
Richard III around the turn of the twentieth century.

Richard, Margaret used these words, her only tool, to bring down a
curse on the House of York.[25] Like the ancient Cassandra, captured
during the Trojan War, taken to a foreign land, and damned with the
power of prophecy, Margaret predicted tragedy for her enemy. "Can
curses pierce the clouds and enter heaven?" she asked. "Why then, give
way, dull clouds, to my quick curses!"[26] She told Elizabeth that her
son Edward would die a youth, as Margaret's own son Edward had,
and that Elizabeth would "die, neither mother, wife, nor England's
queen."[27] For the onlookers at the scene—Lords Rivers, Dorset,
and Hastings—she envisioned early and unpleasant deaths. But for
Richard, she saved her worst curse:

> Stay, dog, for thou shalt hear me.
> If heaven have any grievous plague in store
> Exceeding those that I can wish upon thee,
> O let them keep it till thy sins be ripe,
> And then hurl down their indignation
> On thee, the troubler of the poor world's peace.
> The worm of conscience still begnaw thy soul.
> Thy friends suspect for traitors while thou liv'st,
> And take deep traitors for thy dearest friends.
> No sleep close up that deadly eye of thine,
> Unless it be while some tormenting dream
> Affrights thee with a hell of ugly devils.
> Thou elvish-marked, abortive, rooting hog,
> Thou that wast sealed in thy nativity
> The slave of nature and the son of hell,
> Thou slander of thy heavy mother's womb,
> Thou loathèd issue of thy father's loins,
> Thou rag of honor, thou detested—

RICHARD: Margaret.

MARGARET: Richard!

RICHARD: Ha?

MARGARET: I call thee not.

RICHARD: I cry thee mercy, then, for I did think
> That thou hadst called me all these bitter names.

MARGARET: Why, so I did, but looked for no reply.[28]

The exchange revealed, for a defeated and banished queen, a striking amount of confidence. In short order, Margaret had insulted the king's brother and wife, knowing full well that either could order her immediate death. But by this point in the dynastic wars, Margaret had lost everything, including her fear.[29]

Where Margaret came from or left to would remain a mystery throughout the play. Did Shakespeare (or his boy-player) see her as a person, a supernatural apparition, or some combination of the two?[30] This woman did not seem to live anywhere, need anything, or come with anyone.[31] Before she left the stage to return to the imprecise obscurity whence she came, she again invoked her status as the play's Cassandra, its cursed seer:

> O, but remember this another day,
> When he [Richard] shall split thy very heart with sorrow,
> And say, "Poor Margaret was a prophetess."—
> Live each of you the subjects to his hate,
> And he to yours, and all of you to God's.[32]

And with this last word, not waiting for any further rejoinder from Richard or Elizabeth, she disappeared, not to appear again until the play's fourth act, when the lives of Elizabeth (the queen—for now), Anne (Richard's wife—for now), and Cecily (Richard's mother—alas)—would look quite diffcrent. Margaret's prophecies would soon come true. Yet she would return not to gloat, but to mourn.[33]

In history, Margaret never did return to England. Her appearances in the country under Yorkist rule are wholly the playwright's creation. The historical Margaret mourned her losses in France, probably alone. Shakespeare chose to give her some amount of closure, a choice that also allowed him to revive a widely known, presumably popular character.[34] Besides, the real Margaret's later years were hardly the stuff of high drama.

After Henry VI's death in May 1471, the victorious King Edward kept Margaret in the Tower of London while he and his advisers decided what to do with her. Initially, they merely shuffled her between sites of confinement; first to a prison in Gloucester, then to the riverfront house of Alice de la Pole (widow of the Duke of Suffolk).[35] Following Alice's death three years later, King Edward responded positively to an offer made by the French king, Louis XI, for the former queen's ransom. Louis offered a sum of 50,000 crowns for Margaret's liberty. She was, after all, a French princess, as well as Louis's first cousin. In August, Edward arrived in France and met with the French king on a bridge over the River Somme. The two agreed on Margaret's freedom. Edward stipulated that nowhere in the documentation of the event could Margaret be called a queen or Henry a king. Some have called this event—remembered in history as the Treaty of Picquigny—the final act of the Hundred Years' War between England and France.[36]

Louis had little interest in Margaret's freedom; he wanted her land. The terms of her transfer to France required Margaret to sign away all claims to the property she was set to inherit from her father, giving it to Louis, which she did. In early 1475, Margaret sailed across the English Channel in a fishing boat, which eventually carried her to Rouen—the city where, thirty years earlier, she had been received in joyous celebration as the future queen of England. Contrary to Shakespeare's fabulation, she would never leave France again.[37]

With few resources and no prospects, Margaret made her way south to join René—now an elderly man—in Provence. Like his daughter, René had seen his lands disappear, one by one, to Louis's imperial proclivities. Margaret's mother had died two decades earlier, and René had married a woman three years younger than Margaret herself. When Margaret arrived in Provence—where she had spent many happy years in her childhood—she found her father in Aix-en-Provence, a prosperous market town on the banks of the River Arc, one day's journey from Marseille, on the Mediterranean coast. Had Margaret wished for adventure, she could have roamed the nearby foothills. Had she wished for entertainment in town, there was plenty to be had, as her father had been an active patron of the arts. Had she simply wished for quiet and solitude, Margaret could have gazed out her window, watching the mistral—a strong seasonal wind that blows through Provence and out to the sea—push fog across the plain. Winters in Provence are temperate and summers are full of sun; no doubt she saw more sky and sunlight than she had seen in decades.[38]

Margaret lived with her father and his new wife for a handful of years during which presumably she did little, for nothing was written about it. For the daughter of a king, such a silence in the historical record is telling. Her son, her own power, her reasons to survive had disappeared in the meadows of Tewkesbury, one sad Thursday morning years before.

René of Anjou, once King of Sicily, Naples, and Jerusalem, once brother of the Queen of France, once father of the Queen of England, died in Provence in May of 1480. King Louis inherited claim to all of René's lands except Provence, and he joined them with France. Provence went to René's nephew, who died the following year, allowing Louis to claim yet another territory. With Anjou now subsumed into France, Margaret's home ceased to be. For over seven hundred years, Anjou had been its own kingdom, with its own sovereign and culture. Now it was just another field in France.[39]

René was laid to rest in an elaborate marble tomb of his own design in the Cathédrale Saint-Maurice in Angers. Margaret followed her father's body back north to Anjou, though she no longer had a home in the area. One of her father's supporters apparently took pity on her and offered her lodging on his estate. It was here that she would live out the final quiet, lonely, peaceful years of her life.[40]

By the time Margaret retook the stage, in the fourth scene of the fourth act of the fourth play of this Shakespearean cycle, England had all but fallen apart. "So now prosperity begins to mellow," she declared to her audience, surveying her surroundings, alone onstage for the only time in the play. "And drop into the rotten mouth of death."[41]

Shakespeare had kept Margaret in England for all the long years of Richard's infernal rise. "Here in these confines I have lurked," she continued, "to watch the waning of mine enemies." When they fall, she confided in the groundlings, she "will to France," seeing that her will has been done.[42] The choice to bring back Margaret after a great deal of intervening bloodshed—Richard had orchestrated the murders of his nephews (the "Princes in the Tower"), his brother Clarence, and his wife, Anne, and overseen the (ostensibly natural) death of his other brother, King Edward—revealed her central purpose in this final play of the tetralogy: She was a figure of mourning and of cursing—which is to say, of memory and the profound power it holds.[43]

Soon, voices approached. They belonged to the former Queen Elizabeth (King Edward's widow) and Cecily, the Duchess of York (Edward and Richard's mother). From the throat of Elizabeth came mourning for her two murdered boys; the duchess lamented her two lost grandsons and her three lost sons (Edward, Clarence, and Rutland, whose murder Margaret celebrated in *Henry VI, Part 3*). Amid the lamentations, Margaret, hidden from the two women but not from the audience, spat out acerbic commentary as the elderly duchess elegized with a fluency that her author would later pass on to Lear and Cleopatra: "Dead life, blind sight, poor mortal living ghost, / Woe's scene, world's shame, grave's due by life usurped."[44]

Too full of her own grief to take any more of theirs, Margaret revealed herself. She and the duchess, widows both and fallen matriarchs of the Houses of Lancaster and of York, met at last:

MARGARET
> If ancient sorrow be most reverend,
> Give mine the benefit of seniority,
> And let my griefs frown on the upper hand.
> If sorrow can admit society,
> Tell o'er your woes again by viewing mine.
> I had an Edward, till a Richard killed him;
> I had a husband, till a Richard killed him.
> Thou hadst an Edward, till a Richard killed him;
> Thou hadst a Richard, till a Richard killed him.

DUCHESS
> I had a Richard too, and thou didst kill him;
> I had a Rutland too, thou holpst to kill him.

MARGARET

Thou hadst a Clarence too, and Richard killed him.[45]

Shakespeare's history plays contain precious few female characters; these earliest histories—those in which Margaret appears—possess the lion's share. That so much of what these women do is mourn, and mourn exquisitely, speaks to the importance of the cycle of mortality in these plays.[46] It is the women, in this play and in later histories (like Constance in *King John* and Lady Percy in *Henry IV, Part 2*), who express the human cost that England's rulers exacted in these wars.[47]

As the scene wore on, Elizabeth and the duchess realized that their anguish tied them to Margaret more than their blood feud divided them.[48] "O thou, well skilled in curses, stay awhile," Elizabeth said to Margaret, "And teach me how to curse mine enemies."[49] Margaret, turning to leave, perhaps sensing Richard's impending proximity, obliged, making one final speech to the two attendant women, her former subjects, former enemies, and current allies.

MARGARET

Forbear to sleep the nights, and fast the days;
Compare dead happiness with living woe;
Think that thy babes were sweeter than they were,
And he that slew them fouler than he is.
Bett'ring thy loss makes the bad causer worse.
Revolving this will teach thee how to curse.

QUEEN ELIZABETH

My words are dull. O, quicken them with thine!

MARGARET

Thy woes will make them sharp and pierce like mine.[50]

And with that, with no further goodbye, Margaret left the stage, her part in Shakespeare's story complete.[51]

Yet her presence lingered in the very next scene, as the remaining women resolved to "smother" Richard in "the breath of bitter words."[52] A trumpet sounded. Richard entered. The two women immediately turned on him with their harshest invective. The duchess, Richard's mother, lamented that she had not "strangl[ed] thee in her accursed womb" and (repeating an insult of Margaret's from act 1) decried him as a "toad." Elizabeth went yet further, calling Richard "thou villain-slave" in the same breath as she accused him of murder.[53] Richard, clearly taken aback, hoped that "the heavens" would not "hear these tell-tale women."[54] Yet the duchess pressed on. In her final lines of the play, she again channeled Margaret and bade her son "take with thee my most heavy curse"—that when his "day of battle" comes, her prayer will seal his "bloody" fate.[55]

Armed only with words, these women confronted Richard, behind whom stood an entire army. Yet their words unsettled him, and soon his paranoia would leave him isolated and exposed on the battlefield, where the duchess's curse could at last be realized. Margaret had taught the women well.[56]

In Margaret's final appearance, Shakespeare allowed her, if not her happiness, her catharsis. On Shakespeare's stage, she watched her enemies' depravity destroy them from within. The real Margaret, exiled, humiliated, stripped of resources and alone, never saw the fall of the House of York. She did not live to see King Edward die, the young princes killed by their own flesh and blood in the Tower, or the defeat of Richard and end of the York dynasty. In her final years, Margaret saw little of the world outside of the Loire Valley.

Upon her arrival in Anjou in 1480, Margaret took up residence in the Château de Souzay. The château stood on the south bank of the Loire, just under an hour's walk from the Château de Saumur, where in her childhood Margaret had enjoyed some of the happiest years of her life under the eye of her grandmother Yolande. If Margaret climbed the steps of Souzay's tower, she could look upriver and see Saumur, a grand citadel that still guards the Loire, rising from the river's edge.[57]

A slow-growing illness—possibly cancer—poisoned Margaret in

Edmund Kean as Richard III, a role he played to
great success on both sides of the Atlantic in the
early nineteenth century.

her final years.[58] "Her skin dried up as if it were dust," wrote a chronicler years after her death, "her stomach shriveled, and her eyes, as hollow as if they had been sunk with violence, lost all the fire which had
once shown her soul's great feelings."[59] In the late summer of 1482,
she wrote a short will.

It has been said by some, but confirmed by none, that in her final
days at Souzay, Margaret received a visitor from her past: Jasper Tudor,
half brother of Henry VI, who made his way to Margaret's bedside,
along with his nephew Henry. Allies of the Lancastrian cause, the

two men had spent much of the past two decades in exile on the continent. If the reports of their encounter are true, Margaret used her final modicum of strength to encourage the two men to continue the fight against the Yorkist kings in the name of her beloved son and vanquished husband. Her encouragement would ring in their ears as they planned yet another attempt for the English throne.[60]

Margaret of Anjou died at Morains, a small residence in the hills above Souzay, in August of 1482.[61] England and France would lose their kings the following year; Edward and Louis died and were replaced by their sons, both children at their accession.[62] Almost three years to the day after Margaret's death, Henry Tudor—that same nephew who may have heard Margaret's plea as she lay on her deathbed—led a collection of French, Welsh, and Scottish troops to battle at Bosworth Field, where they cornered and killed the horseless Richard III. Immediately after the battle, Henry Tudor took the throne as King Henry VII, the first monarch of the Tudor dynasty. His son Henry VIII and granddaughter Elizabeth I would enjoy decades-long reigns.

As she requested in her will, Margaret was buried with her father in his elaborate tomb at the Cathédrale Saint-Maurice.[63] And there, beneath the elaborate marble decoration of her family tomb, Margaret would lie forgotten, but for some mentions in English chronicles, for the next hundred years, until a young playwright would resurrect her on the public stage of the capital city of a country she had once ruled.

Shakespeare's decision to return Margaret to the London theatre occurred at the very end of the period in which he is hardest to locate in the historical record—his so-called Lost Years. In the years just after *Richard III* delighted and alarmed and titillated audiences, the young playwright joined a bright new theatrical company, wrote most of his best-known works, and became a rich man. He was obscure no longer. His resuscitation of Margaret is inseparable from his transforming social status; her return was a sign of the young man's confidence, his growing acclaim, his quest for narrative closure, and, quite possibly, his debt to a series of rich benefactors who bought the burgeoning playwright's way into fame and respectability.

First and foremost among these benefactors was Henry Wriothesley (pronounced "Rizley"), the young Earl of Southampton, fabulously wealthy and widely rumored to have homosexual tendencies, a man for whom Shakespeare would write many captivating female characters.[64] At some point toward the end of the Lost Years, Southampton became Shakespeare's "patron," meaning the rich nobleman who supported the playwright financially as he wrote—in exchange for adulation and the pride of being associated with an up-and-coming artist. Shakespeare dedicated first *Venus and Adonis* and then *The Rape of Lucrece* to Southampton, complimenting "your lordship" in increasingly breathless tones. Some have speculated that the erotic parts of the poems were written to titillate the famously sensual Southampton.[65] Still more speculation posits that Southampton is the "Fair Youth" of Shakespeare's sonnets—also written around this time—several of which are, it must be said, quite gay.[66]

Patrons like Southampton exercised an enormous amount of influence over the plays of Elizabethan England. They paid the bills. They lent the prestige of their names. And they did so at a time when almost everyone else in power—especially religious leaders and city fathers—practically vibrated with hatred of the theatre, which was banned within the city limits of London and restricted elsewhere. Actors were purveyors of blasphemy, filth, disloyalty, disorderliness, and sodomy, the critics snarled.[67] The Puritans claimed actors were guilty of idleness—to them, a capital crime.[68] Oxford and Cambridge both banned theatre within a five-mile radius of their respective universities, although this prohibition appears to have been remarkably ineffective.[69] It was the aristocrats who defended the theatre.[70] In fact, just three or four of these rich patrons were principally responsible for protecting Elizabethan players from considerable violence and censure.[71]

These patrons influenced the content of the plays as well. As

Will Shakespeare composed *Richard III*, it certainly appears he was attempting to please his patron—possibly even more than one patron. The play is quite flattering of the ancestors of Lord Strange, who are noted throughout the text by name. This has led some to posit that the play was written, at least initially, for Strange's Men.[72] Yet the play is similarly complimentary of the Earl of Pembroke's ancestors, leading others to propose that it was first performed by Pembroke's Men (perhaps while they toured the country during the plague closures).[73] At least one scholar, meanwhile, has speculated that Shakespeare wrote the light and witty comedy *Love's Labour's Lost* to amuse Southampton and his merry friends.[74]

All this is to say that it's possible that Margaret's ahistorical return was the product of an aristocrat's fancy as much as Shakespeare's own fascination. The deposed queen could have been a favorite of Lord Strange (who had a powerful disgraced mother), the Earl of Pembroke (who had a powerful theatre-loving wife), or even the Earl of Southampton—at whose fine home Shakespeare may have ridden out the plague (and filled his time by writing).[75] This is not mere speculation. Scholars almost uniformly accept the notion that Shakespeare would later revive his bumbling, tragic character of Falstaff to please Queen Elizabeth, who delighted in the character's antics in the *Henry IV* plays. The plays of Shakespeare were art. But art has always reflected the fancies and fantasies of the very rich.

The influence of Shakespeare's patrons did not cease with the success of *Richard III*. In fact, the assistance of a rich friend may have become *more* vital to the young artist in 1594, as plague closures continued to wreak havoc, as bad harvests devastated proletarian audience members, and as both Lord Strange and the Earl of Sussex (another theatrical patron) died, leading to a confusing reshuffling of the companies that bore their names. Several actors fell into poverty; several companies went against custom and sold plays to printers, desperate for some quick cash.[76] The chaos of this era led playing companies to take risks to win over their audiences, inaugurating a series of plays with more radical themes.[77] Margaret—especially in her, ahistorical last act—emerged from the disorder and creativity of the early 1590s.

Yet out of all this turmoil arose, too, a rich, stable William Shakespeare. In June 1594, a new theatrical company began appearing in the records. They were called the Lord Chamberlain's Men, after their patron, the cousin and intimate of Queen Elizabeth. Many of the former Lord Strange's Men moved over to the new company (perhaps making up half their number), as did the star actor Richard Burbage. The Chamberlain's Men took up residence at the Theatre (owned by the Burbage family). By Christmas, they were established enough to play twice before the queen at Greenwich Palace. Among the men splitting the profits of the new company was William Shakespeare. He would remain with the company for the rest of his life.[78]

Somehow, Will had gotten together enough money to buy a share in this new theatrical venture. Rumors would later swirl that Southampton had given the playwright a gift of £1,000, an almost unthinkably large sum of cash. No matter the money's origin, the playwright had invested well. The proceeds from the Chamberlain's Men would help make Shakespeare a wealthy man. Soon, he would purchase a handsome Stratford home and apply for a family coat of arms (in a cute pun, it featured a spear).[79] In return, the Chamberlain's Men gained the rights to his new plays. The company also acquired several of his old ones, apparently including the *Henry VI* scripts, as well as *Richard III*.[80] Some have speculated that this new play, with its captivating antihero and its encore of an antiheroine, was the first play that the new company performed in the summer of 1594.[81] Margaret, a figure from the past, may have inaugurated theatre's future.

· 8 ·

"I Am Fire"

Her Restoration

One day in the early wintry months of 1623, deep in the inky bowels of a printshop not far from the city walls, a workman contemplated Margaret of Anjou.[1] In front of him sat the text of a play—one of Shakespeare's history plays. With his left hand, the workman held a composing stick—basically a small tray—and with his right hand, the workman carefully plucked small metal letters to place in the stick. One by one, the workman assembled the letters that constituted the lines spoken by Margaret. He was reproducing the lines on the page in front of him—but he was also striving to correct typos and improve punctuation. Eventually, the workman had filled the stick to capacity, at which point he transferred its contents into a bigger tray, which would later be pressed into a page of text.[2]

Slowly, imperfectly, the workman was creating a big, beautiful brick of a book—a 908-page behemoth that we now remember as Shakespeare's "First Folio." This was a major project—the First Folio was essentially a collected works of Shakespeare, containing thirty-six plays. The workman's identity has long been lost, but scholars have determined that just two men were responsible for setting the type for all of Margaret's scenes in *Richard III* and all three *Henry VI* plays. In an age when typesetters had considerable liberty to pick their own spellings, these men can be identified by certain typographical tics—one, usually called Compositor A, preferred "doe," "goe," and "here," while the other, Compositor B, liked "do," "go," and "heere."[3]

The two compositors, along with their coworkers, their boss (William Jaggard, an accomplished if slightly crooked and physically ailing printer), and two of Shakespeare's former colleagues (John Heminges and Henry Condell, the last surviving members of the Lord Chamberlain's Men), played outsized roles in shaping the Shakespearean canon following the playwright's death in 1616.[4] Obviously, these men were key to preservation: without the First Folio, it is likely that almost half of Shakespeare's extant plays would now be lost. But, more subtly if no less powerfully, they influenced the way readers and audiences encounter Shakespeare today. In the First Folio, Shakespeare's plays were divided into their modern categories—comedies, histories, and tragedies—for the first time. Further, by denying Shakespeare's coauthors and collaborators any credit, the compilers of the First Folio helped propagate the myth that Shakespeare was a singular genius who wrote alone.[5] Finally, the Folio's creators proudly asserted that its contents contained the *definitive* versions of Shakespeare's plays—a claim that has enjoyed substantial (though certainly not uniform) acceptance for four hundred years, with massive implications for the content of Shakespeare's plays and the contours of his characters—including, of course, Margaret. More than perhaps any other development, the creation of the First Folio determined the reception of Margaret in the centuries to come.

The Folio's assertion of definitiveness was necessary because, in the early 1600s, the texts of Shakespeare's plays changed constantly. His actors may have altered scripts to fit their casts or the tastes of new audiences; they may have called in the playwright to perform this labor, or the playwright may have revised his work of his own initiative.[6] In any case, three different versions of *Henry VI, Part 2* and *Henry VI, Part 3*, along with a whopping six different versions of *Richard III*, had been published and were circulating among the reading public by the time the First Folio hit bookstalls. Today, when audiences attend a performance of Shakespeare's play, it is usually something close to the Folio version that they see (with spellings modernized and stage directions added or adapted by a careful editor). But this represents a choice by modern editors—one with enormous implications for the character of Margaret.

Consider *Henry VI, Part 2*. It was first published in 1594 under the prolix title *The First Part of the Contention Betwixt the Two Famous Houses of Yorke and Lancaster, with the Death of the Good Duke Humphrey: and the Banishment and Death of the Duke of Suffolke, and the Tragical End of the Prowd Cardinall of Winchester, with the Notable Rebellion of Iacke Cade: and the Duke of Yorkes First Clayme to the Crowne* (or, mercifully, just *The Contention* for short). Subsequent versions were published in 1600 and 1619, with similar but not identical texts. Then came the Folio version, titled *The Second Part of King Henry the Sixt*. The Folio version was a full third longer than *The Contention*, and a significant chunk of the difference came from Margaret's lines: she has 341 lines in the Folio, compared with 141 lines in *The Contention*.[7] No other character's lines differ so greatly.[8]

Not only is Margaret's part larger in the Folio than in earlier published versions; she is more assertive, too. In *The Contention*, Margaret is more demure, more passive. In the Folio, she roars and storms and generally bears more responsibility for the play's events. Compare the following lines, first from *The Contention* and then from the Folio, as Margaret urges Henry to flee with her:

The Contention

MARGARET: Away my Lord, and flie to London straight,
    Make hast, for vengeance comes along with them,
    Come stand not to expostulate, lets go.

HENRY: Come then faire Queene to London let vs hast,
    And sommon a Parlament with speede,
    To stop the fury of these dyre euents.

The Second Part of King Henry the Sixt (First Folio)

MARGARET: Away my Lord, you are slow, for shame
away.

HENRY: Can we outrun the Heauens? Good Margaret stay.

MARGARET: What are you made of? You'l nor fight nor fly:
Now is it manhood, wisedome, and defence,
To giue the enemy way, and to secure vs
By what we can, which can no more but flye.
Alarum afarre off.
If you be tane, we then should see the bottome
Of all our Fortunes: but if we haply scape,
(As well we may, if not through your neglect)
We shall to London get, where you are lou'd,
And where this breach now in our Fortunes made May
readily be stopt.

In *The Contention*, Henry readily accedes to Margaret's suggestion; in the Folio, she criticizes him right off the bat, and then—when he hesitates—she denounces his manhood at length. The Margaret of *The Contention* still plots murder and bosses around nobles, but without the hard edge or domineering spirit of the Folio's queen.[9]

What could account for such immense differences? Scholars have skirmished over this question for centuries. One popular theory is that the earlier shorter versions represented actors' (or even bootleggers') attempts to reconstruct entire plays from memory; due to the impossibility of such a task, the texts were inevitably bastardized, leading scholars to label these versions "bad" (as opposed to the "good" Folio version). Another theory holds that the earlier texts represent earlier versions (perhaps drafts) of the plays we know today—versions that Shakespeare may or may not have originally authored or coauthored, but which he later revised, putting his mark on them and transforming them into their Folio texts. Still another proposes that some Folio versions, though published later, were in fact the originals, and those published earlier were the revised texts. Other, more complicated theories suggest some combination of revision and memorial reconstruction, or that there were earlier ur-plays, now lost, from which Shakespeare and others independently drew.[10]

The character of Margaret was never stable—indeed, she almost certainly transformed repeatedly over Shakespeare's lifetime. He may well have written and then rewritten her, such efforts representing a desire to improve or deepen her character. In the earliest surviving version of *Henry VI, Part 3*—originally published in 1595 under the title *The True Tragedie of Richard, Duke of Yorke, and the Death of Good King Henrie the Sixth, with the Whole Contention Betweene the Two Houses Lancaster and Yorke, as it was Sundrie Times Acted by the Right Honourable the Earle of Pembrooke His Seruants*—Margaret has just 156 lines, compared with 281 in the later Folio version.[11] Was *The True Tragedie* an early Shakespeare play, an imperfectly remembered Shakespeare play, an unpolished Shakespeare draft, or a play by other authors altogether, which Shakespeare later revised? Were scholars to ever learn the answer (again, unlikely), this would change our understanding of Shakespeare's feelings toward Margaret. Did these feelings evolve as he wrote? Did they evolve in response to audience reaction? Did he come across an undeveloped character created by others and see the spark of something—someone—he had to foreground and expand?[12]

Alternatively, Shakespeare or a contemporary may have been revising earlier plays or drafts to heighten a sense of continuity, to link these "history" plays together into a consistent narrative (with consistent characters). In *Richard III*, for instance, Margaret changes fairly little between the first published version, from 1597, and the Folio version.[13] But, while all of the pre-Folio versions include the stage direction "Enter Qu[een] Margaret," the Folio states, "Enter old Queene Margaret." The Folio version also adds a question Richard poses to Margaret—"Wert thou not banished, on paine of death?"—not present in the earlier versions. Both of these changes, while subtle, serve to remind a reader of the other plays that include Margaret.

Shakespeare may well have been making her connections across the plays clearer.[14]

The only play in the Margaretsaga that was *not* published before the Folio appeared in 1623 is *Henry VI, Part 1*.[15] Yet many have suggested that this play, too, is a revised version of an earlier text. In fact, as noted briefly in an earlier chapter, a number of scholars have questioned whether Margaret was even present in the original play at all, and whether Shakespeare was a coauthor of the original. Much of the evidence for these views is, it must be noted, strikingly subjective. Some believe the ending of *Part 1* that includes Margaret is so "artistically bad," such an "absurdity," that it simply must have been slapped on later, as Shakespeare was attempting to revise an earlier play into an effective prequel to the other *Henry* plays.[16] Others note, more convincingly, that the play makes more sense without her, since Henry is depicted as a sexless child in almost all of the pre-Margaret scenes (compared with the romantic adult falling head over heels for her, based solely on Suffolk's description), and that Margaret behaves differently than any other character (possessing the ability to overhear another character's asides).[17] Modern scholars have used computer analysis to argue that Thomas Nashe and perhaps Christopher Marlowe wrote the original version performed in 1592, without Shakespeare, and that Shakespeare adapted their play into *Henry VI, Part 1*, linking it to his other plays in part with the addition of his prolific queen—described even in this youthful depiction as possessing "valiant courage and undaunted spirit."[18]

After about two years of preparation, the Folio hit bookstalls in 1623. The thick tome likely cost 15 shillings, almost a pound.[19] Its compilers not only preserved Shakespeare's plays for posterity; they also purged them of curse words and scandalous political references.[20] The Folio apparently sold widely and well. This was an age when many laypeople—women as well as men—began acquiring books (including plays) in significant numbers, storing these within their houses, creating entire shelves or closets or studies just for their reading material.[21] The publication of the Folio allowed readers to encounter Margaret for the first time as a character with some continuity through four different plays. It also transported her out of the playhouse and into the home.

What would a reader of the Folio have made of this bold, belligerent character? One copy of the Folio that still survives today (weathered and yellowed and carefully preserved) provides a hint. The reader of this Folio (apparently a seventeenth-century Scottish man, or a member of his household) scrupulously annotated their copy. Commenting on her first appearance in *Richard III*, the annotator wrote: "Cruell Imprecations by Queene Margaret against the Queene / her Issue Richard and others / reproach of the blind pride of new made noblemen."[22] It's an accurate summary of Margaret's curses, but recorded with a judgmental edge—toward Margaret, for her cruelty, and toward the others, for their pride. Elsewhere, the annotator left even more expressly judgmental comments about many of Shakespeare's female characters, from Lady Macbeth ("hellish wife") to Katherina ("Intolerablie shrewd and scolding").[23] No doubt many early readers encountered Margaret this way—with reproach.

The seventeenth century was the last period in which any of Shakespeare's original audience members could have reflected on his work. Leafing through the Folio, remembering decades-old productions, such audience members could have paused to consider the ways his characters changed over time. In the late 1590s—with Elizabeth fading and a new playhouse, the Globe, rising on the banks of the Thames—Shakespeare created female characters like Rosalind and Viola, who don male clothing to secure an otherwise unattainable power. These women were distinct from his earlier she-wolves, and, in the end, both foreclose their liberatory fantasies and marry, quite unlike Elizabeth.[24] In the early 1600s—with Elizabeth dead and James I, a dedicated fan of the Bard's work, on the throne—Shakespeare's dominant women disappeared from the stage almost entirely, although a fixation on mature female sexuality (*Hamlet*) and adulterous wives (*Othello* and *King Lear*) remained.[25] Only in one of Shakespeare's least-known and least-loved plays, *Cymbeline*, did the aging poet come close to resuscitating the she-wolf in the post-Elizabethan era. In *Cymbeline*, a widowed king marries a character known only as the

Queen, a powerful and evil figure who personally tries to murder her husband and stepdaughter, securing what she believes to be the poison to do so. Like Margaret, the Queen attempts to seize power not by manipulating the men around her (as Lady Macbeth, Cleopatra, or Lear's evil daughters did) but by personally undertaking violence. Like Margaret, the Queen is undone by the death of her son. Unlike Margaret, however, the Queen would have no grand return, no final battle, no spectral vengeance.[26]

Closing the First Folio, replacing the heavy volume on its shelf, this seventeenth-century reader may well have savored Margaret's singularity. In the years to come, with Margaret's plays now secured for posterity, actors—and actresses—would play an ever greater role in dictating her continued transformations.

When Queen Henrietta Maria stepped on-stage, on January 9, 1633, it was almost as if Margaret had returned from the dead. Here was another French-born Queen of England—the first since Margaret herself—another foreign princess who spoke precious little English at the time of her marriage, who assumed the throne as a teenager, whom later chroniclers would indeed compare to her predecessor from Anjou.[27] And now, this controversial queen was challenging the taboos of her era, appearing in a new play, an elaborate seven- or eight-hour masque called *The Shepherd's Paradise*. Like Margaret before her, Henrietta Maria was dressed in men's armor.

Henrietta Maria, just twenty-three years old in 1633, loved the theatre, and she and her husband, King Charles I (son of King James), were enthusiastic patrons, especially of the King's Men, Shakespeare's old company. The queen herself scandalously attended performances at a public playhouse, and her taste influenced the content of many plays—including *The Shepherd's Paradise*, which her friend Walter Montagu wrote specifically for the ladies of the court. For months, Henrietta Maria and her ladies had been rehearsing, an onerous task given the queen's limited English and the play's stupendous length.

The Shepherd's Paradise depicted a strange, utopian society ruled by Belessa, played by the queen herself. A year before, at a different masque dedicated to Henrietta Maria, a female actor had spoken on an English stage for the first time in a century. Now the queen herself took on the all-male theatre. The term "actress" was apparently coined to refer to her.[28]

Just days after the queen performed, William Prynne—a doctrinaire Puritan lawyer—published a massive attack on the theatre,

Queen Henrietta Maria, for whom the term
"actress" was apparently coined, wife of Charles I,
in 1633, the year she appeared in
The Shepherd's Paradise.

denouncing female actors as "notorious whores." In response, the authorities mutilated Prynne's ears, but many were plainly on Prynne's side.[29] The Puritans—a popular movement that sought to "purify" Christian practice—hated theatre, especially performances on Sundays and the Catholic queen's increasing influence.[30] The furor of the Puritans played a significant role in sowing antagonism between King Charles and Parliament, and by the early 1640s legislators were itching to close the theatres, both as an assertion of independence and as a blow struck against deviancy.[31] In 1642, Parliament issued an edict forbidding "publike Stage-plays"—a temporary ban that would become permanent five years later—and, in the mid-1640s, the Globe was demolished.[32]

The enmity between king and Parliament mounted, and both sides mustered armies. Henrietta Maria desperately tried to rally support to her husband's cause, spending a night in Stratford as the guest of Shakespeare's daughter Susannah on one of her journeys to rejoin the king's forces. (Such accommodations, unusual for a queen, may have been a product of Henrietta Maria's avid interest in theatre, but they also undoubtedly reflected the exigencies of wartime.) Charles's opponents seized on the queen's influence to label Charles weak and emasculated, just as Margaret's enemies had mocked Henry centuries before. The parliamentary military soon triumphed, beheading King Charles in 1649 and installing the Puritan Oliver Cromwell as Lord Protector in 1653. Henrietta Maria fled to her native France, where she continued to attend and even appear in dramatic performances. In London, soldiers pulled down several other theatres, and the new regime banned cursing, sports, work on the sabbath, and Christmas.[33]

For most of the 1650s, Cromwell ruled and England's theatres remained officially closed, but the Lord Protector's death in 1658 triggered a political crisis that, to make a long story short, resulted in Parliament inviting the dead king's son to return and rule as Charles II. Not even three months after assuming the throne in 1660, King Charles II officially reopened the playhouses.[34] An aging Henrietta Maria sailed for England, but she soon grew tired of her adopted homeland and returned to the country of her birth—where, like Margaret, she would spend the final years of her life.[35]

The ban on public theatre had lasted almost two decades, and in that time many had forgotten Shakespeare. It had been decades since almost any of his plays had been reprinted, and no complete work of his appears to have been among the plays that were surreptitiously performed during the ban of the 1640s and 1650s.[36] Even among those who remembered Shakespeare, many saw him as a rube or a rustic—old-fashioned, obsolete, even dull.[37] One famous man of letters would report a few years later that the vernacular had become "so much refined since Shakespeare's time that many of his words and more of his phrases are scarcely intelligible," while a diarist would dismiss even *Hamlet* as an "old play" that had begun to "disgust this refined age."[38]

Nonetheless, Shakespeare's plays appealed to the two new theatre companies licensed by King Charles, and they quickly divvied up the Bard's repertory between them.[39] A large part of this attraction was practical; almost two decades had passed without new plays, so the new companies initially had little choice but to draw on existing works. Plus, dead playwrights like Shakespeare did not have to be compensated, and older theatregoers probably retained some nostalgia for familiar works.[40]

Determined, then, to perform Shakespeare's plays, the new companies soon decided that the best thing to do was to update the old works, to "reform" them, to adapt them for modern times.[41] Thus, *The Two Noble Kinsmen* became *The Rivals*; *Measure for Measure* was combined with *Much Ado About Nothing* to become *The Law Against Lovers*. Adapters added several new characters to *The Tempest*, and then the adaptation was itself adapted into an opera. The playwright William Davenant—rumored to be Shakespeare's illegitimate son—sought to update *Macbeth*, making its moral and its language clearer yet far less interesting: for example, changing "The devil damn thee black, thou cream-faced loon" to "Now friend, what means thy change of countenance?" Davenant did give the female characters—Lady Macbeth, Lady Macduff, and especially the witches—bigger parts. For most of the next century, it was Davenant's version, not Shakespeare's, that dominated English stages, with the "singing witches" serving as a particular draw.[42] By the end of the seventeenth century, adaptations of Shakespeare would outnumber the originals onstage.[43]

In the first two decades after public theatre resumed, none of the plays featuring Margaret were among those works of Shakespeare to be performed with any frequency.[44] Slowly but steadily, however, playwrights began to transform them. As early as the 1650s, an instructor at a Jesuit school in what is now northern France had adapted *Henry VI, Part 3* into a Latin play, borrowing from *King John*, *Hamlet*, and *All's Well That Ends Well* as he did so.[45] A decade later, an English playwright staged a popular adaptation of *Richard III*, with its story somewhat simplified and its titular villain's disability downplayed.[46] Significantly, both of these revised versions cut Margaret entirely—inaugurating a trend that would continue for two centuries.[47]

In fact, only one play from the 1660s or 1670s bears any trace of Margaret at all. In the spring of 1667, an adaptation of *The Taming of the Shrew* debuted, rewritten to focus on Grumio, the servant and sidekick of the main male character, Petruchio (he who "tames" the titular "shrew," Katherina). In the adaptation, Grumio (renamed Sauny) is a caricature of a Scotsman, interrupting almost every scene with comic hijinks delivered in a brogue. Interestingly, though—and for no clear reason—this version changed the she-wolf Katherina's name to Margaret. Still, the play ended with her spirit broken, her rebellious nature crushed.[48]

At the same time, however, an innovation even more important than adaptation was changing the way Shakespeare's plays were performed, one with profound implications for the first significant appearance of Margaret in almost half a century. The trend that Henrietta Maria had helped to initiate was shifting the very face of English theatre. Finally, women were appearing on the public stage.

The transition began just months after King Charles II reopened the public playhouses in 1660, with an actress apparently playing Desdemona in a production of *Othello*. Possibly, this was due to a dearth of qualified boy-actresses, or to the fact that the few men with any experience acting at all were well past their prime, or to gains in women's rights, or to Charles and his court's exposure to actresses on French stages during the monarch's exile.[49] Or the scholar Gary Taylor may have had a point when he noted, "Women began appearing on English stages at the same time that pornography began to appear on English bookstalls."[50] In any case, within two years, King Charles had decreed that *only* women could play female parts.[51]

From the beginning, audiences thrilled at the sexual charge that the presence of women engendered. "The very best legs that I ever saw," recorded the diarist Samuel Pepys of one early actress.[52] The sex lives of actresses were much commented upon, and a great many thespians won fame not for their theatrical exploits but for being mistresses to famous men—even King Charles himself.[53] Plays themselves transformed to accommodate female players; some radically foregrounded women's feelings and agency, but others compelled actresses to embody exaggerated stereotypes.[54] "In practical terms," Harold M. Weber has commented, "the freedom women gained to play themselves on stage was to a large extent the freedom to play the whore."[55] Playwrights exorcised or enacted the anxieties of the age onstage, adding a significant number of rape scenes to plays old and new, as well as an astonishing amount of female cross-dressing.[56]

Nonetheless, the increased dramatic opportunities for English actresses allowed many to interpret and embody female characters for the first time in a very long time. The first woman to put her spin on Margaret was the mysterious, compelling Mary Lee.

She was one of the most commented-upon women of her age. Beginning around 1670, Mary Lee burst onto the London stage, taking on dozens of the foremost roles of the era, from *Hamlet's* Gertrude to *King Lear's* Regan. She played the titular female parts in *Troilus and Cressida* and *Antony and Cleopatra*. She was especially renowned for her tragic roles. Lee was probably beautiful, too, as one of her characters from a 1679 play was described in exuberant terms:

"Oh such a skin full of alluring flesh! / Ah, such a ruddy, moist, and pouting lip; / Such Dimples, and such Eyes, such melting Eyes, / Blacker than Sloes, and yet they sparkl'd fire." She married at least twice—first to a minor actor named John Lee, and later to a minor aristocrat named Sir Charles Slingsby—and was once publicly accused of carrying on an affair with a poet.[57]

And, in 1680 and then again in 1681, this accomplished actress played Margaret. Or rather, she played a version of Margaret, an adaptation.

The first time was in a play bearing the topical title *The Misery of Civil War*. It was a combination of *Henry VI, Part 2* and *Part 3*, adapted by the prim playwright John Crowne, a small man, a creator of romantic dramas, a onetime resident of the New World, an early product of Harvard College, and a favorite of King Charles II.[58] Inspired by bitter political fights over whether a Catholic could succeed the king—fights some worried might lead to another civil war— Crowne turned to the Margaret saga for plays about civil strife, as well as ones through which he could insult the Catholic Church. *The Misery of Civil War* contained a few jibes at the pope, but its broader message was straightforwardly political; it was monarchist propaganda, counseling against the kind of uprising implied in its title. A year later, though, actors took up Crowne's prequel, *Henry the Sixth, The First Part* (based, confusingly, on the first four acts of *Henry VI, Part 2*), which was far more rabidly anti-Catholic.[59]

Mary Lee first appeared as Margaret in *The Misery of Civil War*. Outside London's riverside Duke's Theatre, it was wintertime.[60] Inside, audience members clustered on backless benches beneath flickering candles.[61] An increase in the price of tickets had led audiences to become more narrowly prosperous than they'd been in Shakespeare's day, their dress no doubt reflecting their heightened class position.[62] The smell of their perfumes, the scholar John Harold Wilson commented, mixed with animal odors to produce "an atmosphere thick enough to shovel."[63] Backstage, Lee probably spent many minutes preparing herself to appear, splashing her face with cold water, engulfing herself in a corset, teasing her hair, adding some color to her lips or cheeks.[64] Ready, and hearing her cue, she strode past the curtains (a recent innovation) and stepped in front of a painted backdrop (another recent innovation), surrounded by a retinue of other actors—"her Train." She gleefully informed King Henry that the "Villain Cade" was dead.[65] A few minutes later, she told Richard that his "hideous horrid self" was not worth killing.[66]

Crowne's adaptation had reduced Margaret's stage time, but she remained the story's center *of power*.[67] At her command, soldiers hanged so many men and women that she was said to be planting "An Orchard for the Devil."[68] She still baited York, and in the end she still stabbed him. "She-wolf of France!" he called her, "or rather cruel Tygress, / For woman thou art none; women are soft, / Gentle and pitiful, but thou art cruel."[69] Certainly, Margaret wasn't soft. "I am Fire," she announced at one point, leading York to declare that his allies must "wall her in, and keep that fire from spreading."[70] Stop its spread they would, killing her son, Prince Edward, refusing to heed her plaintive command to kill her too, instead leading Mary Lee off-stage and out of the story.[71]

In *The Misery of Civil War*, Crowne added new sexual dimensions to Shakespeare's play by creating a new rival for Margaret and lover for her enemy, Edward, York's son. Lady Elianor Butler was, in fact, a historical figure; she had appeared in a number of chronicles, which Crowne probably consulted.[72] Departing from the available record, however, Crowne made her one of the play's most vivid characters, having her appear on the battlefield "in mans habit" (i.e., armor, something Shakespeare's Margaret possibly got to do as well), goad Edward into fighting on, and die tragically at her lover's hand. In effect, he divided Shakespeare's Margaret into two characters—a diminished original and a compelling variation. Crowne also illustrated the sexual violence of repressive regimes by adding a horrifying scene in which Margaret's soldiers assault two young women as their father weeps.[73]

Due to its sensitive political content, *The Misery of Civil War* may have been performed only once.[74] Yet Mary Lee would soon have another chance to portray Margaret—in early 1681, in Crowne's

Henry the Sixth, The First Part.[75] In this adaptation, Crowne drew even more heavily on Shakespeare's text, yet he departed from his source by filling out Margaret's adulterous relationship with Suffolk, adding greater depth and tenderness to an original "almost barren of romance," in the words of Crowne's biographer.[76] In emphasizing the affair, Crowne made clear that Margaret's unnatural craving for power led directly to Suffolk's undoing: "It was my ambition," his Margaret declares, that "made Suffolk stain his hands in innocent Blood."[77] In this respect, Crowne's Margaret mirrored Charles II's Catholic wife, Queen Catherine of Braganza, often accused of plotting treason and corrupting her husband.[78]

Henry the Sixth, The First Part was apparently well-received in 1681, but clearly it angered someone powerful, for the authorities quickly forbade any further performances.[79] The play's overt anti-Catholic language probably alienated prominent Catholics at court, but its downfall may well have been in its depiction of a weak king manipulated by those around him—including women.[80] Even an adapted Margaret, brought to life almost a century after her Elizabethan debut, may have retained her ability to shock, to appall, and to threaten.

· 9 ·

"A Woman's Glory and the World Avow"

Her Lost Years

nne Oldfield, one of the most famous and infamous women in early eighteenth-century England, swept across the stage of the Theatre Royal—known then, as now, as Drury Lane— wearing gown and crown. The actors playing two cowering nobles, the Earl of Salisbury and the Duke of York, blanched as Oldfield marched downstage, spitting her lines.

"Disdainful men!" Oldfield chided them. "You fight a friendship; you tempt an enmity, discerning neither. You know not Margaret!"

"That England ne'er had known her!" whispered Salisbury, half to York and half to his audience.

"I will be known!" Anne snapped back. She took center stage and, beneath the flickering flames that lit the boards of Drury Lane, the actress proclaimed to her six hundred spectators:

> Is fortitude, and wisdom,
> Given to man, alone? Prove me, in council;
> Prove me, in the Field! In policy, let Salisbury,
> In war, let York, oppose me. But, my lords;
> Be sure, you overmatched this slighted woman!
> Urge me to all Extremes! Friendship and favor,
> I neither ask, nor grant. Success is mine;

If courage claims success. Yet, if we fail;
Your chronicles shall witness to my fame;
Your daughters boast, your sons all emulate,
A woman's glory and the world avow,
England once had a queen deserved to reign![1]

And then Oldfield swept off the stage, not to be seen again until the play's epilogue: a rhyming rumination on whether gender norms are learned or inborn, written especially for her by Ambrose Philips, a Cambridge-educated playwright and politician. Margaret now had—for the first time in her stage history—the final word.

A prodigious performer with a brilliant business mind, Anne Oldfield had risen as high as any woman could in eighteenth-century

Anne Oldfield, one of the first actresses to play
Margaret (in a 1723 adaptation), depicted here as
Rosamund in a play of the same name.

England. By the time she played Queen Margaret in 1723, Oldfield had firmly established herself as one of England's first "celebrity" performers.[2] Not only was she a box office draw, but tales of her extravagant lifestyle, her glittering social circle, her many male admirers, and her considerable wealth spread through London society.[3] She wielded tremendous influence at Drury Lane, she performed for the royals, and she unashamedly carried on affairs with multiple members of Parliament, ultimately bearing these MPs several children. Unlike many other actresses of this era, she had no need to marry—her huge success on the stage had guaranteed her financial security.[4]

Yet Oldfield's offstage renown paled in comparison to her prowess in front of an audience. Onstage, she played at least 102 roles, 68 of which she originated. At her death at age forty-seven, she received a memorial, secured by her lover, a Whig politician, in Westminster Abbey. "So irrepressible was [her] genius," gushed one nineteenth-century critic, "that we should like to imagine her the descendant of one of those inspired actors who played the Globe Theatre, under the watchful eye of Shakespeare and Burbage."[5] Oldfield led English theatre into the eighteenth century, which has been called "the age of the actress."[6]

An artist of Oldfield's stature taking on a new part at Drury Lane, one of only two licensed theatres in London, was certainly an event. Oldfield was about forty years old when she first appeared as Margaret, and by that point in her career, she was the headlining attraction of any theatrical event in which she chose to perform. Such a luminary departing from her famous (usually comedic) roles to embody a historical figure—one of Shakespeare's, no less—undoubtedly attracted the attention of all those who frequented the theatre. But, like *The Misery of Civil War* a half century before, this wasn't Shakespeare's play. Titled *Humfrey, Duke of Gloucester*, the production in which Oldfield played Margaret stretches the term "adaptation" to the breaking point. Philips had created his play from scraps of *Henry VI, Part 2*, and, to satisfy a growing interest in juicy female leading roles, he paid extra attention to Eleanor Cobham and Margaret while ignoring King Henry completely.

In this new play, Margaret was not a side character. Now a role written for a star, Margaret here emerges at the center of the drama, a fierce theatrical force demanding the audience reckon with her. In dispensing with Shakespeare's broad historical perspective and focusing on Margaret and Eleanor, Philips's drama casts the princess of Anjou as not just a lead but a key participant in a complicated conversation about the role of women in English society.[7]

By the time of Philips's *Humfrey*, Shakespeare had been dead just over one hundred years, and actresses had been performing on Restoration stages for about sixty. Theatre was popular among many social classes and all genders. And, if the seventeenth century had been an era in which Shakespeare had disappeared for decades at a time, the eighteenth century was when Shakespeare became Shakespeare: an icon, a beacon, and an industry. The century began with editors poring over and republishing his plays; it continued with translators and travelers taking his work across the globe; and it ended with the tradition of Shakespearean scholarship firmly established. Producers and dramatists shaped and morphed his works to fit their artistic, political, and financial needs. Actors built careers on his characters. It was in the eighteenth century that Shakespeare helped England to develop a national identity even as it consolidated global power. And Margaret, a figure from its medieval past, allowed some of the island's most prominent actresses to grapple with gendered expectations and with the moral conundra of a modernizing empire.[8]

As the seventeenth century gave way to the eighteenth, Londoners poured into the city's playhouses. The capital's population grew considerably, and the theatre was its great mixing place. Actresses like Anne Oldfield worked alongside performer-playwrights who sliced and diced classic plays to create their own dramas. This was not seen as a radical process, nor was it understood as any sort of artistic intervention. Audiences expected to see plays reimagined. Among the most famous of the adapters—and certainly the boldest—was an outspoken and polarizing actor-writer called Colley Cibber. No person—man or woman—would have a greater influence on the trajectory of Margaret through the eighteenth century and far beyond. For, in adapting Margaret's best-loved play, *Richard III*, Cibber would cut her entirely, an excision that would be replicated, again and again, in the centuries to come. As a result, the relatively few adaptations in the eighteenth and nineteenth centuries that did retain Margaret appear—both in retrospect and in their own time—as innovative, even daring works, ones that allowed leading actresses to challenge male dominance onstage.[9]

Born in Bloomsbury in 1671, Colley Cibber worked his way up in the London theatre and, by the late 1690s, had become one of the city's most popular performers. His first great success as a writer came in 1700, when he adapted *Richard III* for a contemporary audience with an eye toward creating an iconic starring role for himself. He shuffled the play's action, included bits of earlier *Henry VI* plays, and cut narrative strands—including Margaret's—to focus the play's attention on his own performance.[10] Shorn of Margaret's two pivotal scenes—in which she challenges the titular monarch and inspires the women of his court to confront and curse him—the play became a work truly dominated by one (male) character.[11]

Colley Cibber was many things: an author, an actor, a manager, his country's poet laureate, and to many, an ostentatious fool. Like his friend Anne Oldfield, he was known for his exertions both on the stage and around town. He made rash business decisions, he was self-serving, and he consistently gave himself plum roles when he was, by all accounts, not terribly good at acting. He made scores of enemies, but he always figured out how to end up on the top of London's theatrical heap. He had twelve children, many of whom entered the theatre as well. His son Theophilus was an actor, a manager, and a participant in a marriage so tempestuous that the resulting gossip and opprobrium all but ended his theatrical career. Colley's youngest, Charlotte Charke, was a novelist and actor who specialized in breeches roles (male characters played by female performers), and later presented as a man in public, leaving the theatre to work as a nobleman's valet, a cleaner, and a tavern keeper. At one point Charke took to the road as a traveling player performing original puppet shows of Shakespeare's history plays.[12]

Despite their popularity during his life, Cibber's own plays have not aged well. His writing style was halting and inconsistent, defects noted by many of the critics of his day.[13] But the warnings of critics fall short when there is money to be made. Cibber did not write his plays for readers but for audiences, and audiences spoke with their wallets. They flocked to see Cibber's sex comedies and over-the-top tragedies; they gorged on the visual feasts he arranged on his stages. His actors wore real jewels, Ophelia's grave bore real dirt, and fresh animal blood subbed for human gore in his *Richard III.*[14]

Colley Cibber's most lasting gift to the theatre was his Margaretless *Richard III*, which dominated English-speaking stages in the eighteenth century. Indeed, it was performed so often that Shakespeare's own play—and the characters therein—was hardly seen until well into the nineteenth century. Though Shakespeare's play eventually retook its place as a classic of the English stage, Cibber's play's influence remained; some of Cibber's text even appears in Laurence Olivier's 1955 film version.[15]

Yet despite the hegemonic influence of this adaptation, Margaret continued to appeal to enterprising actresses and adapters—including, interestingly enough, Cibber's own son Theophilus. Years before Theophilus flamed out of the theatre in spectacular, humiliating, and drunken fashion, he too adapted one of the plays of the Margaretsaga. Theophilus was about seventeen when he wrote *An Historical Tragedy of the Civil Wars Between the Houses of York and Lancaster in the Reign of King Henry the VIth*, drawing from Shakespeare's *Henry VI, Part 3* (which he acknowledged), Crowne's *The Misery of Civil War* (which he did not), and a few other Shakespeare works for good measure.[16] Unlike his father, Theophilus retained Margaret, preserving several large speeches for the queen—and creating several new ones. When rallying her troops to battle, Margaret speaks not the text Shakespeare wrote for her but something else:

> Thus far with Speed, and easy March, we are come!
> Now let us doff our silken Robes of Peace,
> And arm our Minds and Bodies for fell War;
> Stiffen the Sinews, summon up the Blood,
> Disguise fair Nature with hard favour'd Rage.

If this passage sounds familiar to a Shakespearean's ear, it is because this speech is only a light gloss on Shakespeare's Henry V's speech at Harfleur, with that speech's famous introductory phrase, "Once more unto the breach," here becoming Margaret's "Thus far with Speed" and the line about "silken Robes of Peace" being a paraphrase of a line from *Henry VI, Part 1*.[17]

Despite the radical choice to frame Margaret as Henry V (the English hero who, had he lived longer, would have been her father-in-law), Theophilus Cibber did not center Margaret as Ambrose Philips had. Perhaps this was because Anne Oldfield, Philips's Margaret, was a star. By contrast, all that survives of the actress who first played Theophilus's Margaret is her surname: Campbell.

In the end, neither of the two adaptations that kept Margaret had anywhere near the impact of Colley Cibber's *Richard III*. And yet, variations like these were the *only* way one could see Margaret in eighteenth-century London. With just one small exception, the four plays in which Margaret appears, including the Bard's own *Richard III*, were not staged at all in the entire eighteenth century. They existed solely in adaptation. Audiences didn't seem to mind.[18]

By the early eighteenth century, interest in Shakespeare's female characters had begun to swell. Actresses (such as Anne Oldfield) had become genuine celebrities, and alluring modes of performance new to England (such as Italian opera) were generating cult followings for many well-known women. In the midst of this cultural moment, in the late 1730s, a group of female theatregoers assembled to advocate for the increased production of Shakespeare's work in London's major theatres. They called themselves the Shakespeare Ladies Club, and their actions provide vital clues about why Margaret's appearances remained so rare even as the popular appetite for Shakespeare's other great female parts became insatiable.[19]

The Ladies Club's efforts in the 1730s and 1740s made Shakespeare one of the most produced playwrights in England, and the most popular revivals were plays with female protagonists: *As You Like It*, *Twelfth Night*, *All's Well That Ends Well*, and George Lillo's *Marina*, which retold the story of the main female character of *Pericles*—a play that had not been performed in the eighteenth century before the Ladies Club's intercession. So fervent was the interest in female characters that some playwrights even added new roles for women to Shakespeare's plays. The additions were varied: *Henry V* saw the inclusion of Harriet, a young woman who dresses as a boy to fight for England, *Richard II* saw a noblewoman added to carry out an affair, and *Timon of Athens*, a play in which women play practically no part, saw a few different ingenues added in.[20]

Margaret's sole entrée into the Ladies Club's repertory came on March 13, 1738, in the new and gaudily decorated Covent Garden Theatre. It was there that the Duke's Company, still one of only two acting companies permitted to perform in London, put on *Henry VI, Part 1* at the club's request. This was the only unadapted production of any of the *Henry VI* plays recorded in the eighteenth century. And it was a failure, closing after just a single performance.[21]

Given the avid interest in other female characters, Margaret's persistent absence is striking. That she remained offstage, even as other women dominated onstage, was probably due primarily to the simple unpopularity of the *Henry VI* plays; why stage these little-known, uneven works when masterpieces like *Macbeth* or *King Lear* were sure to make money? Meanwhile, the only truly popular play in which Margaret appeared, *Richard III*, had been shorn of her presence by Colley Cibber. An additional explanation, however, may be the lack of clear moralistic statement in the Margaretsaga condemning the female lead's immoral behavior, as in *Macbeth* (with Lady Macbeth, unable to scrub out the damned spot staining her conscience, killing herself) or *Lear* (with Regan succumbing to poison offstage and Goneril likewise dying by suicide). Compelling though she may have been, Margaret was no heroine, and her ultimate survival and scornful vindication would have been tough for many to stomach.

Margaret's eighteenth-century erasure overlapped precisely with the increasing cultural significance of Shakespeare as a literary icon. Thus, even as the Bard's works spread around the globe and took up a central spot within the canon, Margaret remained obscure; she would have to wait decades before returning to the fore of theatrical life.

Shakespeare's rise began with new editions of his plays. In the early eighteenth century, as the old Folio editions and older quartos were decaying, a London publisher named Jacob Tonson cannily bought up the copyright to Shakespeare's plays (not long after the legal concept of copyright emerged). With the assistance of the playwright and poet Nicholas Rowe, Tonson brought out a handsome six-volume set of Shakespeare's writing, delivering the Bard to a truly mass audience. For the first time, character lists, scene breaks, and story locations accompanied Shakespeare's plays, making for a far easier reading experience. The two men's editorial choices did little to change Margaret, though they added introductory text that offhandedly referred to her as Henry's "imperious wife."[22]

This edition was arguably the first portable, accessible version of the plays, and it proved to be so popular that Tonson reprinted it multiple times over the next decade. Soon, other editors decided to get in on the action, and out of their dueling versions and vicious competitiveness emerged the contentious field of Shakespearean scholarship.[23] The Bard's renown soared with the new editions, but his preeminence was truly ensured in 1737, when Parliament enacted the Licensing Act, which gave the lord chamberlain and his assistant, the examiner of plays, the ability to read—and to approve or disapprove—any play written for public performance. New plays were stifled, and old favorites, like those of Shakespeare, became standard fare. The Licensing Act remained in effect, allowing and censoring plays in England, until 1968.[24]

By the mid-eighteenth century, Shakespeare was everywhere in English culture. Academics inaugurated courses on him, and critics—even the rare female critics—started specializing in his work. Few spared a word for Margaret, so thoroughly had she disappeared from the Shakespearean canon. Still, the work of these writers—alongside the now-constant production of Shakespeare's plays—established a literary nationalism that united the kingdom's growing empire. "That Shakespeare was declared to rule world literature at the same time that Britannia was declared to rule the waves," wrote the historian Michael Dodson, "may, indeed, be more than a coincidence."[25]

The Bard's spread across the globe was lubricated with blood. The English victory over France in the Seven Years' War (1756–1763) led to a rise in English cultural exports (and a fall in the French aesthetic reputation). As they had done militarily, the Germans allied themselves culturally with the English against the French, and soon Shakespeare's plays were being translated, printed, and performed from Berlin to Dresden to Prague. Germany had long been a hospitable home for Shakespeare—so hospitable, in fact, that his debut in that country (a 1604 performance of *Romeo and Juliet* in the Bavarian city of Nördlingen) apparently took place while he was still alive.[26] Yet it was in the eighteenth century that Shakespeare became a beloved cultural figure in Germany. New editions blossomed like cornflowers, and by the end of the century one German poet and translator could—almost credibly—call the Bard "completely ours."[27]

Shakespeare's influence extended eastward across Europe, as a distaste for the French—who had dominated theatrical models for the past hundred or so years—grew stronger. Polish and Czech monarchs took in performances of his plays, but it was eighteenth-century Europe's most important female ruler, the Russian Empress Catherine the Great, who did the most to expand Shakespeare's geographic reach. A ruler known for her intellectual ambitions, Catherine even took it upon herself to write four of her own plays influenced by Shakespeare's. Two of these were history plays in Shakespeare's model, complete with portraits of courtly spectacles, everyday soldiers, and royal marriages. Though Catherine's plays were not great works of drama (a fact she freely admitted, as she called them "imitations"), they did help to popularize Shakespeare's work in the Russian theatre. Yet even this female monarch could not muster interest in the plays of Margaret.[28]

As European powers established colonial outposts across the globe, they brought with them not just violence and slavery but also Shakespeare. Records indicate that copies of the Folios existed in colonial libraries as early as 1700 (in Virginia), and they were in use at the Yale and Harvard libraries as early as the 1720s. The earliest known Shakespeare play to be produced in the Americas was *Romeo and Juliet* (New York in 1730), followed by Cibber's *Richard III* in the 1750s. Cibber's adaptation went on to be Shakespeare's most popular play in colonial America; Margaret's antagonist thrilled American audiences as Margaret herself remained absent.[29]

By the second half of the century, Shakespeare's work had become beloved in cities up and down the Atlantic coast, from Philadelphia to Annapolis to Charleston. Many of the individuals involved in the American Revolution even looked to Shakespeare for guidance. Benjamin Franklin, who had seen Anne Oldfield play Shakespeare's Cleopatra in London early in his life, was known to quote Shakespeare from memory. Thomas Jefferson kept printed copies of the plays in his library, and Abigail and John Adams quoted Shakespeare in their letters. (One of John's most cited quotations was from *Richard III*, but though he attributed the phrase to Shakespeare, it actually came from Cibber.) When visiting England a decade after America's independence, Jefferson and Adams traveled to Stratford together to pay homage at Shakespeare's birthplace.[30]

It was at the very start of these revolutionary years, as popular anger simmered, as peasants and patricians alike prepared to throw off the yoke of kings, that one forgotten queen reappeared on the English stage. The year was 1766. *The Earl of Warwick*—Thomas Francklin's adaptation (or, well, *plagiarization*) of a recent French play—was opening at Drury Lane. And one of the decade's best-loved actresses was playing Margaret, pitted as ever against the Yorks. Not Shakespeare's Margaret, to be sure. But one who continued to challenge Londoners' ingrained ideas of gender. After all, this Margaret was about to taunt the audience, prosperous and proletarian, and tell them that women secretly ran the world.

Mary Ann Yates stared out at the throng. She was probably London's preeminent tragic performer, having recently inherited the title from Susannah Cibber (Colley's daughter-in-law). Her performance as Margaret guaranteed the play success. At the performance's end, Yates turned and stared directly at the playgoers. As with Anne Oldfield's epilogue in Ambrose Philips's play or Rosalind's in *As You Like It*, it isn't entirely clear if it's Margaret or Mary Ann speaking.

"Come on!" she yelled to her audience, "now parry Marg'ret if you can." She looked down at the pit, where the merchants, critics, and scholars sat:

> Stand up, ye boasters! don't there sneaking sit;
> Are you for Pleasure, Politics, or Wit?
> The Boxes smile to see me scold the Pit.
> Their turn is next—and though I will not wrong'em,
> A woful havoc there will be among 'em.

As promised, she stared up at the boxes, where the wealthy reclined:

> You, our best friends, love, cherish, and respect us;
> Not take our fortunes, marry, and neglect us.

At this point, it became clear whom she was addressing: men. Men of all classes.

> You think indeed, that as you please, you rule us,
> And with a strange importance often school us!

Yet could they have done all that she had, she wondered?

> What is your boast?—Would you, like me, have done,
> To free a captive wife, or save a son?
> Rather than run such danger of your lives,
> You'd leave your children, and lock up your wives.

The men were not as great as they believed, she concluded:

> When with your noblest deeds a nation rings!
> You are but puppets, and we play the strings.
> We plan no battles—true—but out of sight,
> Crack goes the fan,—and armies halt or fight!
> You have th'advantage, Ladies—wisely reap it,
> And let me hint the only way to keep it.
> Let men of vain ideas have their fill,
> Frown, bounce, stride, strut—while you, with happy skill,
> Like anglers, use the finest silken thread;
> Give line enough—nor check the tugging head:
> The fish will flounder—you with gentle hand,
> And soft degrees, must bring the trout to land.[31]

This Margaret provides a window into a world unlike ours, and unlike Shakespeare's. The Bard's Margaret had not, in fact, been content to stay "out of sight" and pull "the strings"—she had stabbed people! Shakespeare's Margaret had not manipulated her husband—she had abandoned him, taken over his army, and did indeed "plan battles." Francklin, by contrast, cut Henry from his play altogether. Like Ambrose Philips decades before, he wasn't interested in the king. Instead, he used this drama—and Margaret—to play on popular eighteenth-century tropes satirizing marital relations and masculinity itself. Even as the world became more revolutionary, Margaret became more sly.

Slyly, then, Margaret kept finding her way to English audiences. In 1777, *Margaret of Anjou*, a short play (or "interlude") written by

Edward Jerningham, became the first play to bear the queen's name.[32] Jerningham's interlude told the story of Margaret and her son escaping after defeat at the battle of Hexham and, taking little from Shakespeare's text, portrayed the queen as a determined but tragic mother, pathetic and not self-sufficient. A brief sketch perhaps performed alongside a full-length drama, the interlude had little impact on public perception of the character, though it does stand out as the first drama to focus solely on Margaret. Not a decade later, however, in a revival of Thomas Francklin's *The Earl of Warwick*, another actress would seize ownership of the role—and make Margaret her own.[33]

Sarah Kemble was, as traveling vaudevillians would later quip, born in a trunk. The eldest of twelve children, she came into the world in Wales while her father, a traveling player, was on tour. Theatre was the family business, and many of Sarah's siblings later took to the stage; John Philip Kemble, the family's second child, became one of the leading tragedians of his generation and, later, the manager of Covent Garden, one of London's most prestigious theatrical houses. And, like Anne Oldfield before her, Sarah became one of England's most recognizable names as its celebrity culture continued to develop.[34]

Sarah grew to be a tall, striking, and charismatic actor, a figure of such composure that, in the words of one critic, she "should have breathed the formal air of ancient Rome."[35] She married young and, as all women did (regardless of the fame they had accrued under their born name), took her husband's surname; she became Sarah Siddons. By the time she played Queen Margaret in *The Earl of Warwick* in 1784, she was one of London's most popular actresses, having surpassed Yates as the most adulated woman on the English stage, just as Yates had surpassed Susannah Cibber, just as Cibber had surpassed Oldfield. The same year that Siddons played Margaret, she posed for a portrait by Joshua Reynolds, called *Sarah Siddons as the Tragic Muse*, which instantly made her a theatrical icon (and later inspired a key plot point in the film *All About Eve*).[36]

Sarah Siddons had been acting professionally for about ten years when she took on Margaret, and the role came as she entered a more mature phase in her career. "In Margaret of Anjou, I have seen new beauties, and new powers unfold themselves in Mrs. Siddons," wrote a fan of Siddons's performance. "And wondering, I beheld her an object as much to be dreaded as hitherto she excited my admiration and my love."[37] George Bartley, an actor known for his portrayal of Falstaff, wrote of Siddons's magnificent entrance onto the stage at the play's climax: "The giantess burst upon the view, and stood in the centre of the arch motionless. So electrifying was the unexpected impression, that I stood for a moment breathless. . . . I could not but gaze upon her attentively. Her head was erect, and the fire of her brilliant eyes darted upon mine."[38] Siddons's Margaret was a triumph, a "full display of regal majesty," in the words of one biographer.[39]

Sarah Siddons as Margaret in *The Earl of Warwick*, an adaptation by Thomas Francklin. Siddons played the queen in the 1770s, after Mary Ann Yates originated the role in the previous decade.

Elizabeth Whitlock, Sarah Siddons's younger sister, playing Margaret in later productions of *The Earl of Warwick*, an adaptation by Thomas Francklin.

No doubt playing Margaret in Francklin's adaptation prepared Siddons for a role she would play the next year, a role she would also conquer: Lady Macbeth. Indeed, Siddons became known for playing "persecuted queens" like Margaret.[40] She continued to perform—with her brother, for royals, and even as Hamlet, many times—well into the next century. And Margaret would remain something of a family affair; even after Siddons left the role behind, her sister, Elizabeth Whitlock, would take over in not one but two different adaptations of the *Henry VI* plays.[41]

The times—and the tastes of audiences—were changing as the eighteenth century reached its close. Five years after Sarah Siddons took to the stage as Margaret, a different version of the Lancastrian queen appeared on the boards, in a production with extended musical interludes. *The Battle of Hexham*, by the English playwright George Colman the Younger, was a largely fictionalized account of the battle of 1464 that decimated Lancastrian forces. Colman had drawn from Shakespeare—but barely. His story was pastoral: Fleeing from the (unseen) victorious Yorkists to a lively wood replete with peasants, robbers, and a fool singing a "hey ho," Margaret spends time with an unlikely band of rowdy original characters. But Colman's Margaret lacked any dramatic luster. Worrying only for her son, this character has little understanding of the world of war outside this provincial setting. This queen is passive; she even calls herself weak, soft, and idle in her very first speech. This Margaret retained none of the heart of the tiger Shakespeare had given to her.

At the play's debut, Margaret was played by Maria Theresa Kemble, the wife of Charles Kemble, Sarah Siddons's youngest brother. *The Battle of Hexham* was commercially successful and its actors drew plaudits: One critic wrote that "Mrs. Siddons herself could not have surpassed [Kemble] either for spirited animation or melting distress."[42] Still, the latter phrase was significant: Kemble's Margaret was little more than a distressed damsel, melting rather than burning. Colman, it would seem, was more interested in the Wars of the Roses for the quaint medieval setting than he was in their most transgressive figures.[43] Melodrama did not serve Margaret well.

As the nineteenth century began, Colley Cibber's adaptation of Shakespeare's *Richard III* stood unchallenged. A full century after its premiere, the play continued to enthrall audiences on Anglophone stages across the world. Generations of viewers had grown so accustomed to Cibber's cuts and additions that even the most seasoned theatregoers didn't know Shakespeare's text. The *Henry VI* plays were basically ignored. Yet as the century progressed, four actresses brought Margaret back to London audiences: the

Irish-born comedian Julia Betterton Glover, the Scottish tragedian Margaret Agnes Bunn, the brilliant performer and theatre manager Mary Amelia Warner, and the American star Kate Bateman. Theirs was a queen less diminished by adaptation than the Margarets inhabited by Yates, Siddons, or Kemble. Instead, these bright stars of the early nineteenth-century stage revived a fearsome Margaret, one far closer to the Shakespearean original.

Julia Glover was a phenomenon in her day. Like Sarah Siddons and Anne Oldfield, she started in comedies but found great success in tragic roles. She worked consistently despite bearing eight children and enduring a famously difficult personal life (her father confiscated her earnings and then forced her into marriage to a husband who did much the same). But Julia Glover never wavered. She became such a prominent cultural institution that Queen Victoria acted as patron at the actress's retirement benefit performance. Her stage career lasted for over six decades, nearly twice the length of that of the far better-remembered Edmund Kean, the hard-drinking and womanizing actor who captivated English audiences at the start of the nineteenth century. Yet, while many biographical works cover the life of Kean, not a single book about Julia Betterton Glover, England's most prominent actress for over half a century, has been written.[44]

Still, the lives and careers of these two thespians are inextricably connected—and their joint efforts would ultimately have significant ramifications for Margaret. Kean first played Cibber's Richard at Drury Lane in 1814 to a rapturous reception, with Glover appearing opposite him as Elizabeth. This production brought glowing notices from writers like Lord Byron, John Keats, and William Hazlitt, an early figure in the then-nascent field of theatre criticism. A few years later, Kean sought to impress again with another tragic Shakespearean role, and to do so he reached beyond *Richard III*. Working with John Herman Merivale, a playwright with no particularly brilliant plays to his name, he created a new work called *Richard, Duke of York* (this was King Richard III's father). The two assembled their script from scenes taken from the three parts of *Henry VI*, all focused on the life of the elder Richard. It was as if they had a new Shakespeare play, one created by stringing together pieces of forgotten works. When this chimerical production opened in 1817, many in the audience were surely shocked to find Kean playing not King Richard III, as he had just famously done, but rather his father, whose attempts at seizing the crown from the Lancastrian Henry VI set the Wars of the Roses into motion. To play the role of Margaret, Kean called on his friend Julia Glover.[45]

Glover's portrayal of Margaret in *Richard, Duke of York*, signaled that a change was coming—Merivale noted in passing his awe for the "zealous exertions" and "strength of feeling and genius" that Glover poured into a part made difficult by "the imbecility of the wretched Henry."[46] In arranging scenes from the *Henry VI* plays to create a new narrative, Merivale and Kean continued a tradition of adaptation stretching back to Crowne. Their Margaret, personified by Glover, resembled Shakespeare's formidable figure: "Never from her birth / Hath Anjou's Margaret known the taste of fear," Glover declared at the start of the play's fourth act, moments before learning of the death of Margaret's lover, Suffolk. After a century of Cibber, a fearless Margaret was sneaking back into the English theatre.[47]

The next actress to portray Margaret on a London stage was Margaret Agnes Bunn. The daughter of a baker, she learned to act in a small Scottish town by the River Clyde. Despite her provincial origins, however, Bunn impressed observers from a young age, and even before she turned seventeen, she was starring at Drury Lane. By 1821, she was twenty-two, and, just a few years after Glover's turn, Bunn played Margaret in a new adaptation of *Richard III*—an adaptation that, unlike Cibber's, retained her character. This made Bunn the first to perform *Richard III*'s Margaret in well over a century.[48]

This bold new adaptation was the brainchild of William Macready, an upstart actor eager to displace Edmund Kean as the London stage's enfant terrible. He had already found some success playing Cibber's Richard, but now—with Kean busy touring his Richard (and other roles) in America—Macready created his own hybrid version of the play, adding back in a few of Shakespeare's original scenes.[49]

The role of the haunting, lamenting, cursing Queen Margaret

was new to theatregoers. But Bunn's audiences didn't see all that Shakespeare wrote for her. Bunn played Margaret's first scene (her conflict with Richard), but Macready omitted her second (in which Margaret mourns with the other women who had lost husbands and children). Macready claimed that he "reluctantly made" this cut, for though he relished the character's vivid speeches, he feared that audiences would not understand her grief given the rest of the context excised from Shakespeare's story.[50]

To include Margaret at all was to defy not only audience expectations but also critical consensus, as the growing community of Shakespeare critics generally continued to ignore the Margaretsaga (other than *Richard III*). In fact, the editor of *Shakespeare's Plays Abridged and Revised for the Use of Girls* skipped straight from *Henry V* to *Richard III*, justifying the absence with a single sentence: "The Play of Henry VI, being comparatively devoid of interest, has been omitted."[51] Those few critics who mentioned Margaret at all tended to concur that she added little of value to the canon. Anna Jameson, a prolific nineteenth-century art historian and literary critic, admired Margaret's "female spite" but argued that she "is not one of Shakespeare's women"—meaning those more familiar to nineteenth-century audiences: Rosalind, Juliet, Viola, and others from frequently produced plays. The Bard, "who could excite our respect and sympathy even for a Lady Macbeth, would never have given us a heroine without a touch of heroism," she wrote; "he would have redeemed her from unmingled detestation; he would have breathed into her some of his own sweet spirit—he would have given the woman a soul."[52] Decades later, the influential actor-manager Henry Irving added that the Margaret of *Richard III* was "impressive" on the page "but, to the spectator of the acted play, she is only a gloomy kind of chorus, prophesying, with tediously elaborated indignation, events that we are on tenter-hooks to see actually happen."[53]

It took not a critical revolution but a legal one—a massive change in laws governing theatrical production—to clear the way for Margaret to reemerge fully, albeit briefly, in the middle of the century. In 1843, an act of Parliament changed the face of theatre in London, which—for more than a century—had allowed dramatic plays to be staged *only* at Drury Lane and Covent Garden, the two theatres with royal patents. The Theatrical Regulation Act eliminated their duopoly. This was a seismic shift, allowing for the proliferation of Shakespeare's work—and many other plays, classical and contemporary—in playhouses across the capital. Now free to set out on their own, theatrical renegades like the actress Mary Amelia Warner and actor Samuel Phelps broke away from Covent Garden to create a professional company at Sadler's Wells Theatre in Islington, a few miles north of the West End, the longtime home of the more established playhouses. Phelps, Warner, and their compatriots had a dream for their new company: They wanted to bring Shakespeare to the masses. And they would begin by casting aside Cibber entirely and staging Shakespeare's own *Richard III*.[54]

Their production opened at Sadler's Wells on February 20, 1845. Phelps took the role of Richard while Mary Warner claimed Margaret. This production represented the first time in over a century and a half that an adaptation so close to Shakespeare's text had been staged in London. Phelps made some cuts, but both of Margaret's scenes remained. The production was notable not just for its reintroduction of the Bard's words but for its physical splendor. Phelps replaced painted trompe l'oeil scenery with three-dimensional set pieces: staircases and bridges laced his stage. It was a tremendous hit.[55]

Critics (a growing constituency in a London newly awash with newspapers) applauded the material ambition of the production, but what struck them most was, as *The Athenaeum* put it, "the wild and weird Queen Margaret."[56] The *Times* review noted that the presence of Margaret lessened the focus on Richard (the precise reason Cibber cut her all those years before) but nonetheless celebrated the choice:

> What is lost on the side of Richard is more than compensated to the play by the restoration of Queen Margaret. . . . For it is this character that gives unity to the play. . . . She is the incarnate Nemesis,—the revelation of Fate,—almost the Chorus of the Play. Mrs. Warner played her admirably. She entered with

the aspect less of a human enemy than of some supernatural being. The intensity and violence of her hate were terrific.[57]

Warner was an actress of great power on the stage who excelled in dark roles like that of the vituperative, grieving queen. Charles Dickens, an avid theatregoer, said of her more ignoble parts that she was a "defiant splendid sin." She was the "*beau idéal* of a tragic performer," wrote Phelps's nephew after her death, "especially in severe and majestic characters, and greater, perhaps, in them than any other actress of our time." Indeed, her turn as the Lancastrian queen was so definitive that when Phelps revived his production of *Richard III* two decades later, he chose to produce Cibber's play—"I am sure unhappily," the nineteenth-century scholar John Joseph Knight speculated—for he could find no other actress "capable of doing justice to Margaret."[58]

The last of the nineteenth-century stars to return Margaret to the Anglophone stage was the American actress Kate Josephine Bateman, a remarkable artist born—like many of her predecessors as Margaret—into a theatrical family. The daughter of Hezekiah Linthicum Bateman and Sidney Frances Bateman, both performers as well as theatrical managers, Kate was the first of four Bateman daughters to take the stage. Though she would later play Queen Margaret opposite the Richard of Henry Irving, one of England's most popular performers (and a critic who, recall, dismissed Margaret's value), her first appearance in *Richard III* occurred before her tenth birthday.[59] Kate's evolution from child-sized curio in Margaret-less productions to rapturously received adult Margaret exemplifies the character's final nineteenth-century feat: She was starting to become a vehicle for ambitious actors hoping simultaneously to achieve both legitimacy and stardom.

Strange though it may seem to modern theatregoers, children performing Shakespeare constituted a popular entertainment in the mid-nineteenth century, and little Kate played Richmond (later King Henry VII) opposite her sister Ellen's Richard III. Hezekiah and Sidney booked their daughters' production in theatres across the

United States, part of a grueling, yearslong tour lasting essentially the entirety of their childhoods, and eventually attracted the attention of the theatrical impresario P. T. Barnum, who branded the girls talented "freaks" and took their act abroad. The Bateman children were a hit in London and soon enough Kate, Ellen, and the two younger sisters, Virginia and Isabel, were dominating London's biggest houses in both comedic and dramatic roles.[60]

By the time Kate matured into an adult performer, Hezekiah and Sidney assumed the operations of London's Lyceum Theatre alongside Henry Irving, a young man at the start of a meteoric rise (he would ultimately be the first actor to win a knighthood). Following Hezekiah's unexpected death, Sidney took control of the Lyceum and became one of England's most powerful theatrical producers, securing for herself financial gain and top billing, both rarities for women producers in nineteenth-century England. She variously struggled

The Bateman sisters, Ellen and Kate, in costume for their children's production of *Richard III*. Kate Bateman, who would later go on to play Queen Margaret, here played Richmond.

against and capitalized on the outsized ambitions of Henry Irving, who coveted the acclaim of Kean and Macready and sought to match the plaudits they had won playing the great tragic parts. Together, Irving and Sidney Bateman decided to create something exciting and new: They would stage Shakespeare's *Richard III*, Irving would play Richard, and they would go on an extensive press tour to ensure the public knew they were done with Cibber's play once and for all.

The flyers for the Lyceum production of *Richard III* displayed three names in large print: Shakespeare, Irving, and (Kate) Bateman. The first informed audiences that this was Shakespeare's play, performed for the first time since the playwright's lifetime (not entirely true). The second told ticket buyers that Henry Irving would finally take on the role of the Yorkist king, making this a theatrical event not to be missed. And the third, in large capital letters, read: "Miss Bateman as Queen Margaret."[61]

This production thus elevated Kate, and Margaret, to stardom, equal to that of Richard himself. Sidney Bateman was nothing if not canny—she wanted her children to succeed, so she sold this production of a popular property on her daughter's name. The play featured bespoke costumes, florid sets, and a full band. Kate's younger sister Isabel, an actress then building her stage reputation, played Anne. But it was Kate—strutting across the stage as the aged queen, cursing her countrymen with "fearful earnestness," as the *Daily Telegraph* gushed—whose performance made a mark.

Critics lavished praise on this novel *Richard III*; one called it "one of the most interesting revivals the stage has witnessed for a considerable period." Audiences packed the Lyceum "from pit to gallery," noted *Lloyd's Weekly Newspaper.* The papers were especially taken with Kate Bateman, with one calling her "wild and weird" (the same words used in a review of Mary Warner's Margaret) and another noting the great ovations she received.

Yet despite, or perhaps because of, Bateman's prominence in the production, a smattering of contrary takes pierced the consensus, smacking of misogyny. "None of the female characters can at all be praised," sniffed a writer for *The Times*, "and the only time we found cause to regret the change from Cibber to Shakespeare was as we listened to the unintelligible ravings of Queen Margaret in the first scene of the second act." A reviewer from the *Morning Post*, unable to help himself, added: "The imprecations of Margaret of Anjou in this tragedy are violent, but seem wanting in royal dignity." Still, audience adulation rang far louder than dissenting reviews. The production ran on and on, its run extending for many months, a strikingly long engagement for the time; it ended when Kate Bateman left the production to take on another role. The actress—the first American to play the role of Margaret, albeit on an English stage—took her lead billing with her.[62]

The ecstatic reception of both Samuel Phelps's and Sidney Bateman's productions of *Richard III*, each casting aside Cibber and embracing a "pure" text of Shakespeare's, coincided with Shakespeare's ascent to the unquestioned preeminent perch atop Anglophone theatre, a phenomenon George Bernard Shaw later called "Bardolatry." Indeed, following *Richard III*, Phelps's upstart Sadler's Wells Theatre would stage almost all of Shakespeare's works. For her part, Sidney Bateman fell out with Henry Irving almost immediately after Kate played Margaret—the disagreement concerned Irving's attempt to cut professional (and apparently romantic) ties with Isabel Bateman—so mother and daughters left the Lyceum, and Sidney took over management of Sadler's Wells.[63] It was a position she would hold until her death; afterward, Isabel tried her hand at managing the theatre, but years of performing while struggling to get out from under the theatre's mounting debts exhausted her, and she spent the last four decades of her life in a convent. Kate never stopped acting.[64]

Despite Margaret's repeated returns in prominent nineteenth-century productions of *Richard III*, the three *Henry VI* plays continued to be vanishingly obscure. Indeed, though Sadler's Wells produced almost the entire Shakespearean canon in the years following Mary Warner's star turn, the theatre skipped all three parts of

Henry VI.[65] It would take another iconoclastic director, one determined to put his mark on Shakespeare, to bring back those long-neglected works. Not altogether shockingly, that director hailed from Germany, which, in the decades to follow, would be central to Margaret's emergence as a sought-after dramatic role.

For centuries, the Bard had been one of Germany's most celebrated cultural figures, frequently staged, routinely studied, and much discussed. And though they depicted a decidedly English past, Shakespeare's history plays aroused more interest and acclaim in Germany than they did in Britain. Heinrich Heine, the great German literary critic and poet, waxed poetic about the Margaretsaga, devoting lengthy passages to Margaret herself. Even if her depiction was not "founded in fact," Heine contended, "Shakespeare possesses the seers' vision which can often perceive things not contained in chronicles, but which are nonetheless true."[66] Friedrich Schiller, the Enlightenment playwright, went even further: "It would be worthwhile to adapt this series of plays for the contemporary stage," he wrote to his friend Goethe. "This could be a new era for the theatre."[67]

In a series of lectures on drama given in Vienna a decade later, the scholar August Wilhelm Schlegel identified a similar potential:

> The dramas derived from the English history, ten in number, form one of the most valuable of Shakespeare's works . . . I say advisedly *one* of his works, for the poet evidently intended them to form one great whole. It is, as it were, an historical heroic poem in the dramatic form, of which the separate plays constitute the rhapsodies. . . . It furnishes examples of the political course of the world, applicable to all times.[68]

Such scholarly musing presented a provocation—could a director find in these long-neglected plays a sweeping narrative of human history? And could such a director do so in a single theatrical event? Half a century later, an enterprising German director responded in the affirmative.

The year 1864 saw the three hundredth anniversary of Shakespeare's birth. Perhaps deliberately mirroring the extravagant celebration of the

Bard's bicentennial at Stratford a century earlier, Franz Dingelstedt, the director of the Weimar Court Theatre, decided to create a grand, as yet unprecedented spectacle: He produced the history plays, in order, for the first time in history.[69]

Dingelstedt's production was lavish and daring, and he attracted some of Germany's biggest names to participate in the procession of dramatic stories. The director cited Schiller and Schlegel's words specifically as his inspiration; he also liked that the plays had been so long ignored, all the better for him to stand out, to make his mark on the German theatrical world.[70]

Dingelstedt loved how well the plays fit together. When staged as a serial production they were "a single dramatic work constructed according to the strictest artistic rules," he wrote.[71] The most substantial change that he made to Shakespeare's texts was to Margaret. Unlike the English directors—many of whom had cut her lines and shortened her part to serve male actors better—Dingelstedt *enlarged* the role, giving her new speeches and scenes. Specifically, Dingelstedt sought to add more nuance and texture to the adulterous relationship between the queen and the Duke of Suffolk. His project was to "soften" Margaret's harsh edges, to further explain her motivations, which he thought would make her more sympathetic to an audience learning her story for the first time. Dingelstedt claimed that he wanted to give her "light to counterbalance the dark with which the poet [Shakespeare] painted her picture."[72]

To play Margaret, Dingelstedt chose one of Weimar's most beloved actresses, Louise Hettstedt. Already a few decades into a stage career that would last a half century, Hettstedt was adored by audiences and associates alike, remembered by one colleague as a "complete artist" who "never judged her roles" but would accept parts based on their service to the entire artistic project—she rejoiced equally in playing Lady Macbeth or Falstaff's page. Another colleague called her a "gifted actress with rare versatility" who met every part and every collaborator with the "purest, loudest enthusiasm." The history cycle would mark the apex of Hettstedt's artistry. Not only was her performance praised by critics but she also found the wit and humor in Margaret's scenes. Allowed to play all that Shakespeare wrote for Margaret (and a few speeches and scenes that Dingelstedt added, too), Hettstedt was the first actress ever to portray the queen in her entirety—that is, over *all* of the plays that include her—fearsome, clever, and tragic.[73]

Dingelstedt's 1864 production in Weimar proved to be the high-point of his career, as well; he would go on to revive his cycle in Vienna twice in the 1870s. This, in turn, laid the groundwork for many, many productions of Shakespeare's histories as a cycle in the next century—beginning with a similar theatrical experiment, at home, in Stratford.[74]

· 10 ·

"I Rather Like Slightly Nasty Women"

Her Ascendance

In 1901, William Butler Yeats traveled to Stratford-upon-Avon to see a few of Shakespeare's plays. Yeats, a floppy-haired, bespectacled bloke in his mid-thirties and already a leading voice in Irish literature, found Stratford an idyllic anti-London: unpretentious, unfussy, and unspoiled. "One passes through quiet streets, where gabled and red-tiled houses remember the Middle Age," he wrote, "to a theatre that has been made not to make money, but for the pleasure of making it, like the market houses that set the traveller chuckling; nor does one find it among hurrying cabs and ringing pavements, but in a green garden by a river side."[1] Shakespeare's London may have been long lost, but Shakespeare's Stratford still bloomed on the edge of the Arden.

Though Stratford had been connected to London by rail for a half century by the time Yeats visited, industrialization had largely passed by the Warwickshire town, and, thanks to efforts of the local gentry to keep up the town's Tudor appearance, it had become a bit of a tourist draw.[2] Yeats visited Stratford's Shakespeare Memorial Theatre, a small venue then operated by a producer-director-actor by the name of Frank R. Benson, with great input from his actress wife, Constance. Everyone here, Yeats thought, really wanted to be watching these plays, unlike in London, where rich idlers just attended the theatre to kill the after-dinner hours.[3]

Yeats saw a collection of plays unfamiliar to him on that 1901 trip. The Memorial Theatre was putting on a series of shows all about English history; some, like *Richard III* and *Henry V*, he knew, but others he did not. An Irish nationalist, Yeats struggled with these plays, which told tales of English queens and kings as if they were biblical heroes or the flawed protagonists of Greek dramas. He warred, too, with the feeling of agreeable acquiescence that the arcadian town produced in him, a product of the Bensons' efforts to create a pride in the brand of Englishness that Shakespeare represented. He also wondered what these plays were—these plays that, when seen on successive summer evenings, seemed to come together into one narrative, as if Shakespeare had intended to write a serialized historical epic. "The five plays, that are but one play, have, when played one after another, something extravagant and superhuman, something almost mythological," he concluded with awe.[4]

On his trip to Stratford, Yeats saw the earliest English experiment in staging all of Shakespeare's history plays as if they were one continuous drama. When Frank Benson took over the ten-year-old Memorial Theatre in 1889, he decided his mission would be to explore Shakespeare's plays—all of them, even the unloved ones—in his theatre on the banks of the Avon. Armed with an innovative business mind, Benson was a workhorse, but not one known for his, well, grace onstage. "There are, I am sure, thousands of men and women in England who would welcome with the most intense enthusiasm a visit to Shakespeare's birthplace a great interpreter of his plays," wrote one drama critic, "which Mr. Benson certainly is not."[5] Benson had no training as either an actor or a manager, and it showed. "He had nearly every fault of which an actor can be guilty," recalled a colleague. "He mouthed the lines of the great tragic roles until they were meaningless, sang them until they were indistinguishable, and bawled them until they were deafening."[6] And yet, audiences—loyal Stratford locals and Bard-curious tourists like Yeats—loved Benson's shows and returned, year after year, for more.[7]

Though Frank and Constance Benson were tireless in their trips around the country in search of fame, they invariably returned to Stratford, where they, and many of their well-known friends, inhabited some of the greatest roles in Western drama. The Bensons played around with their history plays, producing one or two a season until 1905, when they produced the "earlier" tetralogy (*Richard II*, *Henry IV, Part 1* and *Part 2*, and *Henry V*), and then, in 1906, the Margaretsaga. Newspapers heralded this event, the first serial performance of the two tetralogies in English history. Yet these productions were not

Constance Benson in a studio portrait taken a few years before she played Margaret (and assorted other roles) in the Shakespeare Memorial Theatre's first experiment with serial staging of the history plays.

the lavishly staged, well-rehearsed Shakespeare productions seen in today's professional houses; sometimes, Frank and Constance gave their actors just one day to practice.[8]

The Bensons took the plum roles for themselves; Constance played Margaret in the *Henrys*, of course, but as the character Elizabeth had more stage time in *Richard III*, she switched to that role for the final night of the cycle. Frank also switched roles each night to maximize his time center stage. Despite their shortcomings, the two were beloved as figures of the Stratford stage, and their history plays were some of their greatest successes.[9] The Bensons' productions "showed that something could be made of even the obscure, unrefined *Henry VI* plays," wrote the historian Susan Margaret Kay, "if one was prepared to take risks."[10] No doubt relishing the acclaim, Frank would continue to play Richard on stages across the country for decades to come, eventually attracting the popular actress and classically trained soprano Geneviève Ward to fill the role of Margaret. Ward, who would become the first actress knighted by the King of England, had previously played the queen opposite Henry Irving at the end of his life. All of these actors—Ward, Irving, and Benson—were apparently unable to shake the parts of Margaret and Richard; once they played these characters, they kept returning to them for the rest of their lives.[11]

The Bensons' quarter-century reign as figureheads of the Shakespeare Memorial Theatre on the Avon did more than just introduce English audiences to the Margaretsaga staged in its entirety. It prepared the company housed at the Memorial Theatre for its next iteration, one that would come a few decades following the Bensons' deaths: It would become the Royal Shakespeare Company, a troupe that more than any other would revolutionize the portrayal of Margaret.[12]

Meanwhile, a hundred miles away in London, a theatre to rival the Bensons' was rising. It too would play a role in popularizing Margaret in this new century. The transformation began, as so many

Frank R. Benson, husband to Constance and early figurehead at the Shakespeare Memorial Theatre, in costume as Richard III.

do, with a death. The year was 1912, and the long, productive life of Emma Cons finally ended. Cons was an English suffragist and education activist, who, for many years, had devoted herself to developing Royal Victoria Hall, adjacent to the Waterloo rail station south of the Thames, into a prosperous theatre company. On her death, directorship of the theatre—now known as the Old Vic—passed to her niece, Lilian Baylis. An ambitious woman in her late thirties, a talented musician and veteran performer, Baylis had spent many years assisting her aunt, making her way up the theatre's administrative ladder, and she had grand plans for the Old Vic's future.[13] Foremost among these: that the theatre should perform every one of Shakespeare's plays by 1923, the three hundredth anniversary of the printing of the First Folio.[14]

Baylis was a difficult boss; she knew what she wanted, and she pursued her goals with single-minded focus. When she wanted her friend, the popular actress Sybil Thorndike, to appear in her production of *Hamlet*, she confronted Thorndike even though the actress was confined to her bed, still recovering after giving birth to her daughter Ann. "I can't put it off any more," Baylis told her; they had to start rehearsals. "Ann was late coming," replied the actress. "That's her fault," shot back the producer, "not mine."[15] Baylis got what she wanted. Thorndike would appear in several of her productions—including, repeatedly, as Queen Margaret.

The spiky, demanding role of Margaret was not a natural fit for many Edwardian actresses, especially those accustomed to parts from the classical repertoire, which were less violent and vulgar. But Baylis saw no problem casting her leading lady in such an untraditional female role, for she often cast Thorndike as a man. During the First World War, male performers were in short supply, and Baylis created entire productions with all-female casts, many led by Thorndike. "You won't mind, dear, will you?" Baylis asked her friend. "Because, after all, there should be no sex in acting—you ought to be able to understand men as well as women." Thorndike agreed. "I frankly loved it," the actress recalled. "I've always been jealous of the men in Shakespeare."[16]

Margaret gave Thorndike—an avid socialist, pacifist, and freethinker—everything she wanted from a Shakespearean role. "I love playing a woman who had a touch of masculinity," she said, "because I've always wished I'd been born a boy."[17] And Margaret, with "such wonderful, tearing speeches," as Thorndike put it, proved to be one of her favorite roles, tied, perhaps, with *Twelfth Night*'s Viola, who spends most of her play disguised as a man.[18] Thorndike played Margaret in *Richard III* opposite her brother as the titular king.[19]

Sybil Thorndike returned to the role in 1944, in Laurence Olivier's Old Vic production of *Richard III*. (The program instructed theatre-goers what to do if air-raid sirens sounded.)[20] Thorndike played the part with "an agued intensity," one observer gushed, "her hands, quivering with age and a nervous passion, gave the half-mad queen an added terror"—but Olivier nonetheless chose to cut one of Margaret's two scenes.[21] A critic lamented that Thorndike "poured the vitriol so generously [in her first scene] that we regretted a cut that denied a second draught to us."[22] Unfortunately for the filmgoing public—and for posterity—Thorndike's Margaret does not appear at all in Olivier's influential 1955 film version of *Richard III*.[23]

Olivier apparently had little interest in exploring the nuances of female characters; rather, he filmed the history plays as nationalistic spectacles, and Margaret (a difficult, foreign queen) would have been little help in rousing a nation at war (hot or cold). Propaganda was an approach Olivier perfected but certainly did not originate. Indeed, back in 1935, with fascism still in its adolescence, the Pasadena Playhouse in California staged not just the two tetralogies but all ten of Shakespeare's history plays (including *King John* and *Henry VIII*) in sequence—"the *first time*," the company claimed in promotional materials, this had been accomplished "in the history of the English-speaking stage."[24] For his part, the plays' director proudly proclaimed, "In these plays Anglo-Saxon patriotism was born. Audiences saw in them for the first time the marvelous qualities of the race and learned to glory in them. They embody the gallantry, courage, tenacity, sense of humor and justice which have come to produce the dominant nations of the earth."[25]

While Anglophone theatrical producers were intent on using Shakespeare as a cultural bludgeon, artists elsewhere had their own motivations for continuing to stage the Bard's works. Indeed, for as long as anyone could remember, the residents of Roatán—a long, narrow island about forty miles off the coast of Honduras—had been obsessed with Shakespeare. Just two Shakespeare plays, actually: *Henry VI, Part 3* and *Richard III*. Every year, for many decades, the residents had performed those two plays before rapt throngs of neighbors. The actors, as well as almost everyone in their audiences, were Black—Indigenous islanders and the descendants of enslaved people.

Something about the two plays, depicting centuries-old wars, spoke deeply to the people of Roatán, for they not only revived these plays year after year for much of the twentieth century; they even peppered their everyday speech with Shakespearean dialogue.

Late in 1950, a writer named Louise Wright George traveled to La Ceiba, a port city situated at the base of the Pico Bonito mountains, just across the water from Roatán. One day, her maid, Adela, told her about the native Shakespearean tradition, launching George on a quest to learn more about the Roatán repertory. George would record what she saw and heard in exquisite detail, from the performers' names and backstories to the costumes they lovingly maintained. She would also inject her recollections with casually racist language and sentiments. Since at least the early 1910s, Hondurans told her, the "colored populace" had been staging *Henry VI, Part 3* and *Richard III*, often combining the two into one long performance. Some of the performers were from La Ceiba, though the more dedicated Shakespeareans resided on Roatán. Most worked on banana plantations and in lumber camps, seizing rare moments of leisure for rehearsal and recital. They had no director or printed programs and apparently shared copies of the plays.[26]

Early in 1951, George attended a performance of half the Margaretsaga in an "old, condemned, wooden Methodist Church" in the English-speaking neighborhood of La Ceiba. There was no set and few props; sheets stood in for curtains, bedspreads for backdrops; and a six-piece orchestra introduced the actors. As these performances had for decades, the show began with the entire cast trouping through the audience, each carrying a wooden sword.[27]

A Roatán native named Alva Bennett played Margaret, wearing a white satin dress, trimmed with lace, which she maintained at significant personal expense. To pay her bills, Bennett worked as a cook for a lumberman. Atop her head was a paper crown, and—like everyone else—she clutched a sword.[28] If George's recollections are to be believed, the Hondurans performed abbreviated versions of both plays. Like Colley Cibber before them, and Laurence Olivier a world away, they cut Margaret from *Richard III*. Nonetheless, many of her most spectacular scenes remained in *Henry VI, Part 3*, and Alva Bennett got to divorce Henry, stab York, and insult Richard.[29]

To Louise Wright George, the dedication of poor Black laborers to two of Shakespeare's history plays was a curiosity, an anomaly, and—above all—a source of bemusement. What, one may ask seven decades later, did Shakespeare—and these two history plays in particular—mean to the Hondurans themselves? For the first half of the twentieth century, Honduras was a kleptocracy, with American-controlled fruit companies exploiting the nation and many of its residents forced to endure backbreaking work for the benefit of rich white capitalists who gave orders from afar. Yet resistance permeated the plantations; attempted coups and underground communist organizing roiled the country. Just as George arrived, a rural labor movement was gaining in power and influence; not long after she left, a general strike upended the northern part of the country, including La Ceiba. The Hondurans could well have identified with two plays depicting political turmoil, martial strife, and cruel, charismatic rulers deservedly brought low.[30]

And what did Margaret mean to Alva Bennett? Was she oppressor, collaborator, or empowered icon? She could have been any of these. Or she could have just been a part to play, a vehicle for artistic expression, an escape from drudgery. She was, undeniably, a legitimate excuse to wield a sword.

An ocean away, political events were binding Shakespeare ever closer to violence. Although the Germans had been sporadically performing the history plays for decades—as in Saladin Schmitt's grand 1927 history cycle, exactingly designed to evoke medieval manuscript illustrations—the Nazis' rise to power coincided with a profusion of Shakespeare productions across Germany.[31] Mere months after Hitler took power, his minister of propaganda, Joseph Goebbels, addressed a convention of theatrical directors and producers to tell them that a Nazi theatre was one that embraced "heroic" and "unsentimentally direct" plays steeped in German nationalism.[32]

Though Goebbels might have preferred plays by classic German playwrights, he also embraced *unser Shakespeare*—the German pet name that translated to "our Shakespeare." The same year that the Nazis took control of the country, 235 German theatres produced the Bard's works. Over the next decade, all of Shakespeare's works could be seen in the country. In the 1930s, Nazi Germany produced more plays by Shakespeare than did the rest of the world combined, or so the Nazis claimed.[33]

At a celebration of Shakespeare's birthday in Weimar in 1937, Hans F. K. Günther, a well-known eugenicist nicknamed Germany's *Rassenpapst*, or "race pope," delivered a speech titled "Shakespeare's Girls and Women," in which he argued that Shakespeare wrote his female characters to be Aryan ideals who wanted nothing more than to marry and reproduce. Günther claimed that Shakespeare's women were "entirely female" and that "hardly anything that they express of their own nature could have been spoken by men," forgetting, apparently, that characters like Rosalind and Viola present as men for most of their plays and that Shakespeare wrote these lines to be, as Günther put it, spoken by men. All of Shakespeare's white women were wholly dedicated to raising white children, Günther continued, neglecting to mention Desdemona and Tamora, both of whom partnered with men of color. Günther asserted that these women always married for love, rejecting arranged marriage, citing as proof a line of Suffolk's from *Henry VI, Part 1* about Margaret's strategic marriage. If, as Günther believed, all of Shakespeare's women made love-matches, then Margaret, wed to a stranger for purely diplomatic reasons, could not have been a woman.[34]

Günther and Goebbels were not only devoted to the Bard—or at least, to the idea of him—they were also key to the Reich's plan to use cultural icons to spread ideas of racial purity and white supremacy throughout the population. As the decade wore on and Germany hurtled toward war with England, the Reich banned more and more British cultural imports. Yet Shakespeare—long since absorbed into the German cultural mainstream—retained his position of prominence. In England and the United States, directors continued to stage *Richard III*, depicting the titular villain as increasingly resembling Hitler and Mussolini, a trend reflected by dissenting German artists—but, as the Reich mobilized, at the artists' peril. In 1937, the year of Günther's eugenicist paean (and one year after Goebbels outlawed art criticism, fearing it was too tied to Jewish intellectualism), Jürgen Fehling directed a production of *Richard III* in Berlin that left no room for ambiguity. In his massive five-hour production, Fehling drew clear parallels between Richard's army and the Nazis, even going so far as to dress Richard's henchmen in SS uniforms.[35]

Fehling's *Richard III*, set in a cavernous, barren theatre, reflected the soullessness of the age. Alone on a 120-foot-deep stage, Richard represented the puniness of man against the immense evil of war. The set was mostly bare—just a few simple and necessary props came onstage—and actors made their entrances from two staircases so far upstage that they seemed to wander in from the darkness. The vast hollowness of the production made clear the company's feelings on the regime under which they operated; one critic wrote that Fehling put his "characters into seemingly unlimited, unadorned space and [made] them fill it by sheer power of concentration and the intensity of subdued passion." The link between Richard's depravity and that of the Nazis was hard to miss.[36]

Fehling cast Hermine Körner, one of the most esteemed women of the German stage, as Margaret. Nearing sixty when she took the part, Körner had built so strong a reputation as a performer that she was sure to receive adulation for any role she played. Like Oldfield and Siddons before her, Körner excelled equally in tragedy and comedy. The role of Margaret came at a difficult time for Körner, as she struggled with the demands of being such a popular feature of a rapidly decaying society. Her discomfort with Nazi culture had become clear to her two years earlier, at the wedding of her friend the actress Emmy Sonnemann. Sonnemann was marrying Hermann Göring, a leader in the Nazi party, and at the reception (according to one account) Göring's best man approached Körner to declare his adoration for her work. She was his favorite actress, he said. The man was Adolf Hitler.[37] Not only was the Führer a long-term admirer of

Körner's, he wanted to promote her to a prominent cultural position in the Reich; he even considered giving her a fully funded theatre to run. Terrified by the prospect of working with the ruling party, she excused herself from the festivities and vowed to never again attend a government event.

She returned to the theatre, appearing in plays by Ibsen and Shaw, and in 1937, in Fehling's loudly antifascist *Richard III*. Körner could have chosen a life of comfort among the cultural elite of the Third Reich, but she opted to stay on the stage—a courageous choice, yet one denied others of more suspect heritage.[38] Another celebrated German actress who had once played Margaret, Adele Schönfeld, was half Jewish, and, after coming to the attention of the authorities, she fled to England.[39]

Though little remains of Fehling's *Richard III*—Goebbels's ban on theatrical criticism meant that few records survive—it clearly made an enormous impact on Germany's cultural scene. Furious with the production, Goebbels sprang into action and revoked Fehling's passport. Körner stopped performing in plays altogether (she resumed after the war). Goebbels attempted to ban productions of Shakespeare outright, but he was stopped by, of all people, Hitler himself, who liked the Bard. Once war with England kicked into high gear, Goebbels did the second-best thing: He banned the history plays.[40]

Again, and again, and again, the wail of air-raid sirens pierced the stillness of Cambridge. Smartly dressed students considered darting to the bomb shelter beneath Jesus College; periodically, unpredictably, incendiaries rained down from the sky. It was the early 1940s, and England was at war, but in the cloistered environs of Jesus College, a middle-aged Shakespeare scholar was just trying to work. Eustace Mandeville Wetenhall Tillyard—known professionally (and mercifully) as E. M. W.—had been a resident of Cambridge all his life, a Jesus College fellow for well over a decade, and he was striving mightily to finish what would become *the* paradigm-shifting study of Shakespeare's history plays. Although he sent two of his children away during the blitz, he was not about to let the prospect of falling explosives get in the way of his scholarly work.[41]

Despite this implacability, the experience of war defined Tillyard's life and profoundly affected his scholarship—which, in turn, continues to influence interpretations and depictions of Margaret to this day. When young Eustace was just ten years old, in 1899, the Boer War broke out in South Africa; at home in Cambridge, the Tillyard children playacted the colonial conflict, with the future scholar nicknamed "Corporal Mandeville" (later promoted to "Lieutenant Mandeville"). Tillyard would later fight for real in World War I, and though he spent time in the trenches and his brother was held as a prisoner of war, both Tillyard men emerged from the battlefield safe and victorious; the young scholar had even fallen in love with Shakespeare while on sick leave from the army.[42]

A generation later, in 1944, at the height of an even bloodier global conflict, Tillyard published *Shakespeare's History Plays*, a work that bore the battle scars of an empire at war. Before this book, few scholars had bothered to study the *Henry VI* plays, considering them unpolished and unilluminating.[43] Tillyard disagreed. He argued that the eight plays of the first and second tetralogies—*Richard II*, the *Henry IV* duo, *Henry V*, the *Henry VI* trilogy, and *Richard III*—were a "single unit," collectively narrating the continuous story of a single "unnamed protagonist": England itself.[44] Further, although military violence pulsed through these plays, "order and the natural law" ultimately triumphed, Tillyard wrote, a startling echo of the wartime propaganda and Churchillian rhetoric blaring across England in the early 1940s. The Allies, like the Tudors before them, would end usurpation and restore righteous rule. Order would win out over chaos; moral logic would outmatch bloody anarchy; and unity would bring together a divided Britain, just as it had in Shakespeare's history plays—plays that were, Tillyard argued, themselves a cohesive whole and foundational to a unitary national identity.[45]

Tillyard's conclusions electrified the field, and *Shakespeare's History Plays* quickly became the measuring stick against which almost all subsequent scholarship was assessed.[46] Yet Tillyard had little to say about Margaret. She was "strong-minded and troublesome," playing "the dramatic part of avenging fury." Most importantly, in marrying Henry she set in motion "the troubles between Lancaster and York which otherwise would have lain quiet."[47] In the words of the scholar Randall Martin, Tillyard "reduced Margaret to a personally aggrandizing agent of disorder."[48]

Followers and detractors—nearly all men—did likewise, crediting Margaret as one of the "links" tying the tetralogy together but dismissing her character's complexity, often with sexist undertones.[49] She was a "termagant," a "neurotic and grief-crazed woman," and also "the chief exponent of the philosophy of Providence in the play."[50] She was "ever strong in purpose" yet "fatal to England."[51] She was a "malignant prophetess of God's displeasure."[52] She emblematized "deformity."[53] Indeed, her "grotesque display of 'courage' can only be understood as an inexplicable deviation from nature, a relinquishment of human identity."[54] She was "not as complex and subtle as his later heroines but one gifted with tremendous energy, and even her ghoulishness is an offshoot of her indomitable personality."[55] One mid-century scholar casually labeled Margaret and Elizabeth's altercation a "cat fight."[56] Another wrote that she assumed "an unwomanly dominion over" Henry and possessed a "sanguinary lust for vengeance."[57] Still another, heavily influenced by Freud, wrote of Margaret: "Shakespeare was deeply concerned with the possibility that a woman could drive a man insane."[58] It is not always easy to tell when these men were ventriloquizing the misogyny of Shakespeare and his contemporaries or when they are simply declaring their own, but still—the cumulative effect was not inspiring.

Yet if Tillyard and his ilk were not too interested in Margaret and her nuances, their work did have the effect of spurring directors to start staging the plays more and more, especially in sequence.[59] This, in turn, had the unintended consequence of leading multiple directors and actors to "discover" Margaret—driving further scholarly interest, which in turn shaped still more performances.

The first notable postwar production of the *Henry VI* plays opened in 1951, in Birmingham, England. Barry Jackson—an aging lion of regional theatre—was one of the few working artists old enough (and lucky enough) to have seen the Bensons' 1906 productions at Stratford, and like those earlier theatrical giants, Jackson craved the distinction of staging even Shakespeare's relatively unknown and unloved works.[60] He had serious ambitions for the *Henry VI* trio—he wanted to challenge the idea that they were "unstageable," to rescue them from rumors regarding Shakespeare's authorship, to bring glory to his theatrical company by having them perform *the* story of England. Nationalism was ascendant—memories lingered of the empire's resilience in World War II, the country was in the midst of a memorialization kick (with a celebratory exhibition, the Festival of Britain, set to reach millions that summer), and Tillyard's interpretations were dominant—so Jackson seized his moment, starting with *Part 2*.[61]

The critics loved it, marveling at the novelty of staging such an obscure play and leading Jackson to move on to *Part 3*, then *Part 1*. In particular, critics thrilled at the depiction of Margaret, a role with which few seemed to have any prior familiarity. She is "a superb leader of men in martial enterprise; subtle and brutal," commented the *Birmingham Post*; it would be "difficult to over assess [her] contribution to this fiery chronicle."[62] Rosalind Boxall—a relative newcomer, still in her mid-twenties—played the queen as, above all, physically dominant, towering over the relatively small actor playing Henry and ceaselessly moving about even as Henry stayed mostly still. Though Jackson had eliminated seventeen parts to accommodate his small company, Margaret's lines went almost entirely untouched, and indeed the cuts elsewhere served to emphasize her centrality to the narrative.[63]

Spurred by the critical acclaim, Jackson presented all three *Henry VI* plays in sequence in 1953, a trilogy that opened just days after the coronation of Queen Elizabeth II and then transferred from Birmingham to London.[64] E. M. W. Tillyard, by then the Master of Jesus College and *the* authority on these plays, was delighted as he watched them from the audience. Afterward, he wrote confidently that the performance "greatly confirmed my opinion that Shakespeare was the author and that he constructed massively and with thought." He singled out Margaret's continuous presence as evidence that Shakespeare had the whole tetralogy "roughed out" before he started writing.[65]

At the end of the run, Jackson reflected on why "no major actress ever discovered the tremendous character of Margaret of Anjou, surely one of the greatest feminine roles in the gallery."[66] Decades later, the scholar Irene Dash would propose an answer: The *Henry VI* cycle "offers no male 'star' roles," so few actors, directors, or producers—almost all men—would bother with plays "whose logical emphasis should be on Margaret," a woman.[67] Jackson, who longed to produce the entire Shakespeare canon, was uncowed, leading to a production that marked what one scholar labeled the first time Margaret's "role was credibly staged."[68]

In the years that followed, English companies drew increasingly on Jackson's success, Tillyard's ideas, and Boxall's precedent.[69] In 1957, Douglas Seale—who had served as director under Jackson—put on the *Henry VI* plays at the Old Vic; he departed from Jackson by heavily editing them, essentially combining *Part 1* and *Part 2*, but he left the focus on Margaret, who was played with steely resolve by a sword-wielding Barbara Jefford, her red hair falling freely over her red dress.[70] Three years later, the BBC adapted the *Henry VI* plays into a television series for the first time, turning both tetralogies into what one observer called "a single great unified pageant of English history." Once again, the directors trimmed *Part 1*, which resulted in more attention paid to Margaret (far more present in *Part 2* and *Part 3*), played imperiously by a piercing Mary Morris.[71] No longer could a director simply ignore or casually marginalize Margaret. Indeed, she was ascendant.

Peter Hall was barely twenty when he happened to catch Jackson's production of the *Henry VI* plays at the Birmingham Rep. It was the early 1950s, and Hall resembled nothing so much as a grown-up schoolboy, round-cheeked and eager. He was stunned. The plays positively rippled with "narrative muscularity," Hall would later reflect.

From that moment on, the young man burned to direct this "epic sequence."[72] Remarkably, he would do so within a decade—transforming works that were still little known into one of the most successful, celebrated productions of Shakespeare ever. It was the cycle as staged by Hall that would turn Margaret into a staple for ambitious actresses. And it was one particular actress, the legendary Peggy Ashcroft, who cemented Margaret's evolution into the antihero dominating productions of the first tetralogy, a highly desirable role for actresses trying to establish a reputation.

Hall came of age in war-torn Cambridge, hearing the same explosions that disturbed Tillyard's work across town. He attended the same preparatory school that Tillyard had, and then he was off to Tillyard's university, occasionally journeying from Cambridge to Stratford to see plays at the Memorial Theatre.[73] A brief interlude in the Royal Air Force was the only interruption in an otherwise unencumbered rise; immediately after graduation, Hall became director of the Oxford Playhouse, and in 1955, he directed the English-language premiere of *Waiting for Godot*. The audience booed, but the theatrical world turned its attention to the young man; by the age of twenty-nine, he created the Royal Shakespeare Company in Stratford and became its first artistic director.[74] Hall, a self-described theatrical radical (one scholar compared him to Mick Jagger), appalled some of the RSC's more conservative playgoers by removing the Memorial Theatre's old, dusty curtains, but he ingratiated himself among the actors by winning over their grande dame, Peggy Ashcroft.[75]

Ashcroft too was the product of an empire at war—in 1918, when she was just ten years old, her father died in World War I. The young girl sought refuge in Shakespeare and on the stage, developing a naturalistic acting style at odds with the affected technique of many of her contemporaries. Over the next quarter century, she blazed through almost all of Shakespeare's great female parts, working with Lilian Baylis at the Old Vic and Paul Robeson at the Savoy (the two had an affair, destroying his marriage). By the late 1950s, she was so well-regarded that her embrace of the young Hall was sufficient to win him grudging respect from the rest of the actors. Yet Ashcroft never let Hall forget who was in charge. When, in a 1957 production of *Cymbeline*, Hall tried to dictate Ashcroft's every move, she informed the young man that she would not be bossed around: "That move's wrong," she snapped. Hall gave in—and became more deferential to the RSC's actors moving forward.[76]

In 1962, with the RSC in the throes of an uninspired season and mired in financial crisis, Hall decided to take a risk and stage the first tetralogy.[77] He turned to an old friend from Cambridge, John Barton, a brilliant, eccentric scholar, an expert on Elizabethan speech, albeit one possessed of a disconcerting habit of sucking on razor blades as he worked, sometimes with a trickle of blood escaping one corner of his mouth.[78] The two men met every day that autumn to plan their production, and for the next ten months they furiously prepared the scripts, seeking to turn the four unwieldy, disparate plays into a smooth, comprehensible narrative.[79] Though he edited *Richard III* only slightly, Barton mercilessly cut the three *Henry*s from 12,350 lines to 6,000, and then inserted nearly 1,500 lines of his own, rendered in a faux-Shakespearean idiom. He excised distracting side plots and obliterated unnecessary side characters, adding in text to stitch together what remained. For instance, Barton cut Margaret's father from her first scene, leaving her its central player; he then added a new line for Margaret, justifying her solo appearance and helpfully foreshadowing her character's trajectory: "I'll not go with thee. Knowst thou who I am?" Barton only got away with the bowdlerization because so few playgoers or critics were familiar with the plays. Yet, as with the cuts of Barry Jackson and his followers, these edits served to emphasize Margaret's centrality—Barton and Hall felt she was the vital link connecting the histories.[80] Plus, Hall later reflected, they were working "under the watchful eye of Peggy Ashcroft," who was slated to play Margaret.[81] As a result of the changes, their Margaret appeared onstage earlier and stayed there longer.[82]

Significantly, theirs was a production steeped in postwar scholarship. Tillyard's belief in the unstoppable arc of history and the importance of Elizabethan hierarchy structured the cuts.[83] And on the very first day of rehearsal, Hall's car broke down and he took a train to

Stratford; as he journeyed north, he devoured the page proofs of a forthcoming book by Jan Kott, *Shakespeare Our Contemporary*.[84] Kott, a Polish war refugee, argued that twentieth-century audiences could not help but see Shakespeare's history plays through the lens of their own age's struggles against fascism, totalitarianism, and bomb power. It was the director's imperative, therefore, to be aware of the modern relevance of these plays. History, to Kott—and to Hall—was a pitiless cycle; there are no good kings.[85]

Just two weeks into the rehearsals, Hall suffered a nervous breakdown. It was an awful time for the young director; not only was his theatre in dire economic straits, but his marriage was falling apart amid adultery and mutual alienation. He was plagued with weeping spells and contemplated suicide. The theatre was forced to postpone the productions, yet even this delay did not spare the actors from grueling round-the-clock rehearsals, with doctors appearing periodically to inject them with reviving vitamin shots.[86]

When the cycle—grandly renamed *The Wars of the Roses*—finally opened in Stratford in the summer of 1963, audiences and critics were dumbfounded. Heavily armored actors strode confidently in front of a massive, terrifying, clanging cage of metal; it looked like the end of the world.[87] To almost all viewers, these plays were something "new"—and exciting.[88] One critic called the production "the greatest Shakespearean event within living memory." Another called it "one of the mightiest stage projects of our time . . . a production to remember all our lives."[89] Early in 1964, the company transferred the production to London. Eleven months later, the BBC recorded the cycle and then beamed it all over the world.[90] Over a million people saw the plays on the small screen; one observer called them "the best television productions of Shakespeare's plays in the history of television."[91]

The most lauded actor in this most lauded production was Ashcroft, who played Margaret. By the time the plays opened, she was fifty-six years old, the company's sole star yet one whom many considered to be "past her prime," decades older than the man playing Henry.[92] Nonetheless, she stunned—a "masterly performance of exceptional power," raved *The New York Times*.[93] Ashcroft was the first actor in decades to play Margaret across the entire tetralogy (Jackson had stopped before *Richard III*), and she did so with a memorable (if a touch overdone) French accent. Her range was tremendous. At her first entrance, she proceeded delicately onstage as a young girl with a "Princess Leia" hairdo; by her last, she stormed across the planks in a disheveled gray "fright wig."[94] More than her predecessors, she emphasized her independence from Henry, her agency and culpability, with Barton's alterations highlighting her disillusionment from

Peggy Ashcroft as Margaret in Peter Hall and John Barton's *The Wars of the Roses*, a Royal Shakespeare Company production, in 1964.

what he called her "sexually unsatisfying husband."[95] His Margaret insulted her husband in lines Shakespeare never imagined, taking charge of his court with Barton's fiery words.[96] Ashcroft relished the augmented role. After stabbing York, she drew her hand across her mouth, leaving a bright bloody streak.[97]

The relative novelty of Margaret dominated her reception. To Hall, she was "one of the great undiscovered parts in classic drama."[98] For her part, Ashcroft claimed Margaret among her most favorite roles—"because that was a new part. It was really like doing a new play. . . . I rather like slightly nasty women, having been overfed with ingenues in my youth."[99]

The influence of *The Wars of the Roses* can hardly be overstated. Hall and Barton's style—and, often, their heavily edited scripts—shaped productions in France, Italy, Germany, Japan, Canada, and the United States in the years that followed.[100] In 1976, for instance, the Oregon Shakespeare Festival staged *Henry VI, Part 2*, with a young Jean Smart as Margaret, and the director felt free to cut almost half of the original text.[101] Among Hall and Barton's foremost innovations was the decision to stage the plays in a continuous, daylong "marathon," a feat the RSC only accomplished a handful of times and that was, according to some reports, suggested by Ashcroft herself. This accomplishment (or gimmick) would also appear in many productions in the coming decades.[102]

The Wars of the Roses made Margaret into a Shakespearean hallmark, a character who viewers expected and wanted to see. When Al Pacino played Richard III in Boston in 1973, and then again on Broadway in 1979, Margaret would be omitted from both productions, and *The New York Times* would lament the absence of "old Queen Margaret, who most clearly represents the female forces against Richard."[103] Another critic would claim that these "Margaret-less interpretations were apparently following the precedent set by Colley Cibber, who rewrote the play in 1700 to reinforce the audience's delight in Richard's overweening ambition."[104] When, a decade later, a California production retained Margaret, the reviewer from the *Los Angeles Times* would breathe a sigh of relief: "Often productions of 'Richard III,' for brevity's sake, eliminate a royal lady altogether or rob one of them (frequently Queen Margaret) of a harangue. Not here. The role of the women, a tight, wailing chorus, is restored to its prominence."[105]

· 11 ·

"One of the Greatest Parts Ever Written"

Her Triumph

Even for an audience primed to expect Margaret, few could have predicted the sight of Helen Mirren, dressed in the finery of a princess, striding onto the stage in the summer of 1977. The young actress—still in her early thirties—first appeared draped in soft light, in a form-fitting velvet gown, her presence all the more striking set against a spare black stage with almost no props or scenery beyond a coffin and a throne. What remained were the actors' *bodies*, Margaret's above all others. Later, Mirren would reappear in a metal dress that glittered as she taunted the actor playing York; notably, he forced Mirren to her knees in the midst of the confrontation, and she remained so close that their lips almost touched. As he struggled for freedom, he pushed Mirren beneath him, her legs spread; after stabbing him, she arched her body, luxuriantly, as the scene reached its climax.[1]

This Margaret—sexual if not sexually liberated—was a depiction for a new age. Ashcroft may have made Margaret a star, but Mirren's portrayal transformed the medieval royal into a modern woman, with all the baggage that entailed. She was the first actress to foreground Margaret's sexuality, playing the queen as a sensual subject with intense desires and relationships, rather than as a solely political agent. Her Margaret embodied the explosive power of feminism's righteous second wave—and no small amount of anti-feminist back-lash as well. Hers was a performance that would have been unthinkable without the cutting-edge feminist Shakespeare criticism emerging at this same historical moment—work that, for the first time, turned Margaret from an academic afterthought into a legitimate subject of scholarly inquiry.

The origins of Mirren's Margaret, Margaret the sexual agent, lay in a transformation in who was allowed to write about Shakespeare and his characters. As late as the mid-1960s, women made up just 28 percent of British university students—and under 10 percent of those at Cambridge; women were routinely denied access to high tables or fellows' dinners; dormitories still closed for the night, and students were forbidden to have members of another sex in their rooms. Even in 1972, one woman arriving at Cambridge to teach encountered a college master who informed her, "Well, Miss Finch, I voted against the admission of women."[2] The few Shakespeare scholars who sought to ask questions that foregrounded sex and sexuality were rarely allowed to do so in sessions at professional meetings, their conversations instead consigned to informal interactions between sessions.[3]

Increasingly public and fractious fights over birth control, abortion, forced sterilization, rape, hiring practices, firing practices, unequal pay, and access to childcare exploded into conferences, protests, marches, and collectives. When, in the mid-1970s, female academics insisted on organizing a special session on Feminist Criticism of Shakespeare under the auspices of the Modern Language Association, they received submissions from roughly a hundred scholars—an intense level of interest.[4] The scholar Robert Potter, looking back decades later, recalled an "invading army of feminist critics" who "transformed the Shakespearean battlefield."[5]

Although women had been writing on Shakespeare for centuries, and some had even authored work that today reads as proto-feminist, the liberationist spirit did not become pronounced in Shakespearean criticism until the 1970s. Ironically, one of the first feminist critiques of the history plays appeared in a book by the male critic Leslie Fiedler, who wrote of Shakespeare's "fear of women and his disgust with sex."[6]

Three years later, in 1975, Juliet Dusinberre published a landmark feminist study of Shakespeare, establishing a pattern of early feminist critics calling attention to Shakespeare's own proto-feminism, what Dusinberre called the "modernity in his treatment of women."[7] By the mid-1980s, some feminists were questioning the binary approaches to Shakespeare—either condemning him as a classic chauvinist or celebrating him as a perceptive writer of women—and by the early 1990s, feminist critics were looking beyond Shakespeare's intentions, locating an "oppositional history" in his texts, reading them critically and counterintuitively to discern insights about those "silenced" or "erased" from dominant discourses.[8]

Unlike the scholars who followed in Tillyard's footsteps in the mid-century, the feminist critics lavished attention on Margaret. They devoted whole passages, then entire chapters, to the Lancastrian queen. Unquestionably, high-profile performances like Ashcroft's informed their reappraisals—and were sometimes dissected explicitly.[9] To these second-wave feminists, Margaret provided the "prototype" for all of the terrifying female characters that followed; more than just about any other character in the canon, she embodied Shakespeare's belief that power in women was unnatural, and scary, and destructive.[10] Indeed, the Margaretsaga "helped produce what are now regarded as 'traditional' gender relations" in the first place, Jean E. Howard and Phyllis Rackin concluded. Nonetheless, in demonizing Margaret, the plays—perhaps unintentionally—vested her with "astonishing sensuality and power."[11]

In the wake of the women's liberation movement and the liberation of Margaret from scholarly silence, depictions of Margaret onstage—proliferating in this post-Ashcroft era—morphed in telling ways. First came Mirren's Margaret in 1977. She appeared onstage in an RSC production, this one directed by a young man named Terry Hands. Hands, like Hall before him, had discovered the *Henry*s as a teenager, but unlike his predecessors he sensed in the plays an erotic charge.[12] For Margaret he turned to Mirren, who had already played Anne in a production of *Richard III* that Hands directed for the RSC, in which Mirren had tried to beat Richard with an oversized crucifix.[13] The daughter of an exiled Russian noble, Mirren had spent the last decade performing some of Shakespeare's most iconic female roles: Cleopatra, Cressida, Rosalind, Lady Macbeth. She thrilled at the chance to play Margaret: It was "marvelous" to depict a Shakespearean woman who "keeps developing" over a "long" series of plays, Mirren later told an interviewer, especially since "most of Shakespeare's women are either masculine like Cleopatra, dress up as men for part of the play (like Rosalind and Viola), or are developed with very slight hints in parts that are quite brief (like Lady Macbeth and Desdemona)." Not only does Margaret have more depth and more range as a woman, Mirren added, but she gets to be "physical with every man, really—that's her way." Mirren played her accordingly.[14]

This depiction dismayed many critics, who unfavorably compared Mirren's performance to Ashcroft's.[15] One wrote in *The Guardian* that Mirren "does not develop like Ashcroft into a woman of steel." Later, watching a marathon performance of all three *Henry* plays, the same

Helen Mirren as Margaret in *Henry VI, Parts 1–3*, a Royal Shakespeare Company production, in 1977.

male critic commented, "Helen Mirren's Margaret has now acquired blood-lust as well as body-lust."[16] Indeed, a great many reviewers dwelled on Mirren's body, often describing her in highly sexualized terms; even a critic praising her performance noted the "eroticism" of her "sensuous adolescent body."[17] In one notorious interview from this era, a journalist asked her whether she could truly be a "serious actress" due to her "equipment," with the male journalist glancing meaningfully at her chest. "'Cause serious actresses can't have big bosoms, is that what you mean?" Mirren shot back.[18]

While Mirren's performance should properly be understood as a rejoinder to such reductive attitudes, an argument that powerful female characters could be ones with desire and tenderness, she was also battling against Hands's directorial choices. Although he had cut only 6 percent of the plays' texts (seeking to distinguish himself from Barton and Hall), he had cut 34 percent of Margaret's lines; she was the only character so reduced. Emphasis thus "shifted onto Mirren's body," argued the scholar Kat Hipkiss, "by removing her voice."[19]

Subsequent performances kept the focus on Margaret's sexuality but also emphasized her sexual vulnerability. In a celebrated adaptation staged by the upstart English Shakespeare Company in 1987, director Michael Bogdanov contrasted Suffolk's "seduction" of Princess Margaret with the sexual assault of a peasant girl by a group of soldiers (an event found nowhere in Shakespeare's text). In her very first entrance, Margaret passes the clutch of soldiers pursuing the screaming peasant girl, only to be herself pursued by Suffolk, who points his sword at her in a highly suggestive manner.[20] Two years later, the RSC again staged the Margaretsaga, but this time had Princess Margaret first enter the action wearing a dirty, tattered cloak, looking hungry; the soldiers identify her as a scavenger or looter and nearly kill her, before Suffolk shows up to perform a belated rescue. Once again, Shakespeare never imagined such a scene, but it effectively highlights the danger that Margaret faces.[21] Indeed, in a 1990 *Richard III* at Central Park's Delacorte Theater, the villainous king (played by Denzel Washington) even surprised

Margaret (played by Mary Alice, fresh off a Tony win for Rose in *Fences*) with a kiss; she looked, according to *The New York Times*, "as if she had just tasted poison."[22]

In the decades following the crest of feminism's second wave, directors increasingly placed Margaret at the center of their productions, almost invariably doing so not by giving Margaret more to say, but by allowing her more to do. Sometimes these interpolations were small—in a 1980 American production of *Richard III*, for instance, Margaret smoked a cigar; a decade later, she appeared in the play at London's National Theatre as a "religious fanatic," in the words of one critic, "festooned with rosaries and crucifixes"; in 1992, the Oregon Shakespeare Festival even allowed Margaret to personally wield a sword and fight throughout the *Henry*s (evoking Alva Bennett in Honduras), her dress whipping around her as she sparred with Edward and fended off multiple men.[23]

Sometimes, though, the extratextual additions—especially in productions of *Richard III*—placed Margaret on the stage for far longer than her few lines would suggest. In 1975, for instance, a standalone RSC production of *Richard III* set the play in what looked like a white-walled psychiatric ward, with Margaret resembling nothing so much as Nurse Ratched, the institutional overseer from *One Flew over the Cuckoo's Nest* (a film released just weeks after the RSC's production opened; the novel had been around for a dozen years). She appeared onstage with a whistle, reciting the stage directions and clearing the way for a dead Edward to be wheeled away in a stretcher; she returned to blindfold men about to die, or help them remove a jacket or empty their pockets; she pinned up drawings of Richard's victims on a watchtower and, in fact, spent much of the play viewing his villainy from the watchtower.[24]

Four years later, the Rustaveli Company from Tbilisi, Georgia, put on a gruesome, carnivalesque *Richard III*, a production that toured the globe. Margaret again acted much like a stage manager, brandishing a copy of the script and appearing often to show it to Richard's victims as a sort of "I told you so."[25] A decade afterward, in still another RSC production of *Richard III*, an unkempt Cherry Morris—who had understudied Peggy Ashcroft in 1963—returned to the stage repeatedly to reprise her curses, mark time by tapping a stick, smear dust on her face and sprinkle it around herself to create a spectral clock, and monitor the action from an elevated perch. She even appeared to play a direct role in fulfilling her curses: Amid Richard and Richmond's climactic fight, Richard seems to have the advantage until Margaret appears at his side. He sees her and freezes, his potency leaving him, giving Richmond an opening to recover and then strangle the king to death.[26]

By the late 1980s, the long-ignored *Henry VI* plays had joined *Richard III* as a fixture of the Shakespearean repertory, and by the early 1990s, audiences could count on at least one significant production per year.[27] Margaret, for her part, was finally recognized as a "King Lear for women," in the words of RSC director Adrian Noble.[28] "Surely," added the Australian actress Penny Downie (whom Noble directed as Margaret), "it is one of the greatest parts ever written."[29]

I ncreasingly, however, the part was becoming associated with just one woman, another controversial British leader, one who shared the ancient queen's name. Margaret Thatcher swept into Downing Street with the Tory wave that crashed down upon the United Kingdom in the 1979 general election, which followed frustration with a weak Labour government so widespread that the media borrowed a phrase from *Richard III* and nicknamed the period the "Winter of Discontent." The country was at a crossroads, politically and socially: In 1981, television channels alternated between coverage of a princess's wedding and uprisings for racial justice in London, Liverpool, Birmingham, Leeds, and Manchester. Indeed, dissatisfaction in the wake of financial crises all across the developed world was helping to usher in a cohort of politicians claiming that the solution was to unshackle capitalism and free the market from regulation, with Thatcher as their chief avatar. In the years following her ascent, many directors integrated critiques of policies like hers into the Margaretsaga and modeled their Queen

Margarets after Prime Minister Margaret—even, and especially, the pioneering female directors seizing power at this same moment.

Thatcher and other politicians in her mold believed that there was little the state could do better than the free market, and so they sought to defund public goods—very much including the theatre. Indeed, Thatcher reportedly once asked her arts minister, "When are we going to be able to stop giving money to awful people like Peter Hall?"[30] As early as 1970, the producer of the New York Shakespeare Festival went to war against the austerity regime of the New York City mayor's office, which had withheld the funding needed for the festival to put on a full summer season. Before each performance, the producer spoke directly to the audience, cheekily comparing the "self-serving, unscrupulous politicians" of the Wars of the Roses with the city's own. *The New York Times* noted that Barbara Caruso played Margaret as "a regal Amazon with flame in her heart and ice in her veins"—a warrior to take on wicked men.[31] Nonetheless, the withdrawal of state support for the arts proceeded apace.

Ironically, and perhaps not coincidentally, it was just as theatres descended into financial perma-crisis that women were finally allowed to direct the Margaretsaga. Yet they did not hesitate to use these plays to savage the new political order. First came Pam Brighton. Brighton began her career in the avant-garde; from a working-class Yorkshire family, she traveled to London in the 1960s to study among similarly minded student radicals at the London School of Economics. Soon after leaving university Brighton found herself running the Young People's Theatre Company, which was in the process of becoming the hot spot for daring, cutting-edge drama. She collaborated with other artists of the Left (she acted in socialist filmmaker Ken Loach's television serial *Days of Hope*) and, in the 1980s and 1990s, trained as a barrister to defend political rioters and then moved to Belfast, at the height of the Troubles, to create political theatre.[32]

But before her legal work and her move to Northern Ireland, she decamped, briefly, for Canada. She landed first in Toronto before heading to Ontario's Stratford Festival. Founded in the 1950s, this Stratford Festival—located in a town called Stratford on a river called

Avon—was and is, like the RSC across an ocean, one of the world's preeminent centers for Shakespeare performance. When Brighton arrived in 1980, the town was not ready for the *Henry VI* she would unleash upon it.

Brighton was not only the first director to oversee the *Henry* plays at the Canadian Stratford but also the first woman to direct the *Henry VI* trilogy.[33] Though she condensed the three plays to one, her production still ran four hours long. And Brighton had no difficulty fitting this story of an England in transition to the current moment of a kingdom in crisis. Hers was a gory affair. "Throats are cut, pieces of flesh are thrown towards the audience," wrote one critic. "This production has no respect for the niceties of the theatre." Brighton made discontent visible on her blood-soaked stage.[34] She further asserted the plays' relevance by depicting Henry as a simpleton and a weakling. "In view of the things that Jimmy Carter's opponents are saying about him these days," commented one (Canadian) critic, "this conception of Henry VI may be seen by some to have a macabre aptness."[35]

Reviewers praised Brighton's take on the material, applauding the "awesome clarity" with which her production illuminated these oft-forgotten plays. They did not extend such praise to her Margaret, the Quebecois actress Luce Guilbeault. Critics found the speech of this actress, who spent most of her career performing in French, unpleasant to the ears and ill-equipped for speaking the lines Shakespeare provided (one called her a "bargain-basement Brunhilde"). Like Margaret, Guilbeault was a foreigner in an Anglophone world, and she did not mesh well with the classically trained male actors accustomed to Shakespeare's verse. Yet again, foreignness and femaleness converged to further isolate Margaret from her surroundings.[36]

Fittingly, other directors and performers at this time seized on Margaret's alienation and turned it back on the audience, forcing them to confront the prejudice of this time of conservative governance (while campaigning to become prime minister, Thatcher had lamented the consequences for "the British character" if the country were "swamped by people with a different culture"). In 1989, while preparing for the latest adaptation of the *Henry VI* plays at the RSC, the actress Penny Downie decided her performance would highlight Margaret's foreignness. "As an Australian living in England I think I have a notion of what it is to feel that one doesn't quite fit," she later recalled. The English of the tetralogy, she felt, "hate" Margaret "for being an alien, and especially for being a Frenchwoman." She gave Margaret a noticeable accent and emphasized her distance from Henry, played by a young Ralph Fiennes. The director, Adrian Noble, supported Downie's interpretation, for he too "was very keen to present the sense of English xenophobia in the production," Downie recalled.[37] At the end of the performance, after Richard's defeat, Downie's Margaret removed her crown, picked up her luggage, and departed for France—finally ready to leave this land that had never truly accepted her.[38]

Arguably the most influential production of the Margaretsaga during the Thatcher years was directed by a woman, and her adaptation confronted the Iron Lady head-on, providing a parable for an England being hollowed out by austerity and made mean by jingoism. Like Pam Brighton before her, Jane Howell emerged from the London theatre scene. In fact, Howell had preceded Brighton as the director of the Young People's Theatre Company.[39] Not long after Thatcher's election as prime minister, Howell began capturing all four of Margaret's plays on film. She staged her tetralogy on a winding wooden set composed of bridges, doors, ladders, and balconies reminiscent of those in an Elizabethan playhouse like the Globe. As her televised dramas progressed, the set's clean wood turned gray, scenes became dimmer, costumes got sootier, and actors grew wearier as war destroyed medieval England. Soliloquies and asides, once delivered to the groundlings, were spoken directly to the camera. The result was one long, somber narrative of misplaced ambition and the dangers of nationalism.[40]

Howell's telefilms presented the plays nearly uncut; as such, she gave herself time to explore every side character and subplot (each play ran well over three and a half hours). All of the female characters benefited greatly, Margaret most of all.[41] With hardly any assistance from makeup or wigs, the actress Julia Foster embodied Margaret's transition across the plays using just her body and voice. Though she was a good foot shorter than many of her male costars, Foster was the central planet around whom the four plays orbited. In her first scene with Suffolk, Foster's effervescence emanates from the screen. She played her weeping scene over Suffolk's severed head with an incontrovertible seriousness. And when she leaves Richard's court having cursed all Yorks to hell as a homeless outlaw in *Richard III*, the characters—and perhaps the actors—stand in shocked silence for a (televisual) age.

In the final scene of Howell's *Richard III*, after the victorious Tudors march off-screen, the camera pans across a mound of dead Yorks and Lancasters, bloodied actors piled atop each other. The camera lingers on the heap of corpses, scanning the faces of the dead in reverse order, starting with those who died in *Richard III* and making its way back to the dead of *Henry VI, Part 1*. As the bloody faces pass, a faint laughter grows. As the camera reaches the top of the grisly mass, we see the laughter's source: It is Margaret sitting on a mountain of corpses, her hair wild, the dead body of Richard laid across her lap in some perverse pietà. The wars' only survivor, Margaret, crowns the carnage that she helped to wreak. But she also sits atop her four plays, complete at last, the tetralogy's true protagonist.[42]

Jane Howell's Margaretsaga, aired in 1983, and the similarity between this Margaret and the one then occupying Downing Street was lost on no viewer. Howell deliberately evoked then-iconic images, such as the wedding of Diana and Charles and the Falklands War victory parade in which a martial crowd saluted Thatcher.[43] Other directors and actors from this time went even further. In 1987, Michael Bogdanov's punk-inspired English Shakespeare Company production of the Margaretsaga featured Scottish actress June Watson in a stiff English officer's uniform, her hair exactingly coiffed to resemble the prime minister's.[44] The play's commoners were styled after football hooligans, or else the far-right National Front.[45] After the death of her son, Watson's Margaret reappeared in the tattered remnants of her khaki uniform, her medals and cap askew, her army having deserted her.[46] Bogdanov declared himself to be "burning with anger" over Thatcherism and hoped his production would skewer "Westminster rule."[47]

The presence of another hated Margaret atop the English government proved to be irresistible to those staging the first tetralogy, but ironically their caricatures of the prime minister failed to do justice to either her or her counterpart from Anjou. By depicting the Lancastrian queen as the mere embodiment of bellicosity, productions could not present the character "with any convincing degree of integrity as a mother, or even a woman," commented the scholar Randall Martin. "Seduced by the opportunity to stage political satire, they consciously or unconsciously suppressed the maternal authenticity and political activism by which Shakespeare dignifies his Iron of Naples, since such qualities might inadvertently disturb the prevailing Spitting Image of the modern Iron Lady."[48] And the comparison minimized Thatcher's full impact on the world. True, Margaret of Anjou helped to murder a man with her own hands, but Thatcher's body count was far higher.

Only after Thatcher—the longest-serving prime minister of the twentieth century—resigned in 1990 did Margaret emerge from her long shadow. Yet the Margaretsaga remained ripe for political argumentation. In 1994, for instance, Katie Mitchell—at the time just twenty-nine years old—staged *Henry VI, Part 3* at the Other Place, the RSC's smallest Stratford venue. Separating the play from the others of the Margaretsaga, Mitchell focused her production on the psychic impacts of war on those waging it, drawing clear parallels between this medieval story and the horrors unfolding in the Bosnian War.[49]

Mitchell's production portrayed a history of war that felt strangely like the present. It was not a specifically English history, though. One critic wrote that the play was "less interested in memorializing national history than in releasing different ways of responding to traumatic national, and global, memories."[50] Mitchell drew Margaret and her play away from English lore and toward global themes. It was a neat precursor to Margaret's continued transformations in the new millennium. Indeed, over the last quarter century, Margaret has become a key figure in the canon, joining (and even sometimes supplanting)

Richard as one of Shakespeare's most debated and desired roles, one whose challenging, morally murky narrative provides not merely a mode of self-expression but also a means of exploring gender, race, empire, and geopolitics in an era of unprecedented liberation and backlash. Perhaps more than any other character in Shakespeare, Margaret has a journey that lends itself to such explorations.

For decades, productions of Shakespeare's *Richard III* had all begun the same way—the titular villain, alone, declaring that *now* was the winter of his discontent. In 2007, in Stratford, audiences may have been surprised to find the play open with a woman instead. She wore a full-length black dress adorned with beads. Her "big, open eyes," recorded one chronicler, were "full of tears and anger."[51]

"I am Margaret," the woman intoned. "You needn't be concerned about me. We lost. It is your right to ignore me. I would ignore myself if my history let me." She strode slowly across the stage, picking up pieces of clothing and placing the garments into a suitcase. "I don't want your loans, your gifts, your reconstruction grants. I don't want your pity: we lost. All I ask from you is not to question my thirst for revenge: it is not because I am Arab—I have a degree. And anyway, my name is not Margaret. But our history is so awful, even the victors have changed their names."[52]

Truly, this was a new adaptation for a new century. It was titled *Richard III: An Arab Tragedy*, written by Sulayman Al-Bassam, a young Kuwaiti playwright, and first performed at the RSC. The actors spoke in colloquial Arabic, though audiences could read along with English surtitles. Al-Bassam set his adaptation in the contemporary Arab Gulf and peppered the play with Islamic prayers and references to oil extraction and foreign military invasions.[53] It debuted to considerable acclaim and soon toured widely in Europe, the Middle East, and the United States.[54]

And, at the start of each performance, Margaret assumed center stage. Reflecting this newfound prominence, critics raced to

Amal Omran as Margaret in Sulayman Al-Bassam's
Richard III: An Arab Tragedy, a Royal Shakespeare
Company production, in 2007.

deconstruct her character. She is a vehicle through which the playwright can "present the issue of Arab women's suffering first," argued one scholar, and "not as an afterthought."[55] She is "immediately identifiable as a refugee, dispossessed and rejected, ignored by history and the politics of power," argued another. "She has changed her name, lost her identity, and is insulted and patronised by the fake philanthropy of post-invasion reconstruction. But she retains enough pride to muster a fierce rejection of the audience's 'pity.'"[56] As the play proceeds, this Margaret is "humiliated"—when she reappears onstage to confront Richard, the king orders his men to whip her and then even mount her; "ride the jinn," Richard commands Catesby.[57] Yet she exhibits a kind of grim persistence—in the end, Margaret reappears, marching at the front of a line of those killed throughout the play.[58]

Richard III: An Arab Tragedy was unique in many respects, and its foregrounding of Margaret was among its most innovative decisions. Yet it was also a reflection of its time. Indeed, in the early years of this young millennium—as the character of Margaret entered her fifth century—many theatres began staging adaptations that featured her like never before. Some even turned her into the titular character.

In the summer of 2001, the Colorado Shakespeare Festival staged a play called *Queen Margaret*. It was, the festival's artistic director asserted, "a 'new' Shakespearean play."[59] Robert Potter, a drama professor at the University of California, Santa Barbara, had extracted all of the scenes in which Margaret appeared in *Richard* and the three *Henry* plays and combined them into a single play; a quartet of narrators appeared to bridge the gaps.[60] Potter had been working on this amalgamation for decades: its "world premiere" had been back in 1977, at Temple University.[61] A quarter century later, under a darkening Colorado sky, audiences again got to see Margaret travel from youth to old age, from France to England, from precarity to power to penury.[62]

Potter may have been the first to fuse all of Margaret's scenes into one comprehensive narrative, but he was far from the last. Indeed, at least six different plays premiered between 2011 and 2025 that did much the same. First, *Margaret: A Tyger's Heart* (adapted by Michael Sexton) was staged off-Broadway; then Evanston's Muse of Fire company put on *Queen Margaret* (this version by Jemma Alix Levy); in 2016, two different plays titled *Margaret of Anjou*—one by Lauren Jansen-Parkes and the other by Elizabeth Schafer with Philippa Kelly—graced stages in the Bay Area (the latter had enjoyed readings in Australia and been staged throughout England); two years later, *Queen Margaret* (by Jeanie O'Hare, longtime dramaturge for the RSC) debuted at the Royal Exchange Theatre in Manchester; finally, the Avant Bard Theatre presented *The Margriad*, an adaptation conceived and directed by Séamus Miller, in Arlington, Virginia, in the spring of 2025.[63] Another "new" play—a condensation of *Henry VI, Part 2* and *Part 3*, titled *Henry and Margaret*—was presented at the Oregon Shakespeare Festival (following an adaptation of *Part 1* titled *Talbot and Joan*).[64]

What accounted for this sudden proliferation of Margaretful productions, this profusion of interest in her character and her scenes? The simplest explanation is that, as third and then fourth waves of feminism forced reckonings within and without the theatre, Shakespearean actors and playwrights were hungry for meaty, dramatic female parts. Confronting the limitations of the canon—the unredeemed pugnacity of Lady Macbeth and Cleopatra, the enervating ends of Juliet and Katherina and Ophelia—they dove deeper into the Bard's work, discovering Margaret across four different plays, three of them fairly obscure. *Here* was a real leading lady, a female Lear, a complex woman who could not be dismissed as merely wicked, insipid, or helpless. A female character with *hundreds* of lines. A part to reckon with.

Informed by, and informing, this mounting interest in Margaret is a veritable explosion of scholarly attention. Over the last few decades, academics have continued to spill barrels of ink on Margaret, their excavations uncovering ever more nuance in her character. She exemplifies "both the status quo and the subversion of status quo," argues one scholar.[65] She is one of Shakespeare's "Amazons"—at once "masculine and female, mistaken for men and looked at as women," asserts another.[66]

An additional explanation for the continual rediscovery of Margaret is the mega-hit television show *Game of Thrones*. Based on a fantasy book series by Shakespeare superfan George R. R. Martin, the show transparently drew on the Wars of the Roses, pitting the Stark (i.e., York) family against the Lannisters (i.e., Lancasters).[67] *Many* scholars have noted the parallels between Margaret and Cersei Lannister, the kingdom's powerful, cunning queen.[68] Married to an ineffectual king and unafraid to rule in his absence, widely accused of adultery and widely known to have an iron will to power, marked by a canny political savvy and an implacable dedication to her children, Cersei is nakedly a stand-in for Shakespeare's Margaret. Indeed, directors of new Margaretsaga productions *and* their reviewers have noted the resonances with *Game of Thrones*.[69] No doubt actors and adapters have been inspired by, or at least capitalized on, this ubiquity.

Notably, though, many of the actors, audiences, and academics turning to Margaret in recent years have been unsatisfied with time-worn ways of presenting this long-dead queen. For almost the entirety of the character's existence, every actor and actress playing Margaret was white, but the new century has seen a handful of actors of color trying their turn as the Lancastrian queen—and a larger number using her part or her plays to explore contemporary racial politics. Early groundwork was laid the previous decade, first in 1990 with Mary Alice playing Margaret opposite Denzel Washington in *Richard III*, then in 1991–92 with a multiracial cast performing the *Henry* plays at the Oregon Shakespeare Festival, then between 1999 and 2001, when the RSC controversially cast David Oyelowo, a Black actor, to play Henry VI in a Stratford production. Though color-blind casting was far from new, Oyelowo's selection (opposite Fiona Bell, a white actress, as Margaret) triggered a national scandal, and the actor later recalled commentators denouncing the choice.[70] Still, the production was a massive hit, and in 2006 the RSC revived the adaptation, with another Black actor, Chuk Iwuji, as Henry (and another white actress, Katy Stephens, as Margaret).[71]

In 2016, Sophie Okonedo—a self-described "Jewish Nigerian Brit"—appeared as Margaret in the BBC's influential television adaptation of Shakespeare's history plays, *The Hollow Crown*. Controversy erupted yet again, with conservative commentators decrying the choice in predictably prejudiced terms. Other observers celebrated a Black woman taking on a famously arduous part in one of the highest-profile Shakespeare productions of the new century. Yet the debate about actors of color in Shakespeare plays has never been black-and-white, as it were. The legendary Black American playwright August Wilson once condemned Black actors who chose to play Shakespeare's English kings, claiming they let their bodies "be used in 'the celebration of a culture which has oppressed [Black people].'"[72] Others have decried color-blind casting as an insufficient salve for a structural wound—as even counterproductive, obscuring continued inequities in who receives opportunities and funding.[73]

Still, some sought to use these ancient plays to illuminating ends. *The Hollow Crown*, the scholar Jennie M. Votava has argued, "is at its best when it demonstrates a consciousness of colour." When, for instance, Margaret is hauled offstage after the death of her son at the end of *Part 3*, the director presents the audience with the image of "a dark-skinned woman dragged away by two armed and grinning white men," followed by a shot of Margaret chained to the floor of a cell, forcing viewers to reckon with centuries of racialized violence—especially the legacy of "the transatlantic slave trade that was already under way when this play was originally performed."[74] Another color-conscious approach was taken in 2003 by the Chicago Shakespeare Theater, which staged *Rose Rage*, a brutal adaptation of the Margaretsaga by Roger Warren and Edward Hall (son of Peter

Sophie Okonedo and the cast of *The Hollow Crown: The Wars of the Roses*, a 2016 BBC television production.

Hall). Amid the metal cages and bloody organs of a slaughterhouse, a male actor played Margaret with a strong French accent and skin that was "strikingly paler than any of the other actors," in the words of one observer, all choices that Votava has argued compelled the audience "to interrogate both whiteness and femininity as performed roles."[75]

Indeed, the character of Margaret—and the plays containing her—provided inspiration for many hoping to comment on contemporary politics. Margaret Thatcher may have been old news (especially after her death in 2013), but Queen Margaret remained a useful

Scott Parkinson as Margaret and Timothy Gregory as Suffolk in the Chicago Shakespeare Theater's 2003 production of *Rose Rage*, directed by Edward Hall.

Aysan Celik as Margaret and Jomar Tagatac (kneeling)
as York in the 2018 California Shakespeare Theater
production of *The War of the Roses*, adapted by
Eric Ting and Philippa Kelly.

(and usefully protean) avatar for other women in power. In 2016, a Bay Area company called Those Women Productions put on *Margaret of Anjou*—"The Undiscovered (Feminist!) Shakespeare Play," the company claimed—one of the new productions stitching together Margaret's many scenes. Reviewers and company members alike compared this Margaret to Hillary Clinton, then the Democratic nominee for US president—and "another powerful, ambitious woman who is not a fairytale heroine or the fairytale villainess," in the words of the company's cofounder. The show promoted the (cringeworthy) hashtag #ImWithHerHighness.[76] Another Bay Area Margaretsaga production, this one an adaptation called *The War of the Roses* at the California Shakespeare Theater in 2018, led a reviewer to compare "Holy King Henry" to Barack Obama—"and egomaniac Richard suggests his successor."[77]

Politics takes many forms, and Margaret and her plays have proven irresistible to those seeking to subvert expectations of gender in Shakespearean performance. A considerable number of all-female or cross-cast productions have appeared in the last two decades, including all-female *Richard III*s at the Globe in 2003, the Wales Millennium Centre in 2015, the Seattle Repertory Theater in 2018, and the New York Classical Theater in 2023.[78] Omidaze Productions, the small company in Cardiff that put on the 2015 production, also staged an all-female production of the *Henry VI* trio in 2016, as did Seattle Shakespeare and the delightfully named Upstart Crow Collective the following year.[79]

Critics are divided on the transgressiveness of such productions. One called the 2015 Welsh staging "a brilliant comment on an ancient world ruled by powerful men," while another wrote of the 2016 prequel: "Promotional material had emphasized the subversive nature of the all-female cast, although decades of exposure to largely female Shakespeare productions by undergraduates or high-school pupils have inured me to the sight of women in breeches parts."[80] As with the color-conscious productions that drew attention to racial categories, these gender-bending productions are arguably at their strongest when they use their casting choices to compel audiences to confront gendered assumptions. In the 2003 Globe production, the women playing male characters wore no makeup, while the women playing female characters were costumed to look like Elizabethan boys playing female roles. Gasps echoed across the audience when the actress playing Richard "lingeringly kissed" the actress playing Elizabeth.[81]

A quarter century into a new millennium, Margaret remains at the cutting edge of Shakespearean performance and adaptation, scholarship and criticism. Few other characters in the canon have been so swiftly elevated from obscurity to the titular role. In a culture ovesaturated with the plays and plots of Shakespeare, it is remarkable indeed for a character to retain the ability to shock, to outrage, to draw blood.

Her Future

So what comes next for Margaret? The easiest answer to this question would be to posit a straightforward path of progress, a trajectory of ever greater prominence and prestige. After all, Margaret's last century or so has followed this arc. Yet such a prediction, while it might make for a neat conclusion to this book, would be too simple. The ability of actors to make a living by appearing on Anglophone stages has rarely faced such strong headwinds since the reign of the Puritans; the right of actors to embody transgressive characters—and of critics and scholars to dissect these characters—is in flux around the world.

The truest answer to the question of Margaret's future, then, is inextricable from the future of sex, criticism, and the theatre itself. Artists will likely continue to probe the horizons of gender, but this does not necessarily promise innovation in the depiction of Margaret; indeed, an "all-female, gender-fluid, disability forward" *Richard III* from 2023 cut Margaret altogether.[1] Moreover, *ever* greater experimentation is far from an inevitability. For much of the eighteenth and nineteenth centuries female actors regularly played male parts in England and the United States (there was an especially rich tradition of women playing Richard III); this practice faded in the Victorian era, not to be fully revived for almost a century.[2] As a vicious transphobic backlash currently pulses across the globe, the future of gender experimentation onstage is far from the only thing at stake.

Critical dissections of Margaret may continue to accumulate—we immodestly hope that this book will spur a bit more consideration—but this too cannot be said to be fated. Many of the publications that were home to the most influential theatre criticism of the last century have recently folded or substantially scaled back their coverage.[3] And while many excellent doctoral dissertations and master's theses have recently devoted considerable attention to Margaret—including ones by Sarah Lyons, Rachel Wifall, Gillian Heather Elton, Emily Sloan-Pace, Jane Clay, Sarah E. Pagliaccio, Kat Hipkiss, and Alyssa Renee Miller—sadly none of these has yet been published as a book, limiting the reach of this scholarship.[4] Indeed, as tenure lines wither and academia becomes ever more reliant on overworked, underpaid adjuncts, one fears for the future of Margaret—among, of course, much else. The studies of art and of gender are some of the first to face the chopping block when budget cuts loom. Even more insidiously, discussions of these subjects are the first to be silenced when powerful voices suppress dissent. Margaret's story, in both Shakespeare's play and in history, is one of a woman ultimately unbent amid an onslaught of misogyny and propaganda. Like many other women in Shakespeare's early plays—Joan, Tamora, Katherina—the character of Margaret is a frightening figure to the forces of reaction.

Margaret's chances on the stage may be limited, too. In the United States, the theatre industry is "on the verge of collapse," warned Isaac Butler in *The New York Times* in the summer of 2023. Layoffs and closures have struck theatres across the nation; whole festivals have died off.[5] Similarly, a 2024 report from the Society of London Theatre and UK Theatre warned that 40 percent of the UK's 1,110 theatres are at risk of closure in the next five years.[6] The COVID pandemic dealt a harder blow to theatre than to almost any other sector of society; recovery takes money, which is in short supply. Indeed, one Friday night in May 2025, theatres across the United States received an unsigned email notifying them that their support from the National Endowment for the Arts—an independent agency whose funding represents 0.003 percent of the US federal budget—had been terminated.[7] Who will be left to remember Margaret—the queen, the warrior, the character, the icon—when the drama programs and the theatres have closed?

Shakespeare's Margaret, though she is a fictional character, has always been of this world. Her future is our future. A world with characters like her—a world with art that is free, fathomable, and *funded*—is a world we must fight for.

Yet it would likewise be overly simple for this book to end with such a call to arms—or, worse, a call to give money. It is, of course, vital that engaged individuals attend their local theatre, advocate for greater support for the arts in their community, but such actions are harm reduction, not a meaningful route out of the present polycrisis afflicting the public humanities. Individual action can only advance glancing blows against the structural behemoths of austerity and extraction. In other words, the sort of pleas that theatre attendees hear routinely before performances these days—*we depend on your support!*—are true, and profoundly inadequate.

Still, Margaret herself may provide some wisdom for the present moment. After all, hers is a character that almost invariably leaves an impression on the actors who play her. Peggy Ashcroft, as she aged and people asked her which was the favorite role of her career, responded with Margaret: "one of the most fascinating and demanding characters" in Shakespeare, even though—or perhaps *because*—"she is a sort of monster." Penny Downie, who in the 1980s played the queen opposite Ralph Fiennes, found that the more time she spent with Margaret, the more she found herself: "I spent a lot of time scraping away the preconceptions, coming up against the huge ideas of the mind that created this part, this enormous arc of a role that moves from one play to the next. I know that I had to discover more of myself in taking on the role of this woman who tells us so much about things universal through her particular journey." Tina Packer, actor and director and founder of Shakespeare and Company, a theatre in Lenox, Massachusetts, expressed a similar idea: "My own exploration of Margaret has deepened my creative life. Through her, I understand the passage of time, what remains important, what falls away," Packer wrote. "I understand how love and hate can reside side by side, one person being the focus of both."[8]

Perhaps, then, this is Margaret's legacy—a message of ambivalence or monstrosity is still a message. Margaret, in other words, leaves an impact, makes a mark. There can be no higher compliment than to write that Margaret has scarred the history of performance; hers is a bequest of persistence. Pain recedes, wounds heal, but scars remain. Half a millennium ago, Margaret walked off an Elizabethan stage, marked but not defeated, the only major figure still standing after four plays of bloodshed and war. She then kept walking. This dogged survival despite centuries of institutional sexism, fickle tastes, and literal erasure is the greatest evidence that, however uncertain it may be, a future will be Margaret's.

Acknowledgments

We decided to embark on this project together one sweltering afternoon in 2021 while on our first vacation since the pandemic began. Yet our engagement with Margaret—and the debts we accrued—date back far earlier. She first piqued Scott's interest in a high school English class, when her insults quickened an otherwise halting round-robin reading of *Richard III*. Charlie first noticed the character when he saw his dear friend Arie Levine play the role in her college production of the same play. His scholarly engagement with Margaret began some years later in graduate school, where he very nearly made her the subject of his dissertation. While he eventually decided to focus on an altogether unrelated subject, he was lucky enough to learn from a number of mentors who deepened his engagement with classical drama, including Catherine Sheehy, Paul Walsh, Marc Robinson, Kimberly Jannarone, Tom Sellar, Joe Roach, Jim Leverett, and the dearly missed Gordon Rogoff, who never stopped talking about Peggy Ashcroft wiping the floor with her castmates. Other essential mentors include Elise Morrison, Gabrielle Cody, and Denise Walen. Charlie's fascination with Margaret ultimately persisted beyond the classroom, and his enthusiasm for her character and her arc intrigued Scott, who encouraged him to turn Margaret's story into a book. When Charlie demurred, Scott—who was looking for a new project—proposed that they cowrite it.

In the years that followed, we drew from the generosity and expertise of a great many institutions and individuals. Enormous thanks to the staffs of the Yale University Library, the University of Amsterdam Library, and the Oakland Public Library. We could never have completed this project without the Internet Archive, and the shuttering of its controlled digital lending program is a true blow to intellectual inquiry. We owe thanks to archivists and librarians at the University of Bristol (especially Jill Sullivan), Huntington Library (especially Mina Marciano), University of Birmingham (especially Rosalind MacLachlan), Harvard's Houghton Library (especially Zoë Hill), the University of Texas's Harry Ransom Center (especially Kerri Kilmer), and Syracuse University (especially Amy McDonald). Kari Olmon graciously assisted with securing numerous sources. Stephanie Tillotson generously shared her scholarship (and images of Margaret in performance).

Obtaining the images for this book was an unexpectedly difficult task, but its burdens were diminished by the kindness of many. These include Anna Gubis (Shakespeare Birthplace Trust), Melanie Leung (Folger Shakespeare Library), Tim Noakes (Department of Special Collections, Stanford University), Marie Hawkins and Carmen Holdsworth-Delgado (The Garrick Club), Robert Viglasky, Richard Dobbs-Grove, Peter Huestis (National Gallery of Art), Emma Perrin and Hannah Kennedy (Chicago Shakespeare Theater), Vinota Karunasaagarar (Royal Shakespeare Company), Philippa Kelly and Jay Yamada (California Shakespeare Theater), Jennifer Linhart Wood (*Shakespeare Quarterly*), Anna Schergna and Jack Baker (Bridgeman Images), Karintha Lowe (Harvard Theatre Collection), and Charlotte Fay and Tolulope Karunwi (Carnival Films).

Susan Lee Cohen expertly shepherded this book to W. W. Norton, where we were lucky enough to work with the brilliant editor Alane Salierno Mason. Many thanks to all at Norton, including the excellent editorial assistant YJ Wang, copyeditor Ira Brodsky, designer Jaren Bartman, production manager Julia Druskin, project editor Rebecca Munro, publicist Erin Lovett, and marketing manager Meredith Dowling. Thanks, as well, to the many friends with whom we have discussed this project over the years, including Joshua Blecher-Cohen, Elena Leib, Cody Pomeranz, and Jane Darby Menton.

Finally, our family provided love, support, encouragement, and eventually free childcare during the years we were completing this book. Howard Stern was and is an endless fount of enthusiasm and encouragement. Rhonda Wasserman first introduced Scott to Shakespeare (with an outdoor production of *Macbeth* and then a University of Pittsburgh production of *King Lear*) and years later provided wise commentary on our earliest drafts. Brian and Cynthia O'Malley started Charlie off on a production of *Henry IV, Part 1* when he was barely old enough to follow a story, and he has wondered ever since why everyone's favorite plays aren't the history plays. Thank you for everything. Thanks, also, to Peter O'Malley, Anna Pancoast, Eric Stern, Evan Zuzik, Benny Stern, Hannah Le Comte, and Deborah and Marvin Wasserman. And Harper. Brendan and Nolan—we can hardly wait to share with you the art we love. You are the light and the joy in the darkest of times.

Notes

Introduction

1. *2H6*, IV.iv.5–6; 14–15. Unless otherwise noted, all quotations from Shakespeare's plays and poems are from Stephen Greenblatt, Walter Cohen, Jean E. Howard, and Katharine Eisaman Maus, eds., *The Norton Shakespeare* (W. W. Norton, 1997). Throughout this book, we quote from this edition in narrativizing the plays' original performances on the Elizabethan stage. Although modern, edited play texts undoubtedly differ from the words first spoken more than four centuries ago, such texts nonetheless provide a decent approximation of the Elizabethan playgoing experience. We discuss the instability of Shakespeare's plays, and the evolution of their texts, at length throughout the book, especially in chapter 8.

2. *2H6*, IV.iv.55.

3. The specific word and line counts vary based on the specific text one is using (i.e., which edition of the plays). For this calculation, we've used the *Shakespeare's Words* web project, adding together all of Margaret's lines across her four plays. See "Characters by Part Sizes," *Shakespeare's Words* (2017).

4. Two minor characters also appear in four Shakespeare plays, Mistress Quickly and Bardolph, yet their characterization is highly inconsistent.

5. Irene Dash, *Wooing, Wedding, and Power: Women in Shakespeare's Plays* (Columbia Univ. Press, 1981), 157, 193.

6. Phyllis Rackin, "Women's Roles in the Elizabethan History Plays," in Michael Hattaway, ed., *The Cambridge Companion to Shakespeare's History Plays* (Cambridge Univ. Press, 2002), 76.

7. Patricia-Ann Lee, "Reflections of Power: Margaret of Anjou and the Dark Side of Queenship," *Renaissance Quarterly* 39.2 (summer 1986), 183–84.

8. Rory Loughnane and Andrew J. Power, "Introduction: Beginning with Shakespeare," in Rory Loughnane and Andrew J. Power, eds., *Early Shakespeare, 1588–1594* (Cambridge Univ. Press, 2020), 11–12.

9. Rachel Wifall, "Swords and Curses: The Power of Female Power in Shakespeare's Early History Plays" (PhD diss., New York University, 1999), 36–37; Jean E. Howard and Phyllis Rackin, *Engendering a Nation: A Feminist Account of Shakespeare's English Histories* (Routledge, 1997), 24; Leslie Fiedler, *The Stranger in Shakespeare* (Stein and Day, 1972), 78; Carol Banks, "Warlike Women: 'Reproofe to These Degenerate Effeminate Dayes'?" in Dermot Cavanagh, Stuart Hampton-Reeves, and Stephen Longstaffe, eds., *Shakespeare's Histories and Counter-Histories* (Manchester Univ. Press, 2006), 169.

10. Juliet Dusinberre, *Shakespeare and the Nature of Women* (Palgrave Macmillan, 1975), 19; David Mann, *Shakespeare's Women: Performance and Conception* (Cambridge Univ. Press, 2008), 154–55.

11. Jane Austen, *History of England* (1791, Penguin, 1995), 4.

12. John D. Cox and Eric Rasmussen, eds., *King Henry VI, Part 3* (Arden, 2001), 148.

Chapter 1: Daughter of Warfare, Princess of Peace

1. John Lydgate, appendix: "Margaret of Anjou's Entry into London," in Claire Sponsler, ed., *Mummings and Entertainments* (Medieval Institute Publications, 2010), 157–66 (spelling modernized).

2. Bertram Wolffe, *Henry VI* (Yale Univ. Press, 2001, 1st ed. 1981), 182; Helen Castor, *She-Wolves: The Women Who Ruled England Before Elizabeth* (Faber and Faber, 2010), 326; Lauren Johnson, *The Shadow King: The Life and Death of Henry VI* (Pegasus, 2019), 196–98; Helen E. Maurer, *Margaret of Anjou: Queenship and Power in Late Medieval England* (Boydell, 2003), 19; Gordon Kipling, *Enter the King: Theatre, Liturgy, and Ritual in the Medieval Civic Triumph* (Clarendon, 1998), 188–201; Ralph A. Griffiths, *The Reign of King Henry VI: The Exercise of Royal Authority, 1422–1461* (Univ. of California Press, 1981), 488–490.

3. Lydgate, appendix, 157–66 (spelling modernized).

4. C. N. L. Brooke and V. Ortenberg, "The Birth of Margaret of Anjou," *Historical Research* 61 (1988), 357–58.

5. Michael Jones, "The Crown and the Provinces in the Fourteenth Century," in David Potter, ed., *France in the Later Middle Ages 1200–1500* (Oxford Univ. Press, 2002), 61–89.

6. Jock Haswell, *The Ardent Queen: Margaret of Anjou and Lancastrian Heritage* (Peter Davies, 1976), 15–22.

7. Keith Dockray, *Henry VI, Margaret of Anjou, and the Wars of the Roses* (Sutton, 2000), 1; Peter Saccio, *Shakespeare's English Kings: History, Chronicle, and Drama* (Oxford Univ. Press, 1999), 87–88; J. R. Lander, *Conflict and Stability in Fifteenth-Century England* (Hutchinson, 1969), 59–63.

8. John Watts, *Henry VI and the Politics of Kingship* (Cambridge Univ. Press, 1996), 111–13; Saccio, *Shakespeare's English Kings*, 98.

9. George Duby, *France in the Middle Ages, 987–1460: From Hugh Capet to Joan*

of Arc, trans. Juliet Vale (Blackwell, 1987), 77; J. J. Bagley, *Margaret of Anjou: Queen of England* (Herbert Jenkins, 1948), 24–25; Pierre Charbonnier, "Society and the Economy: The Crisis and Its Aftermath," in Potter, *France in the Later Middle Ages*, 117–29.

10. Castor, *She-Wolves*, 321–23. See also Howard and Rackin, *Engendering a Nation*, 51.

11. Castor, *She-Wolves*, chap. 5.

12. Bagley, *Margaret of Anjou*, 23–25.

13. Duby, *France in the Middle Ages*, 317; Haswell, *The Ardent Queen*, 24–28; Castor, *She-Wolves*, 321; Margaret Lucille Kekewich, *The Good King: René of Anjou and Fifteenth Century Europe* (Palgrave Macmillan, 2000), 57–58.

14. Zita Eva Rohr, *Yolande of Aragon (1381–1442) Family and Power: The Reverse of the Tapestry* (Palgrave Macmillan, 2016), 190–96; Edmond Pognon, *Les Très Riches Heures du Duc de Berry* (Liber, 1987).

15. Theresa Earenfight, *Queenship in Medieval Europe* (Red Globe, 2013), 200–201; Haswell, *The Ardent Queen*, 21–22.

16. Haswell, *The Ardent Queen*, 28; Bagley, *Margaret of Anjou*, 25–26; Nicholas Orme, *Medieval Children* (Yale Univ. Press, 2001), 242–46; Sonja Drimmer, "Beyond Private Matter: A Prayer Roll for Queen Margaret of Anjou," *Gesta* 53.1 (March 2014), 95–120.

17. Kekewich, *The Good King*, 86–87; Johnson, *The Shadow King*, 192–93.

18. Kekewich, *The Good King*, 87; Haswell, *The Ardent Queen*, 3; Paul B. Newman, *Growing Up in the Middle Ages* (McFarland, 2007), 101–3.

19. Dockray, *Henry VI, Margaret of Anjou*, 11; Haswell, *The Ardent Queen*, 32–33.

20. Agnes Strickland, *Lives of the Queens of England* (George Barrie, 1902), 3.177–79.

21. Griffiths, *The Reign of King Henry VI*, 482–84; B. M. Cron, "The Duke of Suffolk, the Angevin Marriage, and the Ceding of Maine, 1445," *Journal of Medieval History* 20.1 (1994), 78; Wolffe, *Henry VI*, 170–72; Johnson, *The Shadow King*, 193; Haswell, *The Ardent Queen*, 36.

22. Cron, "The Duke of Suffolk," 77–78; Haswell, *The Ardent Queen*, 39–41; Helen E. Maurer and B. M. Cron, *The Letters of Margaret of Anjou* (Boydell Press, 2018), 237; Wolffe, *Henry VI*, 175–76.

23. Haswell, *The Ardent Queen*, 44; Maurer, *Margaret of Anjou*, 18; Cron, "The Duke of Suffolk," 78; Maurer and Cron, *The Letters of Margaret of Anjou*, 177; Johnson, *The Shadow King*, 194.

24. Griffiths, *The Reign of King Henry VI*, 487; Haswell, *The Ardent Queen*, 45–48.

25. Margaret may have met Alice earlier. See Gwyn Williams, "Suffolk and Margaret: A Study of Some Sections of Shakespeare's Henry VI," *Shakespeare Quarterly* 25 (summer 1974), 313.

26. Kekewich, *The Good King*, 98–100; Johnson, *The Shadow King*, 195.

27. Maurer, *Margaret of Anjou*, 40.

28. Wolffe, *Henry VI*, 182; Castor, *She-Wolves*, 326; Johnson, *The Shadow King*, 198.

29. Johnson, *The Shadow King*, 196; Strickland, *Lives of the Queens of England*, 3.189–91; Maurer, *Margaret of Anjou*, 19; Barbara A. Hanawalt, *The Ties That*

Bound: Peasant Families in Medieval England (Oxford Univ. Press, 1986), 203; Kipling, *Enter the King*, 188–201.

Chapter 2: "Of Witte and Wilinesse She Lacked Nothyng"

1. Andrew Gurr, *The Shakespearean Stage, 1574–1642* (Cambridge Univ. Press, 1994), 197–98.
2. Peter Holland, "Openings," in Stuart Hampton-Reeves and Bridget Escolme, eds., *Shakespeare and the Making of the Theatre* (Palgrave Macmillan, 2012), 16.
3. *2H6*, I.i.21–35.
4. Watts, *Henry VI and the Politics of Kingship*, 364.
5. A 2025 article claims that Anne may have lived in London with Will, though possibly not until 1599 or so. Matthew Steggle, "The Shakspaires of Trinity Lane: A Possible Shakespeare Life-Record," *Shakespeare* 21.2 (2025), 450–94.
6. Russell Fraser, *Young Shakespeare* (Columbia Univ. Press, 1988), 86–88; D. M. Palliser, *The Age of Elizabeth: England Under the Later Tudors, 1547–1603* (Longman, 1992), 248–50; René Weis, *Shakespeare Revealed: A Biography* (John Murray, 2007), 95.
7. Weis, *Shakespeare Revealed*, 95–96; E. K. Chambers, *The Elizabethan Stage* (Clarendon, 1945), 2.377.
8. Park Honan, *Christopher Marlowe: Poet & Spy* (Oxford Univ. Press, 2005), 161; Peter Thomson, *Shakespeare's Professional Career* (Cambridge Univ. Press, 1999), 67; Gurr, *The Shakespearean Stage, 1574–1642*, 116.
9. Stephen Greenblatt, *Will in the World: How Shakespeare Became Shakespeare* (Jonathan Cape, 2004), 183.
10. Terence G. Schoone-Jongen, *Shakespeare's Companies: William Shakespeare's Early Career and the Acting Companies, 1577–1594* (Ashgate, 2008), 59–60.
11. Chambers, *The Elizabethan Stage*, 2.385, 2.393; Richard Dutton, *Shakespeare's Theatre: A History* (Wiley, 2018), 92–93; Michael Hattaway, *Elizabethan Popular Theatre: Plays in Performance* (Routledge, 2005), 11; Fraser, *Young Shakespeare*, 114–15; Tiffany Stern, *Making Shakespeare: From Stage to Page* (Routledge, 2004), 11–12.
12. Greenblatt, *Will in the World*, 183; Chambers, *The Elizabethan Stage*, 2.527–28, 2.544; Gurr, *The Shakespearean Stage*, 121; Christine Eccles, *The Rose Theatre* (Routledge, 1990), 2; Hattaway, *Elizabethan Popular Theatre*, 22; Fraser, *Young Shakespeare*, 115–16.
13. Chambers, *The Elizabethan Stage*, 2.358; Glynne Wickham, Herbert Berry, and William Ingram, eds., *English Professional Theatre, 1530–1660* (Cambridge Univ. Press, 2000), 337; Dutton, *Shakespeare's Theatre*, 97, 99.
14. Weis, *Shakespeare Revealed*, 94–95, 100; Chambers, *The Elizabethan Stage*, 2.385–88; Gurr, *The Shakespearean Stage*, 31; Fraser, *Young Shakespeare*, 110.
15. Gurr, *The Shakespearean Stage*, 89–90.
16. Wickham et al., *English Professional Theatre*, 348, 404–11; Schoone-Jongen, *Shakespeare's Companies*, 61; Chambers, *The Elizabethan Stage*, 2.400–402,

2.524, 2.546; Hattaway, *Elizabethan Popular Theatre*, 12, 40; William Ingram, "Henry Lanman's Curtain Playhouse as an 'Easer' to the Theatre, 1585–1592," in Herbert Berry, ed., *The First Public Playhouse: The Theatre in Shoreditch 1576–1598* (McGill-Queen's Univ. Press, 1979), 17–28; Stern, *Making Shakespeare*, 16.

17. Eccles, *The Rose Theatre*, 18 (discussing the Rose).

18. Eccles, *The Rose Theatre*, chaps. 1, 3–4; Chambers, *The Elizabethan Stage*, 1.358, 2.405–9, 2.524–25, 2.531; Thomson, *Shakespeare's Professional Career*, 67–81; Schoone-Jongen, *Shakespeare's Companies*, 61; Ernest L. Rhodes, *Henslowe's Rose: The Stage and Staging* (Univ. Press of Kentucky, 1976); Carol Chillington Rutter, ed., *Documents of the Rose Playhouse* (Manchester Univ. Press, 1999); Wickham et al., *English Professional Theatre*, 419–21.

19. Samuel Schoenbaum, *William Shakespeare: A Documentary Life* (Oxford Univ. Press, 1975), 111–13.

20. Stanley Wells, *Shakespeare and Co.* (Pantheon, 2006), 2, 62–105; Bart Van Es, *Shakespeare in Company* (Oxford Univ. Press, 2013), 2; Fraser, *Young Shakespeare*, 136, 138–39.

21. Weis, *Shakespeare Revealed*, chap. 8; Chambers, *The Elizabethan Stage*, 3.418–19; Wells, *Shakespeare and Co.*, 75–78, 104–5; Stephen Greenblatt, *Dark Renaissance: The Dangerous Times and Fatal Genius of Shakespeare's Greatest Rival* (W. W. Norton, 2025), chaps. 5–7 and 10; F. P. Wilson, *Marlowe and the Early Shakespeare* (Clarendon, 1953), 14–17; Honan, *Christopher Marlowe*, 187–90, 293; Hattaway, *Elizabethan Popular Theatre*, 92–96; Van Es, *Shakespeare in Company*, 2–3; G. B. Harrison, *Shakespeare at Work, 1592–1603* (Univ. of Michigan Press, 1963), 36–40.

22. Glynne Wickham, *Early English Stage, 1300 to 1660* (Routledge, 1959); William Tydeman, *English Medieval Theatre, 1400–1500* (Routledge, 1986); chapters by Greg Walker, Richard Beadle, David Mills, Peter Meredith, and Alan J. Fletcher in Richard Beadle and Alan J. Fletcher, eds., *The Cambridge Companion to Medieval English Theatre* (Cambridge Univ. Press, 2008); Rosemary Woolf, *The English Mystery Plays* (Routledge, 1972); John Gassner, *Medieval and Tudor Drama* (Applause Books, 1987).

23. David Riggs, *The World of Christopher Marlowe* (Henry Holt, 2004), 114; Andrew Gurr, *The Shakespearian Playing Companies* (Clarendon, 1996), 218–28; Chambers, *The Elizabethan Stage*, 1.378–80.

24. Wickham et al., *English Professional Theatre*, 153; Gurr, *The Shakespearean Stage*, 85–87; M. C. Bradbrook, *The Rise of the Common Player* (Cambridge Univ. Press, 1962), 96–98.

25. Chambers, *The Elizabethan Stage*, 2.77–103; Gurr, *The Shakespearian Playing Companies*, 58–59, 167–84.

26. Scott McMillin and Sally-Beth MacLean, *The Queen's Men and Their Plays* (Cambridge Univ. Press, 1998), especially chaps. 1–3; Chambers, *The Elizabethan Stage*, 1.267, 1.312, 2.104–115; Gurr, *The Shakespearian Playing Companies*, 19–35, 58–62, 64, 200–217; Gurr, *The Shakespearean Stage*, 32–33; E. K. Chambers, *William Shakespeare* (Clarendon, 1930), 1.28–31; Schoone-Jongen, *Shakespeare's*

Companies, 53–54; Wickham et al., *English Professional Theatre*, 208; Wells, *Shakespeare and Co.*, 6; Riggs, *The World of Christopher Marlowe*, 197; Brian Walsh, *Shakespeare, the Queen's Men, and the Elizabethan Performance of History* (Cambridge Univ. Press, 2009), 30–35; Helen Ostovich, Holger Schott Syme, and Andrew Griffin, introduction to *Locating the Queen's Men, 1583–1603: Material Practices and Conditions of Playing* (Routledge, 2016), 1–26.

27. Schoone-Jongen, *Shakespeare's Companies*, 87–101; McMillin and MacLean, *The Queen's Men*, 52–53, 86, 160–66.

28. Gurr, *The Shakespearian Playing Companies*, 231–34; Chambers, *The Elizabethan Stage*, 2.134; Schoone-Jongen, *Shakespeare's Companies*, 65.

29. Riggs, *The World of Christopher Marlowe*, 159, 201–31; Weis, *Shakespeare Revealed*, 100–102; Wilson, *Marlowe and the Early Shakespeare*, 26–27, 38, 105; Wells, *Shakespeare and Co.*, 83–85; Greenblatt, *Dark Renaissance*, chap. 9; Chambers, *The Elizabethan Stage*, 2.134–38; Honan, *Christopher Marlowe*, 164–77, 184–86; Robert Logan, *Shakespeare's Marlowe: The Influence of Christopher Marlowe on Shakespeare's Artistry* (Ashgate, 2007), 49; Greenblatt, *Will in the World*, 189–90; McMillin and MacLean, *The Queen's Men*, 155–60; Van Es, *Shakespeare in Company*, 24–26; A. D. Wraight, *Christopher Marlowe and Edward Alleyn* (Adam Hart, 1993), 1–64; Bradbrook, *The Rise of the Common Player*, 127–28; Andrew Gurr, *Shakespeare's Workplace: Essays on Shakespeare's Theatre* (Cambridge Univ. Press, 2017), 81–85.

30. Andrew Gurr, *Playgoing in Shakespeare's London* (Cambridge Univ. Press, 2004), 143–70; Gurr, *The Shakespearian Playing Companies*, 59–60, 200, 218–26; McMillin and MacLean, *The Queen's Men*, 121–24, 155–60; Robert Y. Turner, *Shakespeare's Apprenticeship* (Univ. of Chicago Press, 1974), 5; Bradbrook, *The Rise of the Common Player*, chap. 5; Schoone-Jongen, *Shakespeare's Companies*, 57–58; Peter Berek, "*Tamburlaine*'s Weak Sons: Imitation Before 1593," *Renaissance Drama* 13 (1982), 55–82; Cook, "Audiences," 318; Fraser, *Young Shakespeare*, 102.

31. Chambers, *The Elizabethan Stage*, 2.118–24, 2.161–64, 4.164–65, 4.387; Schoone-Jongen, *Shakespeare's Companies*, 66–67, 103–17; Lawrence Manley and Sally-Beth MacLean, *Lord Strange's Men and Their Plays* (Yale Univ. Press, 2014), 30–36, 46; Dutton, *Shakespeare's Theatre*, 62; Gurr, *The Shakespearian Playing Companies*, 258–60; Gurr, *Shakespeare's Workplace*, 94–95; Wickham et al., *English Professional Theatre*, 332; E. A. J. Honigmann, *Shakespeare: The "Lost Years"* (Manchester Univ. Press, 1998), 59–62; Riggs, *The World of Christopher Marlowe*, 260–63, 282–83.

32. Schoone-Jongen, *Shakespeare's Companies*, 43–44; Gurr, *The Shakespearian Playing Companies*, 47–48; Siobhan Keenan, *Acting Companies and Their Plays in Shakespeare's London* (Bloomsbury, 2014), 26–28.

33. Schoone-Jongen, *Shakespeare's Companies*, 49; Siobhan Keenan, *Travelling Players in Shakespeare's England* (Palgrave Macmillan, 2002), 11, 15; Gurr, *The Shakespearian Playing Companies*, 44–45.

34. Wells, *Shakespeare and Co.*, 22; Gurr, *The Shakespearean Stage*, 198. See also Fraser, *Young Shakespeare*, 107–8.

35. Weis, *Shakespeare Revealed*, 93.

36. Ralf Hertel, *Staging England in the Elizabethan History Play: Performing National Identity* (Ashgate, 2014), 25–26.

37. Gurr, *The Shakespearian Playing Companies*, 100–101; Gurr, *The Shakespearean Stage*, 42, 102.

38. Honan, *Christopher Marlowe*, 187; E. A. J. Honigmann, *Shakespeare's Impact on His Contemporaries* (Barnes and Noble Books, 1982), 23–24; Schoenbaum, *William Shakespeare*, 184.

39. Schoone-Jongen, *Shakespeare's Companies*, 35–39; Gary Taylor and Gabriel Egan, eds., *The New Oxford Shakespeare: Authorship Companion* (Oxford Univ. Press, 2017), 493–94; Gary Taylor et al., eds., *The New Oxford Shakespeare: Modern Critical Edition* (Oxford Univ. Press, 2017), 254; Ronald Knowles, ed., *King Henry VI Part 2* (Arden, 1999), 111–15. See also Hanspeter Born, "The Date of *2, 3 Henry VI*," *Shakespeare Quarterly* 25 (1974), 323–34.

40. G. E. Bentley, *The Profession of Dramatist in Shakespeare's Time, 1590–1642* (Princeton Univ. Press, 1971), 63–64, 114–20; Roslyn Lander Knutson, *Playing Companies and Commerce in Shakespeare's Time* (Cambridge Univ. Press, 2001), 49–54.

41. Gurr, *The Shakespearian Playing Companies*, 102; Keenan, *Acting Companies and Their Plays*, 60–62; Bentley, *The Profession of Dramatist*, 228–34; Thomson, *Shakespeare's Professional Career*, 83; Carol Chillington, "Playwrights at Work: Henslowe's, Not Shakespeare's, Book of *Sir Thomas More*," *English Literary Renaissance* 10 (1980), 449; Brian Vickers, *Shakespeare, Co-Author: A Historical Study of Five Collaborative Plays* (Oxford Univ. Press, 2004), 21–23, 27–30; Grace Ioppolo, *Dramatists and Their Manuscripts in the Age of Shakespeare, Jonson, Middleton and Heywood: Authorship, Authority and the Playhouse* (Routledge, 2006), 32–33; Tiffany Stern, *Documents of Performance in Early Modern England* (Cambridge Univ. Press, 2009), 1–2.

42. Van Es, *Shakespeare in Company*, 278–84; John Jones, *Shakespeare at Work* (Oxford Univ. Press, 1996), chap. 1; Chillington, "Playwrights at Work," 439 79; Vickers, *Shakespeare, Co-Author*, 34–42; Schoone-Jongen, *Shakespeare's Companies*, 112–13.

43. Robert Miola, *Shakespeare's Reading* (Oxford Univ. Press, 2000), 8.

44. Jonathan Bate, *Soul of the Age: The Life, Mind and World of William Shakespeare* (Viking, 2008), 144–45; Miola, *Shakespeare's Reading*, 11–12.

45. Lucille King, "The Use of Hall's Chronicles in the Folio and Quarto Texts of *Henry VI*," *Philological Quarterly* 13.4 (October 1934), 321–32; Bate, *Soul of the Age*, 148; Kavita Mudan Finn, *The Last Plantagenet Consorts: Gender, Genre, and Historiography, 1440–1627* (Palgrave Macmillan, 2012), 88–93, 103–4.

46. E. M. W. Tillyard, *Shakespeare's History Plays* (Chatto and Windus, 1944), 47–56.

47. Dockray, *Henry VI, Margaret of Anjou*, xxxiii; Miola, *Shakespeare's Reading*, 45–63; Bate, *Soul of the Age*, 148; Lucille King, "*2 and 3 Henry VI*—Which Holinshed?" *PMLA* 50 (1935), 745–52; Nina S. Levine, *Women's Matters: Politics, Gender, and Nation in Shakespeare's Early History Plays* (Univ. of Delaware Press, 1998), 74; Finn, *The Last Plantagenet Consorts*, 90–94.

48. Knowles, *King Henry VI Part 2*, 438–39; Chambers, *William Shakespeare*, 1.289; Emrys Jones, *The Origins of Shakespeare* (Clarendon, 1977), 164–70, 173–75; Lucille King, "Text Sources of the Folio and Quarto *Henry VI*," *PMLA* 51.3 (September 1936), 702–18; Saccio, *Shakespeare's English Kings*, 115–16.

49. Miola, *Shakespeare's Reading*, 44.

50. Paola Pugliatti, *Shakespeare the Historian* (Macmillan, 1996), 32.

51. Pugliatti, *Shakespeare the Historian*, 32–33; Cyndia Susan Clegg, "Censorship and the Problems with History in Shakespeare's England," in Richard Dutton and Jean E. Howard, eds., *A Companion to Shakespeare's Work: The Histories* (Blackwell, 2006), 48–69; Levine, *Women's Matters*, 74.

52. Edward Hall, *The Union of the Two Noble and Illustre Famelies of Lancastre and York* (1548; Johnson et al., 1809), 234.

53. W. G. Boswell-Stone, *Shakespeare's Holinshed: The Chronicle and the Historical Plays Compared* (Chatto and Windus, 1907), 242.

54. Hall, *The Union*, 249.

55. Lawrence Stone, *The Family, Sex, and Marriage in England, 1500–1800* (Weidenfeld and Nicolson, 1977), 175–76.

56. Park Honan, *Shakespeare: A Life* (Oxford Univ. Press, 2008), 18–19, 23.

57. Lois Potter, *The Life of William Shakespeare: A Critical Biography* (Wiley-Blackwell, 2012), 10; Weis, *Shakespeare Revealed*, 329–30.

58. Weis, *Shakespeare Revealed*, 14.

59. Honan, *Shakespeare*, 5–6; Fraser, *Young Shakespeare*, 24.

60. Wallace T. MacCaffrey, *The Shaping of the Elizabethan Regime* (Princeton Univ. Press, 1968), 17.

61. Jane Clay, "Performing Queenship in Premodern England: Gender, Politics, and Drama" (PhD diss., St. John's University, 2016), chap. 3.

62. Hertel, *Staging England in the Elizabethan History Play*, 80–81, 194; Dominique Goy-Blanquet, "Elizabethan Historiography and Shakespeare's Sources," in Hattaway, *The Cambridge Companion to Shakespeare's History Plays*, 57–70; Levine, *Women's Matters*, 75–79.

63. Hertel, *Staging England in the Elizabethan History Play*, 212; Levine, *Women's Matters*, 69; Louis Adrian Montrose, "'Shaping Fantasies': Figurations of Gender and Power in Elizabethan Culture," in Stephen Greenblatt, ed., *Representing the English Renaissance* (Univ. of California Press, 1988), 47–55.

64. Barbara Hodgdon, *The End Crowns All: Closure and Contradiction in Shakespeare's History* (Princeton Univ. Press, 1991), 62–63; Chris Fitter, "Emergent Shakespeare and the Politics of Protest: *2 Henry VI* in Historical Contexts," *ELH* 72.1 (spring 2005), 129–30.

65. Helen Hackett, "The Rhetoric of (In)fertility: Shifting Responses to Elizabeth I's Childlessness," in Jennifer Richards and Alison Thorne, eds., *Rhetoric, Women and Politics in Early Modern England* (Routledge, 2007).

66. Hertel, *Staging England in the Elizabethan History Play*, 221; Peter Lake, *How Shakespeare Put Politics on the Stage: Power and Succession in the History Plays* (Yale Univ. Press, 2016), 70–71.

67. Susan Doran, *Monarchy and Matrimony: The Courtships of Elizabeth I* (Routledge 1996), chap. 7; Hertel, *Staging England in the Elizabethan History Play*, 8–10, 196, chap. 9; Leah Marcus, *Puzzling Shakespeare: Local Reading and Its Discontents* (Univ. of California Press, 1988), 60.

68. Andy Kesson, "'It Is a Pity You Are Not a Woman': John Lyly and the Creation of Woman," *Shakespeare Bulletin* 33.1 (spring 2015), 33–47; Andy Kesson, *John Lyly and Early Modern Authorship* (Manchester Univ. Press, 2014), 132–33.

69. Darren Freebury-Jones, *Shakespeare's Tutor: The Influence of Thomas Kyd* (Manchester Univ. Press, 2022), 93–96.

70. Wells, *Shakespeare and Co.*, 25 (citing Eric Rasmussen, "Collaboration," in Michael Dobson and Stanley Wells, eds., *The Oxford Companion to Shakespeare* [Oxford Univ. Press, 2001]); Gurr, *The Shakespearian Playing Companies*, 102; Bentley, *The Profession of Dramatist*, 199; Jeffrey Masten, "Playwrighting: Authorship and Collaboration," in John D. Cox and David Scott Kastan, eds., *A New History of Early English Drama* (Columbia Univ. Press, 1997), 357–58; Vickers, *Shakespeare, Co-Author*, 18–21.

71. Bentley, *The Profession of Dramatist*, 204.

72. Van Es, *Shakespeare in Company*, 27–28, 36n6; Grace Ioppolo, *Revising Shakespeare* (Harvard Univ. Press, 1991), 86.

73. Van Es, *Shakespeare in Company*, chap. 1, especially 30–31; Masten, "Playwrighting: Authorship and Collaboration," 367.

74. Van Es, *Shakespeare in Company*, 50; Ioppolo, *Dramatists and Their Manuscripts*, chap. 4.

75. Gurr, *The Shakespearean Stage*, 4–6, 20–21; Van Es, *Shakespeare in Company*, 54; Ioppolo, *Dramatists and Their Manuscripts*, 31; Wells, *Shakespeare and Co.*, 152.

76. Keenan, *Acting Companies and Their Plays*, 56–58; Bentley, *The Profession of Dramatist*, 87; Wells, *Shakespeare and Co.*, 23. But see Chambers, *The Elizabethan Stage*, 3.198.

77. Bentley, *The Profession of Dramatist*, 82–87. But see Ioppolo, *Dramatists and Their Manuscripts*, 26.

78. Taylor and Egan, *The New Oxford Shakespeare: Authorship Companion*, 493, 496; John V. Nance, "'We, John Cade': Shakespeare, Marlowe, and the Authorship of 4.2.33–189 *2 Henry VI*," *Shakespeare* 13.1 (2016), 30–51; John Jowett, "Shakespeare as Collaborator," in Stanley Wells and Paul Edmondson, eds., *Shakespeare Beyond Doubt* (Cambridge Univ. Press, 2013), 91. But see Darren Freebury-Jones, *Shakespeare's Borrowed Feathers: How Early Modern Playwrights Shaped the World's Greatest Writer* (Manchester Univ. Press, 2024), 53–63.

79. H. C. Hart, ed., *The Second Part of King Henry VI* (Arden, 1909); John Dover Wilson, ed., *The Second Part of King Henry VI* (Cambridge Univ. Press, 1952); Hugh Craig, "The Three Parts of *Henry VI*," in Hugh Craig and Arthur F. Kinney, eds., *Shakespeare, Computers, and the Mystery of Authorship* (Cambridge Univ. Press, 2009), 40; Knowles, *King Henry VI Part 2*, 116–21.

80. Paul Vincent, "Unresolved Mysteries in *Henry VI, Part Two*," *Notes and Queries* 48 (2002), 270–74; Gary Taylor and John Jowett, "Appendix II: 'O' and 'Oh' in

English Renaissance Dramatists," in *Shakespeare Reshaped, 1600–1623* (Oxford Univ. Press, 1993), 248–59; Taylor and Egan, *The New Oxford Shakespeare: Authorship Companion*, 495.

81. Santiago Segarra et al., "Attributing the Authorship of the *Henry VI* Plays by Word Adjacency," *Shakespeare Quarterly* 67.2 (2016), 232–56; Brian Vickers, "Shakespeare and Authorship Studies in the Twenty-First Century," *Shakespeare Quarterly* 62 (2011), 106–40.

82. Honan, *Christopher Marlowe*, 193; Greenblatt, *Will in the World*, 195–96.

83. Honan, *Christopher Marlowe*, 192; Nicholas Brooke, "Marlowe as Provocative Agent in Shakespeare's Plays," *Shakespeare Survey* 14 (1961), 34–44; James Shapiro, *Rival Playwrights: Marlowe, Jonson, Shakespeare* (Columbia Univ. Press, 1991), 90; Greenblatt, *Will in the World*, 192; Maurice Charney, "The Voice of Marlowe's Tamburlaine in Early Shakespeare," *Comparative Drama* 31.2 (summer 1997), 213–23; J.A.K. Thomson, *Shakespeare and the Classics* (George Allen, 1952), 89. But see Kazuaki Ota, "Was Marlowe Shakespeare's Collaborator? Computational Stylometry and the Authorship of the Three Parts of *Henry VI*," *Studies in Languages and Cultures* 50 (2023), 17.

84. Taylor and Egan, *The New Oxford Shakespeare: Authorship Companion*, 496; Segarra et al., "Attributing the Authorship of the *Henry VI* Plays," 246.

85. Wells, *Shakespeare and Co.*, 25.

86. Greenblatt, *Will in the World*, 189; Honigmann, *Shakespeare's Impact on His Contemporaries*, 54.

87. Chillington, "Playwrights at Work," 447; Frederick Gard Fleay, *A Chronicle History of the London Stage 1559–1642* (Reeves and Turner, 1890), 118.

88. Keenan, *Acting Companies and Their Plays*, 58–60; Vickers, *Shakespeare, Co-Author*, 24. See also Van Es, *Shakespeare in Company*, 42–43, 50; Bentley, *The Profession of Dramatist*, 88–110; Wells, *Shakespeare and Co.*, 23–24.

89. Van Es, *Shakespeare in Company*, 44, 50; Vickers, *Shakespeare, Co-Author*, 30–32; Chillington, "Playwrights at Work," 445.

90. Bentley, *The Profession of Dramatist*, 76–78; Wells, *Shakespeare and Co.*, 24–25; Tiffany Stern, *Rehearsal from Shakespeare to Sheridan* (Oxford Univ. Press, 2007), 59–61.

91. Bentley, *The Profession of Dramatist*, 79–82.

92. Gurr, *The Shakespearian Playing Companies*, 55–57; Gurr, *The Shakespearean Stage*, 72–73; W. R. Streitberger, *The Masters of the Revels and Elizabeth I's Court Theatre* (Oxford Univ. Press, 2016), chap. 4; Chambers, *The Elizabethan Stage*, 1.88–96, 1.319; Bentley, *The Profession of Dramatist*, 148–52; Richard Dutton, "Censorship," in Cox and Kastan, *A New History of Early English Drama*, 296; Richard Dutton, *Mastering the Revels: The Regulation and Censorship of English Renaissance Drama* (Macmillan, 1991), 41–53.

93. Gurr, *The Shakespearean Stage*, 74–76; Chambers, *The Elizabethan Stage*, 1.318, 1.320–24; Bentley, *The Profession of Dramatist*, 145–49, 154–56, 167–93; Rutter, *Documents of the Rose Playhouse*, 17; Keenan, *Acting Companies and Their Plays*,

70–72; Dutton, *Mastering the Revels*, 53–55, 81–89; Dutton, "Censorship," 297–98; Ioppolo, *Revising Shakespeare*, 78–81.

94. Bentley, *The Profession of Dramatist*, 157. But see Gurr, *Playgoing in Shakespeare's London*, 144; Dutton, "Censorship," 297–98.

95. McMillin and MacLean, *The Queen's Men*, 13–17; Dutton, *Mastering the Revels*, 52.

96. Rutter, *Documents of the Rose Playhouse*, 17–18; Bentley, *The Profession of Dramatist*, 194–96.

Chapter 3: "Were I a Man"

1. Naomi C. Liebler and Lisa Scancella Shea, "Shakespeare's Queen Margaret: Unruly or Unruled?" in Thomas A. Pendleton, ed., *Henry VI: Critical Essays* (Routledge, 2001), 79–80; Kavita Mudan Finn, "Tragedy, Transgression, and Women's Voices: The Case of Eleanor Cobham and Margaret of Anjou," *Viator* 47.2 (2016), 277–304.

2. Saccio, *Shakespeare's English Kings*, 118.

3. *2H6*, I.ii.1–16

4. *2H6*, I.ii.63–67.

5. *2H6*, V.iv.3–6.

6. Marilyn French, *Shakespeare's Division of Experience* (Ballantine, 1981), 62.

7. Nicholas Grene, *Shakespeare's Serial History Plays* (Cambridge Univ. Press, 2002), 114; Hertel, *Staging England in the Elizabethan History Play*, 206; Sandra Logan, *Shakespeare's Foreign Queens: Drama, Politics, and the Enemy Within* (Palgrave Macmillan, 2018), especially chap. 5.

8. Liebler and Shea, "Shakespeare's Queen Margaret," 85.

9. *2H6*, I.iii.121–51.

10. Lawrence Manley, "From Strange's Men to Pembroke's Men: *2 Henry VI* and *The First part of the Contention*," *Shakespeare Quarterly* 54 (2003), 273–81; Manley and MacLean, *Lord Strange's Men and Their Plays*, 308–11.

11. Manley, "From Strange's Men to Pembroke's Men," 265.

12. Saccio, *Shakespeare's English Kings*, 119; Pugliatti, *Shakespeare the Historian*, 160–61.

13. Knowles, *King Henry VI Part 2*, 441.

14. J. A. Sharpe, *Instruments of Darkness: Witchcraft in England, 1550–1750* (Hamish Hamilton, 1996), 108–9.

15. Anthony Harris, *Night's Black Agents: Witchcraft and Magic in Seventeenth-Century English Drama* (Manchester Univ. Press, 1980); John D. Cox, "Devils and Power in Marlowe and Shakespeare," *Yearbook of English Studies* 23 (1993), 46–64.

16. Deborah Willis, *Malevolent Nature: Witch-Hunting and Maternal Power in Early Modern England* (Cornell Univ. Press, 1995), 166–67. See also Lake, *How Shakespeare Put Politics on the Stage*, 86; Kristin M. Smith, "Martial Maids

and Murdering Mothers: Women, Witchcraft and Motherly Transgression in *Henry VI* and *Richard III*," *Shakespeare* 3.2 (2007), 143–60.

17. Ralph Griffiths, *King and Country: England and Wales in the Fifteenth Century* (Hambledon, 1991), chap. 15; Gemma Hollman, *Royal Witches: Witchcraft and the Nobility in Fifteenth-Century England* (Pegasus, 2020), chaps. 7–8.

18. Lily B. Campbell, *Shakespeare's "Histories": Mirrors of Elizabethan Policy* (Huntington Library, 1947), 109–10; Finn, *The Last Plantagenet Consorts*, 119–20.

19. *2H6*, III.i.233.

20. Williams, "Suffolk and Margaret," 318–19; Geoffrey Bullough, ed., *Narrative and Dramatic Sources of Shakespeare: "Henry VI," "Richard III," "Richard II"* (Columbia Univ. Press, 1966), 203. But see Finn, *The Last Plantagenet Consorts*, 53–54, 112–13.

21. Fraser, *Young Shakespeare*, 117; Stern, *Making Shakespeare*, 12. But see Dutton, *Shakespeare's Theatre*, 94.

22. William Montgomery, "The Original Staging of *The First Part of the Contention* (1594)," *Shakespeare Studies* 41 (1988), 14.

23. *2H6*, III.ii.3–4.

24. Haswell, *The Ardent Queen*, 63–68; Saccio, *Shakespeare's English Kings*, 120–23.

25. *2H6*, III.ii.390, 404.

26. *2H6*, I.ii.54–8.

27. *2H6*, III.ii.341–58.

28. Cf. James L. Calderwood, "Shakespeare's Evolving Imagery: *2 Henry VI*," *English Studies* 48 (1967), 493.

29. Gwyn Williams, "Suffolk and Margaret: A Study of Some Sections of Shakespeare's *Henry VI*," *Shakespeare Quarterly* 25.3 (summer 1974), 318; *2H6*, III.ii.413–15.

30. Honor Matthews, *Character and Symbol in Shakespeare's Plays: A Study of Certain Christian and Pre-Christian Elements in Their Structure and Imagery* (Schocken Books, 1962), 18.

31. Taylor and Egan, *The New Oxford Shakespeare: Authorship Companion*, 490–91.

32. Hazel Isobel Craig, "Shakespeare's Women: A Comparison of Shakespeare's Female Characters with the Originals" (master's thesis, University of Wyoming, 1932), 62.

33. *Titus Andronicus*, II.iii.10–16.

34. *Titus Andronicus*, II.iii.7.

35. Joan Lord Hall, *Sexual Desire and Romantic Love in Shakespeare* (Edinburgh Univ. Press, 2021), 75.

36. Chambers, *William Shakespeare*, 1.289; Williams, "Suffolk and Margaret," 318; Bullough, *Narrative and Dramatic Sources of Shakespeare*, 31, 94; Finn, *The Last Plantagenet Consorts*, 90, 114, 149.

37. Wifall, "Swords and Curses," 112–13.

38. Williams, "Suffolk and Margaret," 318; Maurer and Cron, *The Letters of Margaret of Anjou*, 191; Maurer, *Margaret of Anjou*, 27–38.

39. Dockray, *Henry VI, Margaret of Anjou*, xxviii.

40. Pugliatti, *Shakespeare the Historian*, chap. 9, 158–59; Finn, *The Last Plantagenet Consorts*, 91.

41. Edna Zwick Boris, *Shakespeare's English Kings, the People, and the Law* (Fairleigh Dickinson Univ. Press, 1978), 63.

42. Roger Virgoe, "The Death of William de la Pole, Duke of Suffolk," *Bulletin of the John Rylands Library* 47.2 (1965), 489–95; Haswell, *The Ardent Queen*, 76–81. See also Wolffe, *Henry VI*, 228–30.

43. Haswell, *The Ardent Queen*, 76; Dockray, *Henry VI, Margaret of Anjou*, xxiii; Alison Basil, "Henry VI and Margaret of Anjou: Madness, Gender Dysfunction and Perceptions of Dis-ease in the Royal Body," in Sean McGlynn and Elena Woodacre, eds., *The Image and Perception of Monarchy in Medieval and Early Modern Europe* (Cambridge Scholars, 2014), 168–82.

44. Watts, *Henry VI and the Politics of Kingship*, 205.

45. Michael Hicks, *The Wars of the Roses* (Yale Univ. Press, 2010), chap. 5; Haswell, *The Ardent Queen*, 75–97; Kekewich, *The Good King*, 127–32; Castor, *She-Wolves*, 332–33; Maurer, *Margaret of Anjou*, 57–58, 67–74.

46. Bagley, *Margaret of Anjou*, 54–57; Maurer, *Margaret of Anjou*, 66; Dockray, *Henry VI, Margaret of Anjou*, 1, 5; Wolffe, *Henry VI*, 135–45; Johnson, *The Shadow King*, 253.

47. See Annabel Patterson, *Shakespeare and the Popular Voice* (Basil Blackwell, 1989), 34–38, 50–51; Roger B. Manning, *Village Revolts: Social Protest and Popular Disturbances in England, 1509–1640* (Oxford Univ. Press, 1988), 187–219; Marjorie Garber, *Shakespeare After All* (Anchor, 2004), 102–3; Ronald Knowles, "The Farce of History: Miracle, Combat, and Rebellion in *2 Henry VI*," *Yearbook of English Studies* 21 (1991), 176–77.

48. *2H6*, IV.iv.1–4.

49. *2H6*, IV.iv.18–9.

50. *2H6*, IV.iv.19.

51. Finn, *The Last Plantagenet Consorts*, 156–57.

52. Catherine Grace Canino, "'From These, our Henry Lineally Descends': Textuality and Topicality in Shakespeare's Henry VI Plays" (PhD diss., Arizona State University, 1999), 183–216.

53. Howard and Rackin, *Engendering a Nation*, 79.

54. Craig, "The Three Parts of *Henry VI*," 73–74, 76; Vickers, *Shakespeare, Co-Author*, 42–43; John Velz, "*Sir Thomas More* and the Shakespeare Canon: Two Approaches," in T. H. Howard-Hill, ed., *Shakespeare and "Sir Thomas More": Essays on the Play and Its Shakespearian Interest* (Cambridge Univ. Press, 1989), 171–74; R. W. Chambers, *Man's Unconquerable Mind: Studies of English Writers, from Bede to A. E. Housman and W. P. Ker* (Jonathan Cape, 1939), 215–21.

55. Knowles, "The Farce of History," 176; Hertel, *Staging England in the Elizabethan History Play*, 174; Greenblatt, *Will in the World*, 167. But see Thomas Cartelli, "Jack Cade in the Garden: Class Consciousness and Class Conflict in *2 Henry VI*," in Richard Burt and John Michael Archer, eds., *Enclosure Acts:*

Sexuality, Property, and Culture in Early Modern England (Cornell Univ. Press, 1994), 52–53, 56–57, 62; Patterson, *Shakespeare and the Popular Voice*, 3.

56. *2H6*, IV.x.70–71; Pugliatti, *Shakespeare the Historian*, 170.

57. Dutton, *Mastering the Revels*, 85.

58. *2H6*, V.i.112–19.

59. *2H6*, V.i.155–6.

60. Saccio, *Shakespeare's English Kings*, 132–33.

61. Wolffe, *Henry VI*, 267–86; Griffiths, *The Reign of King Henry VI*, 715–18; J. L. Laynesmith, *The Last Medieval Queens: English Queenship 1445–1503* (Oxford Univ. Press, 2004), 77, 93–116; Dockray, *Henry VI, Margaret of Anjou*, xxvii–xxix; Johnson, *The Shadow King*, 308–19; Earenfight, *Queenship in Medieval Europe*, 214; Carole Rawcliffe, "The Insanity of Henry VI," *The Historian* 50 (1996), 8–12.

62. Maurer, *Margaret of Anjou*, 90, 96, 99–111; Johnson, *The Shadow King*, 323–25; Bagley, *Margaret of Anjou*, 76.

63. Haswell, *The Ardent Queen*, 107; Anthony Goodman, *The Wars of the Roses: Military Activity and English Society, 1452–97* (Routledge, 1981), 22; Christine Carpenter, *The Wars of the Roses: Politics and the Constitution in England, c.1437–1509* (Cambridge Univ. Press, 1997), 134–35; Griffiths, *The Reign of King Henry VI*, 738–39; Maurer and Cron, *The Letters of Margaret of Anjou*, 203–7; Johnson, *The Shadow King*, 328.

64. Griffiths, *The Reign of King Henry VI*, 738–45; Maurer and Cron, *The Letters of Margaret of Anjou*, 203–7; Johnson, *The Shadow King*, 328–39; Bagley, *Margaret of Anjou*, 79–80; Saccio, *Shakespeare's English Kings*, 132–33; P. A. Johnson, *Duke Richard of York, 1411–1460* (Oxford Univ. Press, 1988), 156–58.

65. Bagley, *Margaret of Anjou*, 80–81, 88–90, 94; Maurer, *Margaret of Anjou*, 127–41, 151–57, 165; Castor, *She-Wolves*, 356–58; Watts, *Henry VI and the Politics of Kingship*, 337–39; Johnson, *Duke Richard of York*, 184–85; Carpenter, *The Wars of the Roses*, 142–43; Carole Levin, "Margaret of Anjou: Passionate Mother," in Aidan Norrie et al., eds., *Later Plantagenet and the Wars of the Roses Consorts: Power, Influence, and Dynasty* (Palgrave Macmillan, 2023), 201–3.

66. *2H6*, V.ii.72–74; Lake, *How Shakespeare Put Politics on the Stage*, 85.

67. Dockray, *Henry VI, Margaret of Anjou*, xx, xxiii–xxiv.

68. Howard and Rackin, *Engendering a Nation*, 77, 82; Levine, *Women's Matters*, 81–82.

Chapter 4: "Tiger's Heart Wrapped in a Woman's Hide"

1. *3H6*, I.i.212–15.

2. *3H6*, I.i.231–35.

3. Jeremy Lopez, *Theatrical Convention and Audience Response in Early Modern Drama* (Cambridge Univ. Press, 2003), 79.

4. Holland, "Openings," 21.

5. Gurr, *Playgoing in Shakespeare's London*, 67–68, 71–72, 76–77.

6. Keenan, *Acting Companies and Their Plays*, 138; Howard and Rackin, *Engendering a Nation*, 33–35; Stephen Orgel, *Impersonations: The Performance of Gender in Shakespeare's England* (Cambridge Univ. Press, 1996), 10; Chambers, *The Elizabethan Stage*, 2.549.

7. Chambers, *The Elizabethan Stage*, 2.548–49.

8. Gurr, *Playgoing in Shakespeare's London*, 38; Michael J. Hirrel, "Duration of Performances and Lengths of Plays: How Shall We Beguile the Lazy Time?" *Shakespeare Quarterly* 61.2 (summer 2010), 161–62; Ann Jennalie Cook, *The Privileged Playgoers of Shakespeare's London, 1576–1642* (Princeton Univ. Press, 1981), 172.

9. Cook, *The Privileged Playgoers*, 147–48; Stern, *Making Shakespeare*, 7–8.

10. Hattaway, *Elizabethan Popular Theatre*, 46.

11. Gurr, *Playgoing in Shakespeare's London*, 45–46; Chambers, *The Elizabethan Stage*, 2.548–49; Fraser, *Young Shakespeare*, 108–9.

12. Stern, *Making Shakespeare*, 16.

13. Paul Menzer, "Crowd Control," in Jennifer A. Low and Nova Myhill, eds., *Imagining the Audience in Early Modern Drama, 1558–1642* (Palgrave Macmillan, 2011), 24.

14. Gurr, *Playgoing in Shakespeare's London*, 45.

15. Wells, *Shakespeare and Company*, 10–11; Chambers, *The Elizabethan Stage*, 1.317–18; Alfred Harbage, *Shakespeare's Audience* (Columbia Univ. Press, 1941), 92, 97, 105–10; Cook, *The Privileged Playgoers*, 205–7, 249–52, 256–59; Gurr, *The Shakespearean Stage*, 206–9. But see Thomson, *Shakespeare's Professional Career*, 101; Hattaway, *Elizabethan Popular Theatre*, 44–45; Lopez, *Theatrical Convention and Audience Response*, 19–20.

16. Ann Jennalie Cook, "'Bargaines of Incontinencie': Bawdy Behavior at the Playhouses," *Shakespeare Studies* 10 (1977), 271–90; Cook, *The Privileged Playgoers*, 157–62, 202–4; Harbage, *Shakespeare's Audience*, 96–97, 100–101.

17. Gurr, *Playgoing in Shakespeare's London*, 42.

18. Howard and Rackin, *Engendering a Nation*, 32; Hattaway, *Elizabethan Popular Theatre*, 41, 46; Ann Jennalie Cook, "Audiences: Investigation, Interpretation, Invention," in Cox and Kastan, *A New History of Early English Drama*, 310; Phyllis Rackin, *Stages of History: Shakespeare's English Chronicles* (Cornell Univ. Press, 1990), 26–27.

19. Gurr, *The Shakespearean Stage*, 209; Gurr, *Playgoing in Shakespeare's London*, 52–55; Keenan, *Acting Companies and Their Plays*, 147–48.

20. Quoted in Bradbrook, *The Rise of the Common Player*, 101.

21. Cook, *The Privileged Playgoers*, 196–99; Gurr, *Playgoing in Shakespeare's London*, 43; Gurr, *The Shakespearean Stage*, 160.

22. Stern, *Rehearsal from Shakespeare to Sheridan*, 14.

23. Keenan, *Acting Companies and Their Plays*, 147.

24. Keenan, *Acting Companies and Their Plays*, 130–41; Gurr, *The Shakespearean Stage*, 198–200; Gurr, *Playgoing in Shakespeare's London*, chap. 3; Thomson, *Shakespeare's Professional Career*, 100–102; Harbage, *Shakespeare's Audience*,

12, 18, 53–91; Cook, *The Privileged Playgoers*, 150–51, chap. 6; Chambers, *The Elizabethan Stage*, 2.532–37.

25. Gurr, *Playgoing in Shakespeare's London*, 46–49; Bradbrook, *The Rise of the Common Player*, 104–5; Cook, *The Privileged Playgoers*, 152–54; Cook, "Audiences: Investigation, Interpretation, Invention," 309.

26. Dusinberre, *Shakespeare and the Nature of Women*, 9–11.

27. Orgel, *Impersonations*, 10–11; Gurr, *Playgoing in Shakespeare's London*, 71–72; Richard Levin, "Women in the Renaissance Theatre Audience," *Shakespeare Quarterly* 40.2 (summer 1989), 165–74.

28. Cf. Jean E. Howard, *Shakespeare's Art of Orchestration: Stage Technique and Audience Response* (Univ. of Illinois Press, 1984), 8.

29. Cox and Rasmussen, *King Henry VI, Part 3*, 9–10; Schoenbaum, *William Shakespeare*, 121.

30. Mann, *Shakespeare's Women*, 156.

31. Mann, *Shakespeare's Women*.

32. Orgel, *Impersonations*, 74–78, 82.

33. *3H6*, I.i.243, 254.

34. Levine, *Women's Matters*, 88. As with *Part Two*, Shakespeare drew on the Tudor chronicles of Hall and Holinshed, among many others and much else, for *Part Three*. Cox and Rasmussen, *King Henry VI, Part 3*, 81–87; King, "Text Sources of the Folio and Quarto *Henry VI*," 702–18.

35. *3H6*, I.i.248–49.

36. Levine, *Women's Matters*, 88.

37. Howard and Rackin, *Engendering a Nation*, 85.

38. *3H6*, I.i.256–63.

39. Stern, *Rehearsal from Shakespeare to Sheridan*, 113–20.

40. Taylor and Egan, *The New Oxford Shakespeare: Authorship Companion*, 496–98; Taylor et al., *The New Oxford Shakespeare: Modern Critical Edition*, 334; John Burrows and Hugh Craig, "The Joker in the Pack? Marlowe, Kyd, and the Co-Authorship of *Henry VI, Part 3*," in Taylor and Egan, *The New Oxford Shakespeare: Authorship Companion*, 194–217, especially 217; Cox and Rasmussen, *King Henry VI, Part 3*, 3, 44–49.

41. Shapiro, *Rival Playwrights*, 90–95; Brooke, "Marlowe as Provocative Agent," 37–38; Riggs, *The World of Christopher Marlowe*, 282–84; Honan, *Christopher Marlowe*, 293–95.

42. Stern, *Rehearsal from Shakespeare to Sheridan*, 56–57.

43. Thomson, *Shakespeare's Professional Career*, 83–85; David Bradley, *From Text to Performance in the Elizabethan Theatre: Preparing the Play for the Stage* (Cambridge Univ. Press, 1992), 89–91; Stern, *Rehearsal from Shakespeare to Sheridan*, 62.

44. Thomson, *Shakespeare's Professional Career*, 85.

45. Stern, *Rehearsal from Shakespeare to Sheridan*, 10, 64–65, 77–78; John Astington, *Actors and Acting in Shakespeare's Time: The Art of Stage Playing* (Cambridge Univ.

Press, 2010), 140–42; Wells, *Shakespeare and Co.*, 22; Hattaway, *Elizabethan Popular Theatre*, 53–54.

46. Scott McMillin, "Casting for Pembroke's Men: The *Henry VI* Quartos and *The Taming of a Shrew*," *Shakespeare Quarterly* 23 (1972), 155–57; T. J. King, *Casting Shakespeare's Plays: London Actors and Their Roles, 1590–1642* (Cambridge Univ. Press, 1992), 78–79. But see Schoone-Jongen, *Shakespeare's Companies*, 125–26.

47. Gurr, *The Shakespearean Stage*, 39; Chambers, *The Elizabethan Stage*, 2.324, 2.339.

48. Wells, *Shakespeare and Co.*, 51–53; Gurr, *The Shakespearian Playing Companies*, 72n36. But see Allison Gaw, "John Sincklo as One of Shakespeare's Actors," *Anglica* 49 (1925), 289–303.

49. Chambers, *The Elizabethan Stage*, 2.341.

50. Hattaway, *Elizabethan Popular Theatre*, 52–53.

51. Stern, *Rehearsal from Shakespeare to Sheridan*, 87–88; Gurr, *The Shakespearian Playing Companies*, 271.

52. Larry S. Champion, *Perspective in Shakespeare's English Histories* (Univ. of Georgia Press, 1980), 48–52.

53. Cox and Rasmussen, *King Henry VI, Part 3*, 1.

54. Cox and Rasmussen, *King Henry VI, Part 3*, 1.

55. Irving Ribner, *The English History Play in the Age of Shakespeare* (Routledge, 1957), 8.

56. Campbell, *Shakespeare's "Histories,"* 125.

57. Lee, "Reflections of Power," 216; Levine, *Women's Matters*, 92.

58. *3H6*, I.ii.49–52.

59. *3H6*, I.iv.1–5.

60. Mark Van Doren, *Shakespeare* (Holt, 1939), 21, 41.

61. Hattaway, *Elizabethan Popular Theatre*, 56; Gurr, *The Shakespearean Stage*, 101. See also Joseph R. Roach, *The Player's Passion: Studies in the Science of Acting* (Univ. of Delaware Press, 1985), 42.

62. Hattaway, *Elizabethan Popular Theatre*, 54–60; Thomson, *Shakespeare's Professional Career*, 86–87

63. Gurr, *The Shakespearean Stage*, 97–99, 110; Peter Thomson, "Rogues and Rhetoricians: Acting Styles in Early English Drama," in Cox and Kastan, *A New History of Early English Drama*, 329.

64. But see Frank Kermode, *The Age of Shakespeare* (Modern Library, 2004), 54.

65. *3H6*, I.iv.67–79.

66. David Riggs, *Shakespeare's Heroical Histories: "Henry VI" and Its Literary Tradition* (Harvard Univ. Press, 1971), 134.

67. *3H6*, I.iv.80–84.

68. *3H6*, I.iv94–103.

69. Bullough, *Narrative and Dramatic Sources of Shakespeare*, 178.

70. *3H6*, I.iv.108–9.

71. *3H6*, I.iv.112–45.

72. *3H6*, I.iv.177.

73. Chambers, *The Elizabethan Stage*, 3.53; Gurr, *The Shakespearean Stage*, 166.

74. Brett Gamboa, *Shakespeare's Double Plays: Dramatic Economy on the Early Modern Stage* (Cambridge Univ. Press, 2018), 52, also chap. 2.

75. Gamboa, *Shakespeare's Double Plays*, 240.

76. Wells, *Shakespeare and Co.*, 30.

77. Hattaway, *Elizabethan Popular Theatre*, 84.

78. Chambers, *The Elizabethan Stage*, 1.362; Bentley, *The Profession of Player*, 118–24, 128–29; Gurr, *The Shakespearean Stage*, 93; Wells, *Shakespeare and Co.*, 57; Hattaway, *Elizabethan Popular Theatre*, 83–84.

79. Bentley, *The Profession of Player*, 131–34, 145–46.

80. Wells, *Shakespeare and Co.*, 54–55.

81. Orgel, *Impersonations*, 69–70.

82. James H. Forse, *Art Imitates Business: Commercial and Political Influences in Elizabethan Theatre* (Bowling Green State Univ. Popular Press, 1993), 98–99.

83. David Kathman, "How Old Were Shakespeare's Boy Actors?" *Shakespeare Survey* 58 (2007), 220; Marvin Rosenberg, "The Myth of Shakespeare's Squeaking Boy Actor—Or Who Played Cleopatra?" *Shakespeare Bulletin* 19.2 (2001), 5–6; Mann, *Shakespeare's Women*, 58; Gamboa, *Shakespeare's Double Plays*, chap. 6.

84. Courtney Bailey Parker, *Spectrums of Shakespearean Crossdressing: The Art of Performing Women* (Routledge, 2020), 7.

85. Hattaway, *Elizabethan Popular Theatre*, 84; Kathman, "How Old Were Shakespeare's Boy Actors?" 221–22; Richard Rastall, "Female Roles in All-Male Casts," *Medieval English Theatre* 7 (1985), 28–35; Herbert Moller, "The Accelerated Development of Youth: Beard as a Biological Marker," *Comparative Studies in Society and History* 29.4 (1987), 752–53.

86. Quoted in Gamboa, *Shakespeare's Double Plays*, 183.

87. Thomson, *Shakespeare's Professional Career*, 94.

88. Thomson, *Shakespeare's Professional Career*, 94; M. Channing Linthicum, *Costume in the Drama of Shakespeare and His Contemporaries* (Clarendon, 1936), 177–88, 265.

89. Gurr, *The Shakespearean Stage*, 183. One rare drawing of a Shakespearean queen from 1595 shows her wearing such a crown. R. A. Foakes, *Illustrations of the English Stage, 1580–1642* (Stanford Univ. Press, 1985), 48–51.

90. Marcus, *Puzzling Shakespeare*, 93.

91. Gurr, *The Shakespearean Stage*, 171–72, 178–82; Thomson, *Shakespeare's Professional Career*, 93–94; Fraser, *Young Shakespeare*, 117; Jean MacIntyre and Garrett P. J. Epp, "'Cloathes Worth All the Rest': Costumes and Properties," in Cox and Kastan, *A New History of Early English Drama*, 279.

92. Fraser, *Young Shakespeare*, 117–18.

93. Linthicum, *Costume in the Drama of Shakespeare*, 13–15, 21, 24.

94. G. E. Bentley, *The Profession of Player in Shakespeare's Time, 1590–1642* (Princeton Univ. Press, 1984), 5–9; Chambers, *The Elizabethan Stage*, 1.351; Gurr, *The Shakespearean Stage*, 85; Wells, *Shakespeare and Co.*, 47–48.

95. James Stokes, "The Ongoing Exploration of Women and Performance in Early Modern England," *Shakespeare Bulletin* 33.1 (spring 2015), 9–31; James Stokes, "Women and Performance in Medieval and Early Modern Suffolk," *Early Theatre* 15.1 (2012), 27–43; Orgel, *Impersonations*, 5.

96. Michael Shapiro, *Gender in Play on the Shakespearean Stage: Boy Heroines and Female Pages* (Univ. of Michigan Press, 1996), 31–33; Orgel, *Impersonations*, 1–2.

97. Shapiro, *Gender in Play on the Shakespearean Stage*, 29–30. But see David Cressy, "Gender Trouble and Cross-Dressing in Early Modern England," *Journal of British Studies* 35.4 (1996), 438–65.

98. Orgel, *Impersonations*, 38 (citing Alan Bray and Bruce Smith).

99. Kathman, "How Old Were Shakespeare's Boy Actors?," 221; Shapiro, *Gender in Play on the Shakespearean Stage*, 38–39; Bentley, *The Profession of Player*, 114–15, 136; Wells, *Shakespeare and Co.*, 57–58; Chambers, *The Elizabethan Stage*, 1.362n2.

100. Astington, *Actors and Acting in Shakespeare's Time*, 116; Terri Bourus, "Arden of Faversham, Richard Burbage, and the Early Shakespeare Canon," in Loughnane and Power, *Early Shakespeare*, 209–11.

101. Bate, *Soul of the Age*, 101.

102. Kathleen McCluskie, "The Act, the Role, and the Actor: Boy Actresses on the Elizabethan Stage," *New Theatre Quarterly* 10 (May 1987), 120–30; Carol Chillington Rutter, "Learning Thisby's Part—or—What's Hecuba to Him?" *Shakespeare Bulletin* 22.3 (fall 2004), 5–30; Parker, *Spectrums of Shakespearean Crossdressing*, 12; Lisa Jardine, *Still Harping on Daughters: Women and Drama in the Age of Shakespeare* (Harvester, 1983), 10–12.

103. Orgel, *Impersonations*, 70.

104. Jean E. Howard, "Crossdressing, the Theatre, and Gender Struggle in Early Modern England," *Shakespeare Quarterly* 39.4 (winter 1988), 435; Catherine Belsey, "Disrupting Sexual Differences: Meaning and Gender in Comedies," in John Drakakis, ed., *Alternative Shakespeares* (Methuen, 1985), 166–90; Laura Levine, *Men in Women's Clothing: Anti-Theatricality and Effeminization, 1579–1642* (Cambridge Univ. Press, 1994), 1, 3–6; Simone Chess, *Male-to-Female Crossdressing in Early Modern English Literature* (Routledge, 2016), 4, 8.

105. Jardine, *Still Harping on Daughters*, 20–21, 33; Dympna Callaghan, *Shakespeare Without Women: Representing Gender and Race on the Renaissance Stage* (Routledge, 2000), 32.

106. Graham Holderness, ed., *Shakespeare's History Plays: "Richard II" to "Henry V"* (Macmillan, 1992), 14.

107. Lake, *How Shakespeare Put Politics on the Stage*, 89.

108. Roberta Barker, "'Not One Thing Exactly': Gender, Performance and Critical Debates over the Early Modern Boy-Actress," *Literature Compass* 6.2 (2009), 460–81.

109. This paraphrases John Crow paraphrasing Desmond McCarthy. Takashi Kozuka and J. R. Mulryne, eds., *Shakespeare, Marlowe, Jonson: New Directions in Biography* (Routledge, 2006), 3.

110. Bagley, *Margaret of Anjou*, 113; Maurer, *Margaret of Anjou*, 192–94. But see Johnson, *The Shadow King*, 429–30.

111. Laynesmith, *The Last Medieval Queens*, 80; Haswell, *The Ardent Queen*, 145–46. But see Johnson, *The Shadow King*, 436.

112. Goodman, *The Wars of the Roses*, 49–50; Lander, *The Wars of the Roses*, 96–97; Lander, *Conflict and Stability in Fifteenth-Century England*, 85–86; Griffiths, *King and Country*, 83–85; Saccio, *Shakespeare's English Kings*, 138–40; William Huse Dunham Jr. and Charles T. Wood, "The Right to Rule in England: Depositions and the Kingdom's Authority, 1327–1485," *American Historical Review* 81 (1976), 753–54.

Chapter 5: "You Fight in Justice"

1. *3H6*, II.ii.84.

2. *3H6*, II.ii.102–4.

3. *3H6*, II.ii.135–38.

4. *3H6*, II.ii.139, 145, 146, 154.

5. Philippe de Commines, quoted in Haswell, *The Ardent Queen*, 152.

6. Maurer, *Margaret of Anjou*, 201–4; Castor, *She-Wolves*, 381–82.

7. Haswell, *The Ardent Queen*, 147–48.

8. *3H6*, II.iii.1.

9. G. L. Harriss, *Shaping the Nation: England 1360–1461* (Clarendon, 2005), 644–45; Charles Ross, *Edward IV* (Univ. of California Press, 1974), 36–47; Carpenter, *The Wars of the Roses*, chaps. 7 and 8; George Goodwin, *Fatal Colours: Towton 1461—England's Most Brutal Battle* (W. W. Norton, 2012).

10. This is likely when *Henry VI, Part 3* debuted. Schoone-Jongen, *Shakespeare's Companies*, 35–39; Taylor and Egan, *The New Oxford Shakespeare: Authorship Companion*, 496–99; Born, "The Date of *2, 3 Henry VI*," 323–34.

11. Honan, *Christopher Marlowe*, 223.

12. Wells, *Shakespeare and Co.*, 81–82; Constance Brown Kuriyama, *Christopher Marlowe: A Renaissance Life* (Cornell Univ. Press, 2002), 81–85; Riggs, *The World of Christopher Marlowe*, 250–52, 255; Honan, *Christopher Marlowe*, 225–30; Mark Eccles, *Christopher Marlowe in London* (Harvard Univ. Press, 1934), 9–10, 57–59, 69.

13. Gurr, *Playgoing in Shakespeare's London*, 161–62; Anthony Holden, *William Shakespeare: His Life and Work* (Little, Brown, 1999), 82.

14. Marcus, *Puzzling Shakespeare*, 80.

15. Palliser, *The Age of Elizabeth*, 350.

16. Pugliatti, *Shakespeare the Historian*, 1–2; Fitter, "Emergent Shakespeare and the Politics of Protest," 136–37.

17. Harrison, *Shakespeare at Work*, 9–12; Fitter, "Emergent Shakespeare and the Politics of Protest," 132–33.

18. John D. Cox, *Shakespeare and the Dramaturgy of Power* (Princeton Univ. Press,

1989), 83; Pugliatti, *Shakespeare the Historian*, 3–4; Campbell, *Shakespeare's "Histories,"* 11.

19. Marcus, *Puzzling Shakespeare*, 55, 93; Levine, *Women's Matters*, 89; Lake, *How Shakespeare Put Politics on the Stage*, 95. But see John Guy, *Elizabeth: The Forgotten Years* (Viking, 2016), 107.

20. Although there are many conflicting versions of this speech, this famous line (or something quite similar) appears in the most accurate-seeming accounts.

21. The iconoclastic writer A. D. Wraight noted the "well-known connotation of extreme cruelty and deceitfulness which the image of the tiger held for the Elizabethan mind." Wraight, *Christopher Marlowe and Edward Alleyn*, 134, see also 159.

22. Quoted in Marcus, *Puzzling Shakespeare*, 89; Williams, "Suffolk and Margaret," 311–12; Grene, *Shakespeare's Serial History Plays*, 112.

23. Rohr, *Yolande of Aragon*, 95.

24. *3H6*, II.v.94–96, 103–12. See also Harold Goddard, *The Meaning of Shakespeare* (Univ. of Chicago Press, 1951), 30–31.

25. Haswell, *The Ardent Queen*, 159–63; Johnson, *The Shadow King*, 466–69.

26. Bagley, *Margaret of Anjou*, 146–47; Haswell, *The Ardent Queen*, 163; Johnson, *The Shadow King*, 471–72.

27. Laynesmith, *The Last Medieval Queens*, 168–69; Carpenter, *The Wars of the Roses*, 159–61; Haswell, *The Ardent Queen*, 165.

28. Lander, *The Wars of the Roses*, 116.

29. Haswell, *The Ardent Queen*, 166–67; Madame d'Aulnoy, *The history of the Earl of Warwick* [. . .] (J. Woodward, 1708), 72–73, Rare Books Collection, Huntington Library, San Marino, CA; Enguerrand De Monstrelet, *The chronicles of Enguerrand de Monstrelet* [. . .], trans. Thomas Johnes (William Smith, 1810), 2.290.

30. Bagley, *Margaret of Anjou*, 155; Lander, *The Wars of the Roses*, 117–19.

31. Maurer, *Margaret of Anjou*, 206–7.

32. Griffiths, *The Reign of King Henry VI*, 889–90; Haswell, *The Ardent Queen*, 181–83; Lander, *The Wars of the Roses*, 118–25; John Gillingham, *The Wars of the Roses: Peace and Conflict in Fifteenth-Century England* (Weidenfeld and Nicolson, 1981), chap. 10.

33. *3H6*, III.iii.186–98.

34. *3H6*, III.iii.229–30.

35. Gillingham, *The Wars of the Roses*, 179–88; Griffiths, *The Reign of King Henry VI*, 885–92; Haswell, *The Ardent Queen*, chap. 11; Bagley, *Margaret of Anjou*, chap. 10; Castor, *She-Wolves*, 383–89.

36. Gillingham, *The Wars of the Roses*, 179.

37. Bagley, *Margaret of Anjou*, 204–5.

38. Bagley, *Margaret of Anjou*, 207–14; Castor, *She-Wolves*, 395–96.

39. Gillingham, *The Wars of the Roses*, 196–201; Johnson, *The Shadow King*, 519–20;

Goodman, *The Wars of the Roses*, 79–80; Haswell, *The Ardent Queen*, 195–96; Saccio, *Shakespeare's English Kings*, 148.

40. *3H6*, V.iii.4.

41. Hodgdon, *The End Crowns All*, 71.

42. *3H6*, V.iv.1–38.

43. *H5*, III.i.1, IV.iii.61–62.

44. Saccio, *Shakespeare's English Kings*, 149; Castor, *She-Wolves*, 398; Bagley, *Margaret of Anjou*, 222–26.

45. Maurer and Cron, *The Letters of Margaret of Anjou*, 280; Gillingham, *The Wars of the Roses*, 214.

46. Haswell, *The Ardent Queen*, 12, 198–204.

47. Haswell, *The Ardent Queen*, 204; Carpenter, *The Wars of the Roses*, 180; Goodman, *The Wars of the Roses*, 81–83; Lander, *The Wars of the Roses*, 152–55.

48. Taylor and Egan, *The New Oxford Shakespeare: Authorship Companion*, 498; Burrows and Craig, "The Joker in the Pack," 195.

49. *3H6*, V.iv.73–82.

50. *3H6*, V.iv.73–82.

51. Haswell, *The Ardent Queen*, 204, 206; Levin, "Margaret of Anjou," 210; Johnson, *The Shadow King*, 534.

52. Katherine Duncan-Jones, *Ungentle Shakespeare: Scenes from His Life* (Arden, 2001), 14–16.

53. *3H6*, V.v.78–79, 81.

54. Howard and Rackin, *Engendering a Nation*, 98.

55. Marcus, *Puzzling Shakespeare*, 94; Hodgdon, *The End Crowns All*, 74–75.

56. Maurer, *Margaret of Anjou*, 208; Laynesmith, *The Last Medieval Queens*, 170.

57. W. H. St. John Hope, "The Discovery of the Remains of King Henry VI in St. George's Chapel, Windsor Castle," *Archaeologia* 62.2 (1911), 537, 541.

58. Bagley, *Margaret of Anjou*, 229–30; Haswell, *The Ardent Queen*, 206–8; Wolffe, *Henry VI*, 347–48; Johnson, *The Shadow King*, 534–35.

Chapter 6: "As Lightning from the Sky"

1. R. A. Foakes, ed., *Henslowe's Diary*, 2nd ed. (Cambridge Univ. Press, 2002), 16. The "ne" demarcation in Henslowe's diary (accompanying the March 3, 1592, performance of "harey the vj") did not necessarily mean "new"—it might have meant "newly revised," for instance. Further, some have argued that "harey the vj" might refer to another of the *Henry VI* plays, or even the work of another playwright. Schoone-Jongen, *Shakespeare's Companies*, 109–11, 151–54; Allison Gaw, *The Origin and Development of 1 Henry VI* (AMS, 1971, originally published 1926), especially 162–68; Honigmann, *Shakespeare's Impact on His Contemporaries*, 76–77; Edward Burns, ed., *King Henry VI Part 1* (Arden, 2000), 71. On balance, though, it seems by far most likely that some version of the play we now call *Henry VI, Part 1* debuted then. Manley and MacLean, *Lord Strange's Men and Their Plays*, 280–82; Paul Vincent, *When "harey" Met Shake-*

speare: The Genesis of "The First Part of Henry the Sixth" (VDM Verlag, 2008), especially 16–54.

2. Rhodes, *Henslowe's Rose*, 2.

3. Burns, *King Henry VI Part 1*, 8–9; Harrison, *Shakespeare at Work*, 13; Eccles, *The Rose Theatre*, 133–36.

4. Gurr, *The Shakespearian Playing Companies*, 259; Manley and MacLean, *Lord Strange's Men and Their Plays*, 49; Chambers, *The Elizabethan Stage*, 2.120–21; Harrison, *Shakespeare at Work*, 2.

5. Gurr, *The Shakespearian Playing Companies*, 259; Eccles, *The Rose Theatre*, 27–28; Dutton, *Shakespeare's Theatre*, 62; Manley and MacLean, *Lord Strange's Men and Their Plays*, 62; Burns, *King Henry VI Part 1*, 3.

6. Eccles, *The Rose Theatre*, 28–29, 93–94, 138–41; Burns, *King Henry VI Part 1*, 10–11; Harrison, *Shakespeare at Work*, 1–2; Rhodes, *Henslowe's Rose*, 12; Manley and MacLean, *Lord Strange's Men and Their Plays*, 59–63.

7. Eccles, *The Rose Theatre*, 136.

8. Manley and MacLean, *Lord Strange's Men and Their Plays*, chap. 2; Wraight, *Christopher Marlowe and Edward Alleyn*, 240–41.

9. Harrison, *Shakespeare at Work*, 3, 6–8, 14; Wraight, *Christopher Marlowe and Edward Alleyn*, 238–39; Eccles, *The Rose Theatre*, 29; Gaw, *The Origin and Development of 1 Henry VI*, 2–3; Gurr, *The Shakespearian Playing Companies*, 86–87.

10. Rhodes, *Henslowe's Rose*, 32–34.

11. Eccles, *The Rose Theatre*, 94; Thomson, *Shakespeare's Professional Career*, 74.

12. Chambers, *The Elizabethan Stage*, 3.76–77.

13. Eccles, *The Rose Theatre*, 132.

14. *2H6*, I.i.1.

15. Gaw, *The Origin and Development of 1 Henry VI*, 56–58; Burns, *King Henry VI Part 1*, 15–16; Charles Edelman, *Brawl Ridiculous: Swordfighting in Shakespeare's Plays* (Manchester Univ. Press, 1992), chap. 4.

16. Cox and Rasmussen, *King Henry VI, Part 3*, 7–8; Eccles, *The Rose Theatre*, 92.

17. Thomson, *Shakespeare's Professional Career*, 61; Burns, *King Henry VI Part 1*, 2.

18. Burns, *King Henry VI Part 1*, 8–9; Cox and Rasmussen, *King Henry VI, Part 3*, 5.

19. Gaw, *The Origin and Development of 1 Henry VI*, 4–6; Walsh, *Shakespeare, the Queen's Men*, 110; Holden, *William Shakespeare*, 93; Marcus, *Puzzling Shakespeare*, 51.

20. Marcus, *Puzzling Shakespeare*, 77.

21. Charles Wilfrid Scott-Giles, *Shakespeare's Heraldry* (Dutton, 1950), 136–41; Dockray, *Henry VI, Margaret of Anjou*, ix; Burns, *King Henry VI Part 1*, 57–60, 180.

22. Potter, *The Life of William Shakespeare*, 91.

23. Taylor and Egan, *The New Oxford Shakespeare: Authorship Companion*, 513–17; Taylor et al., *The New Oxford Shakespeare: Modern Critical Edition*, 926; Freebury-Jones, *Shakespeare's Tutor*, chap. 4; Warren Chernaik, "Shakespeare as Co-Author: The Case of 1 Henry VI," *Medieval and Renaissance Drama in*

England 27 (2014), 210–14; Vincent, *When "harey" Met Shakespeare*, 173–74 and chap. 5; Craig, "The Three Parts of *Henry VI*," 41–42.

24. Gaw, *The Origin and Development of 1 Henry VI*, 27–35; Clifford Leech, "The Two-Part Play: Marlowe and the Early Shakespeare," *Shakespeare Jahrbuch* 94 (1985), 104; Paul Vincent, "Structuring and Revision in *1 Henry VI*," *Philological Quarterly* 84 (2005), 379–80.

25. *1H6*, I.vi.3.

26. Burns, *King Henry VI Part 1*, 25–30, 291–94. Burns looks to Marina Warner, *Joan of Arc: The Image of Female Heroism* (Univ. of California Press, 1999), 22–26; Gary Taylor, "Shakespeare and Others: The Authorship of *Henry the Sixth, Part One*," *Medieval and Renaissance Drama in England* 7 (1995), 154–55.

27. David M. Bevington, "The Domineering Female in *1 Henry VI*," *Shakespeare Studies* 2 (1966), 51.

28. *1H6*, I.i.68–69.

29. Phyllis Rackin, "Anti-Historians: Women's Roles in Shakespeare's Histories," *Theatre Journal* 37.3 (October 1985), 329–44; Gabriele Bernhard Jackson, "Topical Ideology: Witches, Amazons, and Shakespeare's Joan of Arc," *English Literary Renaissance* 18.1 (winter 1988), 40–65; Richard F. Hardin, "Chronicles and Mythmaking in Shakespeare's Joan of Arc," *Shakespeare Survey* 42 (1990), 25–36.

30. Hattaway, *Elizabethan Popular Theatre*, 85.

31. Marilyn L. Williamson, "'When Men Are Rul'd by Women': Shakespeare's First Tetralogy," *Shakespeare Studies* 19 (1987), 42. See also Nancy A. Gutierrez, "Gender and Value in *1 Henry VI*: The Role of Joan de Pucelle," *Theatre Journal* 42.2 (1990), 183.

32. Burns, *King Henry VI Part 1*, 36.

33. Howard and Rackin, *Engendering a Nation*, 45.

34. *1H6*, V.iii.7.

35. Cf. Jones, *The Origins of Shakespeare*, 121.

36. *1H6*, III.vii.44–57.

37. Taylor and Egan, *The New Oxford Shakespeare: Authorship Companion*, 514; Burns, *King Henry VI Part 1*, 83. See also Marcus, *Puzzling Shakespeare*, 52; Craig, "Three Parts of *Henry VI*," 67–68.

38. Levine, *Women's Matters*, 34, 39.

39. Marcus, *Puzzling Shakespeare*, chap. 2; Hodgdon, *The End Crowns All*, 55; Pugliatti, *Shakespeare the Historian*, 200–201.

40. Marcus, *Puzzling Shakespeare*, 52–53, 66–74. But see Kathryn Schwarz, "Fearful Simile: Stealing the Breech in Shakespeare's Chronicle Plays," *Shakespeare Quarterly* 49.2 (summer 1998), 151–52.

41. *1H6*, V.iv.5, 13.

42. Tillyard, *Shakespeare's History Plays*, 169; Marcus, *Puzzling Shakespeare*, 89.

43. Schwarz, "Fearful Simile," 144; Finn, *The Last Plantagenet Consorts*, 150.

44. *1H6*, V.v.2–5.

45. *1H6*, V.v.41.

46. Cf. Bevington, "The Domineering Female in *1 Henry VI*," 56–57.

47. Gaw, *The Origin and Development of 1 Henry VI*, 31.

48. *1H6*, V.v.34–35.

49. Thomson, *Shakespeare's Professional Career*, 63.

50. Foakes, *Henslowe's Diary*, 16; Dutton, *Shakespeare's Theatre*, 64.

51. Harrison, *Shakespeare at Work*, 20.

52. Chambers, *The Elizabethan Stage*, 2.296–97; Gurr, *Playgoing in Shakespeare's London*, 165; Harrison, *Shakespeare at Work*, 3; Manley and MacLean, *Lord Strange's Men and Their Plays*, 55–56.

53. Manley and MacLean, *Lord Strange's Men and Their Plays*, 283, 288–89.

54. Wells, *Shakespeare and Co.*, 70–73; Chambers, *The Elizabethan Stage*, 3.450–56.

55. Vincent, *When "harey" Met Shakespeare*, 24–28; Cox and Rasmussen, *King Henry VI, Part 3*, 5–6. See also Born, "The Date of *2, 3 Henry VI*," 324; Andrew Cairncross, ed., *Henry VI, Part One* (Arden, 1962), xi; Pugliatti, *Shakespeare the Historian*, 5–6.

56. Gary Taylor, "Shakespeare and Others: The Authorship of *Henry the Sixth, Part One*," *Medieval and Renaissance Drama in England* 7 (1995), 174–77.

57. Vincent, *When "harey" Met Shakespeare*, 26 and n33.

58. Wells, *Shakespeare and Co.*, 73. Nashe is more often credited as the author of act 1. Taylor and Egan, *The New Oxford Shakespeare: Authorship Companion*, 513–14.

59. Charles W. Crupi, *Robert Greene* (Twayne, 1986), chap. 1; Harrison, *Shakespeare at Work*, 3; John Clark Jordan, *Robert Greene* (Columbia Univ. Press, 1915), 2; Brenda Richardson, "Robert Greene's Yorkshire Connexions: A New Hypothesis," *Yearbook of English Studies* 10 (1980), 160–80.

60. Harrison, *Shakespeare at Work*, 4.

61. Wraight, *Christopher Marlowe and Edward Alleyn*, 130–31, 140.

62. Greenblatt, *Will in the World*, 216–220.

63. Harrison, *Shakespeare at Work*, 21.

64. Greenblatt, *Will in the World*, 210–11; Crupi, *Robert Greene*, 27–31; Jordan, *Robert Greene*, 3–4; G. B. Harrison, *The Elizabethan Journals: Being a Record of Those Things Most Talked of During the Years 1591–1603* (Univ. of Michigan Press, 1955), 158; Chambers, *William Shakespeare*, 1.58.

65. Schoone-Jongen, *Shakespeare's Companies*, 18–19; Harrison, *Shakespeare at Work*, 23–24.

66. Alexander Dyce, ed., *The Dramatic Works of Robert Greene* (William Pickering, 1831), 1.81.

67. Some have suggested that the passage alludes not to Shakespeare but to another playwright (possibly Marlowe) or even to Alleyn (assuming the actor was also a playwright). Schoone-Jongen, *Shakespeare's Companies*, 27–32; John Semple Smart, *Shakespeare: Truth and Tradition* (Edward Arnold, 1928), 196; Honigmann, *Shakespeare's Impact on His Contemporaries*, 2–6.

68. Schoone-Jongen, *Shakespeare's Companies*, 32–35; Warren B. Austin, "A Supposed Contemporary Allusion to Shakespeare as a Plagiarist," *Shakespeare Quarterly* 6.4 (autumn 1955), 373–80; Brian Vickers, "'Upstart

Crow'? The Myth of Shakespeare's Plagiarism," *Review of English Studies* 68.284 (April 2017), 244–67; Peter Berek, "The 'Upstart Crow,' Aesop's Crow, and Shakespeare as a Reviser," *Shakespeare Quarterly* 35.2 (summer 1984), 205–7; Bate, *Soul of the Age*, 40; Sophie Chiari, "Upstart Crow vs. University Wit: Shakespeare 'Beautified,'" *World Literature Studies* 6 (2014), 141–42; Honan, *Shakespeare*, 158.

69. Gaw, *The Origin and Development of 1 Henry VI*, 75.

70. Carol Chillington Rutter, "Of 'Tygers' Hearts and Players' Hides," in Cavanagh, Hampton-Reeves, and Longstaffe, *Shakespeare's Histories and Counter-histories*, 185.

71. Howard and Rackin, *Engendering a Nation*, 95–96.

72. Jordan, *Robert Greene*, 195–99.

73. Schoone-Jongen, *Shakespeare's Companies*, 20–26.

74. Cox and Rasmussen, *King Henry VI, Part 3*, 7.

75. Schoone-Jongen, *Shakespeare's Companies*, 21–22.

76. Taylor, "Shakespeare and Others," 186.

77. Chambers, *The Elizabethan Stage*, 2.121–22; Eccles, *The Rose Theatre*, 29.

78. Gurr, *The Shakespearian Playing Companies*, 259. See also Harrison, *Shakespeare at Work*, 2; Chambers, *The Elizabethan Stage*, 2.121.

79. Dutton, *Shakespeare's Theatre*, 62; Manley and MacLean, *Lord Strange's Men and Their Plays*, 64.

80. Harrison, *Shakespeare at Work*, 19–20; Chambers, *The Elizabethan Stage*, 4.310–11; Harrison, *The Elizabethan Journals*, 138, 140, 142–43; Guy, *Elizabeth*, 192–93; Eccles, *The Rose Theatre*, 29.

81. Harrison, *Shakespeare at Work*, 20; Ian W. Archer, *The Pursuit of Stability: Social Relations in Elizabethan London* (Cambridge Univ. Press, 1991), 9–17; Harrison, *The Elizabethan Journals*, 175; F. P. Wilson, *The Plague in Shakespeare's London* (Clarendon, 1927), 49–50; Guy, *Elizabeth*, 193–94.

82. Chambers, *The Elizabethan Stage*, 4.347–48.

83. Fraser, *Young Shakespeare*, 164.

84. Paul Slack, *The Impact of Plague in Tudor and Stuart England* (Routledge & Kegal Paul, 1985), 285.

85. Slack, *The Impact of Plague*, 208–12, 274, 277–78; Fraser, *Young Shakespeare*, 163–64; Wilson, *The Plague in Shakespeare's London*, 8–10.

86. Wilson, *The Plague in Shakespeare's London*, 51–55; Chambers, *The Elizabethan Stage*, 1.331.

87. Eccles, *The Rose Theatre*, 32.

88. Schoone-Jongen, *Shakespeare's Companies*, 216.

89. Chambers, *The Elizabethan Stage*, 1.332–33; Thomson, *Shakespeare's Professional Career*, 52–53; Gurr, *The Shakespearean Stage*, 38–40.

90. Fraser, *Young Shakespeare*, 167–68.

91. Germaine Greer, *Shakespeare's Wife* (HarperCollins, 2007), 187; Weis, *Shakespeare Revealed*, 140. But see Holden, *William Shakespeare*, 111–12.

92. Fraser, *Young Shakespeare*, 167; Schoenbaum, *William Shakespeare*, 127; Thomson, *Shakespeare's Professional Career*, 54.

93. Foakes, *Henslowe's Diary*, 19.

94. Riggs, *The World of Christopher Marlowe*, 309–10.

95. Harrison, *Shakespeare at Work*, 26; Riggs, *The World of Christopher Marlowe*, 315; Chambers, *The Elizabethan Stage*, 2.122–23, 4.313; Dutton, *Shakespeare's Theatre*, 64; Honan, *Christopher Marlowe*, 277, 313 (noting the winter cold).

96. Honan, *Shakespeare*, 169–70; A.L. Beier, *Masterless Men: The Vagrancy Problem in England, 1560–1640* (Methuen, 1985), 6.

97. J.E. Neale, *Elizabeth and Her Parliaments, 1504–1601* (Jonathan Cap, 1957), 2.241–323; Harrison, *Shakespeare at Work*, 48–49.

98. Gurr, *The Shakespearian Playing Companies*, 264.

99. Duncan-Jones, *Ungentle Shakespeare*, 100.

100. Katherine Duncan-Jones and H. R. Woudhuysen, eds., *Shakespeare's Poems* (Arden, 2007), 13–15.

101. Honigmann, *Shakespeare's Impact on His Contemporaries*, 28–29.

102. Thomson, *Shakespeare and the Classics*, 41–44.

103. *VA*, 343–48.

104. Cf. *3H6*, I.iv.143, with *VA*, 199. Cf. also *RJ*, I.v.116–21, with *VA*, 207–10.

105. See Barbara Hodgdon, ed., *The Taming of the Shrew* (Arden, 2010), 7–23; John V. Nance, "Early Shakespeare and the Authorship of *The Taming of the Shrew*," in Loughnane and Power, *Early Shakespeare*, 261–83; Holden, *William Shakespeare*, 124–28; Eric Sams, *The Real Shakespeare: Retrieving the Early Years, 1564–1594* (Yale Univ. Press, 1995), xii–xiii, 136–45; Weis, *Shakespeare Unbound*, 121–28; T. W. Baldwin, *On the Literary Genetics of Shakespeare's Plays* (Univ. of Illinois Press, 1959), chap. 3; Tori Haring-Smith, "The Taming of the Shrew: A Stage History, 1594–1978" (PhD diss., University of Illinois at Urbana-Champaign, 1980), 9–12.

106. Mann, *Shakespeare's Women*, 154.

107. Mann, *Shakespeare's Women*, 155.

108. David Underdown, *Revel, Riot, and Rebellion: Popular Politics and Culture in England 1603–1660* (Oxford Univ. Press, 1985), 36–40, 48. See also Banks, "Warlike Women," 172–73; Bernard Capp, "Separate Domains? Women and Authority in Early Modern England," in Paul Griffiths, Adam Fox, and Steve Hindle, eds., *The Experience of Authority in Early Modern England* (Palgrave Macmillan, 1996), 119–21; Orgel, *Impersonations*, 17–18.

109. Andy Kesson, "His Fellow Dramatists and Early Collaborators," in Paul Edmondson and Stanley Wells, eds., *The Shakespeare Circle: An Alternative Biography* (Cambridge Univ. Press, 2015), 241 (quoting Frank S. Hook's 1962 edition of *Edward I*).

110. Lesley Wade Soule, "Tumbling Tricks: Presentational Structure and 'The Taming of the Shrew,'" *New Theatre Quarterly* 20.2 (May 2004), 176.

111. Bate, *Soul of the Age*, 42–43.

112. Thomson, *Shakespeare's Professional Career*, 114–15.

Chapter 7: *"Dead Life, Blind Sight, Poor Mortal Living Ghost"*

1. Stern, *Making Shakespeare*, 72; James R. Siemon, ed., *Richard III* (Arden, 2009), 83–84.
2. Siemon, *Richard III*, 79.
3. *R3*, I.i.1–8.
4. Thomson, *Shakespeare's Professional Career*, 105. But see Van Es, *Shakespeare in Company*, 63.
5. E. Pearlman, "The Invention of Richard of Gloucester," *Shakespeare Quarterly* 43 (1992), 411.
6. But see Alice I. Perry Wood, *The Stage History of Shakespeare's King Richard the Third* (Columbia Univ. Press, 1909), 4–5, 8; G. B. Churchill, *Richard the Third up to Shakespeare* (Mayer and Muller, 1900); J. Dover Wilson, "Shakespeare's *Richard III* and *The True Tragedy of Richard the Third*, 1594," *Shakespeare Quarterly* 3.4 (autumn 1952), 299–306; Robert J. Lordi, "The Relationship of *Richardus Tertius* to the Main *Richard III* Plays," *Boston Univ. Studies in English* 5 (1961), 149–53.
7. Howard and Rackin, *Engendering a Nation*, 217.
8. Alyssa Renee Miller, "Acting Up: Age, Women, and Power in Shakespeare's Elizabethan England" (PhD diss., University of Colorado, Boulder, 2022), chap. 2.
9. On the date: Siemon, *Richard III*, 44–50; Taylor and Egan, *The New Oxford Shakespeare: Authorship Companion*, 507–8; Honigmann, *Shakespeare's Impact on His Contemporaries*, 88; John Jowett, ed., *The Tragedy of King Richard III* (Oxford Univ. Press, 2000), 4–7; John Jowett, "'Derby,' 'Stanley,' and Memorial Reconstruction in Quarto *Richard III*," *Notes and Queries* 245 (2000), 75–79; Schoone-Jongen, *Shakespeare's Companies*, 37–38; Manley and MacLean, *Lord Strange's Men and Their Plays*, 314; Wood, *The Stage History*, 8, 25–26. On the acting company: Taylor and Egan, *The New Oxford Shakespeare: Authorship Companion*, 507–8; Manley and MacLean, *Lord Strange's Men and Their Plays*, 313–15, 319–20; Van Es, *Shakespeare in Company*, 64; Katherine Duncan-Jones, "'Three Partes Are Past': The Earliest Performances of Shakespeare's First Tetralogy," *Notes and Queries* 50.3 (March 2003), 21; Siemon, *Richard III*, 49; John Dover Wilson, ed., *Richard III* (Cambridge Univ. Press, 1968), x.
10. Thomson, *Shakespeare's Professional Career*, 105–8.
11. Hertel, *Staging England in the Elizabethan History Play*, 112–13.
12. Campbell, *Shakespeare's "Histories,"* 333; Arthur Colby Sprague, *Shakespeare's Histories: Plays for the Stage* (Society for Theatre Research, 1964), 140.
13. Hertel, *Staging England in the Elizabethan History Play*, 103.
14. On Marlowe's death: Charles Nicholl, *The Reckoning: The Murder of Christopher Marlowe* (Harcourt, 1994), 17–20, 91; Riggs, *The World of Christopher Marlowe*, 332–36; Honan, *Christopher Marlowe*, 343–55; Kuriyama, *Christopher Marlowe*,

135–41; Harrison, *Shakespeare at Work*, 50–51. On the summer disquiet: Guy, *Elizabeth*, 194–96; Harrison, *Shakespeare at Work*, 48–49, 58; Harrison, *The Elizabethan Journals*, 222–23, 235.

15. Logan, *Shakespeare's Marlowe*, chap. 2. On Marlowe's influence: Brooke, "Marlowe as Provocative Agent"; Charney, "The Voice of Marlowe's Tamburlaine in Early Shakespeare," 214–16; Jonathan Bate, *The Genius of Shakespeare* (Picador, 1997), 116–20, 307–9.

16. Logan, *Shakespeare's Marlowe*, 39 (glossing G. Blakemore Evans).

17. On these sources: Siemon, *Richard III*, 51–52, 60, 66; Daniel Kinney, "The Tyrant Being Slain: Afterlives of More's *History of King Richard III*," in Neil Rhodes, ed., *English Renaissance Prose: History, Language and Politics* (Medieval and Renaissance Texts and Studies, 1997), 35–56; Greenblatt, *Will in the World*, 33–34.

18. Rackin, *Stages of History*, 161.

19. Howard, *Shakespeare's Art of Orchestration*, 57–59.

20. Parker, *Spectrums of Shakespearean Crossdressing*, 133–34.

21. Howard, *Shakespeare's Art of Orchestration*, 58–59.

22. *R3*, I.iii.158–62.

23. *3H6*, V.v.43.

24. Garber, *Shakespeare After All*, 124.

25. *R3*, I.iii.212.

26. *R3*, I.iii.192–93.

27. *R3*, I.iii.206.

28. *R3*, I.iii.213–35.

29. Dash, *Wooing, Wedding, and Power*, 193.

30. Garber, *Shakespeare After All*, 147; Liebler and Shea, "Shakespeare's Queen Margaret," 92; Parker, *Spectrums of Shakespearean Crossdressing*, 133–34; Hodgdon, *The Crown Ends All*, 107.

31. Tillyard, *Shakespeare's History Plays*, 212.

32. *R3*, I.iii.297–301.

33. Nicholas Brooke, *Shakespeare's Early Tragedies* (Methuen, 1968), 69; Wifall, "Swords and Curses," 156; Donald G. Watson, *Shakespeare's Early History Plays: Politics at Play on the Elizabethan Stage* (Univ. of Georgia Press, 1990), 4.

34. But see W. Gordon Zeefeld, "The Influence of Hall on Shakespeare's English Historical Plays," *English Literary History* 3 (1936), 350; Bullough, *Narrative and Dramatic Sources of Shakespeare*, 236–37.

35. Haswell, *The Ardent Queen*, 208–9.

36. Haswell, *The Ardent Queen*, 208–9; Laynesmith, *The Last Medieval Queens*, 172; Maurer, *Margaret of Anjou*, 208.

37. Haswell, *The Ardent Queen*, 210–11; Bagley, *Margaret of Anjou*, 236–37; Johnson, *The Shadow King*, 543; Mary Ann Hookham, *The Life and Times of Margaret of Anjou, Queen of England and France* (Tinsley, 1872), 2.338.

38. Hookham, *The Life and Times*, 2.337–38; Bagley, *Margaret of Anjou*, 238–39.

39. Bagley, *Margaret of Anjou*, 239; Hookham, *The Life and Times*, 443–46.

40. Haswell, *The Ardent Queen*, 212; Bagley, *Margaret of Anjou*, 239.

41. *R3*, IV.iv.1–2.

42. *R3*, IV.iv.3–4, 6.

43. Denise A. Walen, "Exiling Margaret in Shakespeare's *Richard III*," *Shakespeare Bulletin* 38.4 (winter 2020), 635–58.

44. *R3*, IV.iv.26–30; Nicole Loraux, *Mothers in Mourning*, trans. Corinne Pache (Cornell Univ. Press, 1998), 6.

45. *R3*, IV.iv.35–46.

46. Coppelia Kahn, *Man's Estate: Masculine Identity in Shakespeare* (Univ. of California Press, 1981), 63; Siemon, *Richard III*, 18.

47. Katharine Goodland, *Female Mourning and Tragedy in Medieval and Renaissance English Drama* (Routledge, 2006), 9, 10.

48. Madonne M. Miner, "'Neither Mother, Wife, Nor England's Queen': The Roles of Women in *Richard III*," in Carolyn Ruth Swift Lenz, Gayle Greene, and Carol Thomas Neely, eds., *The Woman's Part: Feminist Criticism of Shakespeare* (Univ. of Illinois Press, 1980), 45.

49. *R3*, IV.iv.116–17.

50. *R3*, IV.iv.118–25.

51. Emily Sloan-Pace, "Articulating Agency: Women in Shakespeare's History Plays" (PhD diss., University of California, Santa Cruz, 2012), 160–61.

52. *R3*, IV.iv.133.

53. *R3*, IV.iv.138–45.

54. *R3*, IV.iv.150.

55. *R3*, IV.iv.184–96.

56. Williamson, "'When Men Are Rul'd by Women,'" 56; Fiedler, *The Stranger in Shakespeare*, 51; Cristina León Alfar, "Speaking Truth to Power as Feminist Ethics in *Richard III*," *Social Research* 86.3 (fall 2019), 798–801.

57. Haswell, *The Ardent Queen*, 212–13.

58. Haswell, *The Ardent Queen*, 212–13.

59. Jean-François Bodin, *Recherches historiques sur la ville de Saumur, ses monuments et ceux de son arrondissement*, 2d ed. (Dubosse and Godft, 1845), vol. 1 (translation original).

60. Haswell, *The Ardent Queen*, 215–16; Hookham, *The Life and Times*, 376.

61. Cf. Maurer, *Margaret of Anjou*, 208; Castor, *She-Wolves*, 401; and Bagley, *Margaret of Anjou*, 240 (August 25) with Haswell, *The Ardent Queen*, 213–14 (August 20).

62. Haswell, *The Ardent Queen*, 214.

63. Bodin, *Recherches historiques sur la ville de Saumur*, 261.

64. G. P. V. Akrigg, *Shakespeare and the Earl of Southampton* (Harvard Univ. Press, 1968), 1–188; Alan H. Nelson, "His Literary Patrons," in Edmondson and Wells, *The Shakespeare Circle*, 275, 281; Fraser, *Young Shakespeare*, 177–78; Sams, *The Real Shakespeare*, 100; Weis, *Shakespeare Revealed*, 113–16, 145; Honan, *Shakespeare*, 176–77; Schoenbaum, *William Shakespeare*, 128;

Potter, *The Life of William Shakespeare*, 109–10; Greenblatt, *Will in the World*, 227–30.

65. Akrigg, *Shakespeare and the Earl of Southampton*, 196, 200; Greenblatt, *Will in the World*, 244–45.

66. Sams, *The Real Shakespeare*, chaps. 19–20; Weis, *Shakespeare Revealed*, 116–17, 120–21, 144–45; Schoenbaum, *William Shakespeare*, 134; Potter, *The Life of William Shakespeare*, 125–31; Greenblatt, *Will in the World*, 230–31, 237–40.

67. Bradbrook, *The Rise of the Common Player*, 67, 74, 78–82; Hattaway, *Elizabethan Popular Theatre*, 42–44; Chambers, *The Elizabethan Stage*, 1.313–14; Gurr, *The Shakespearean Stage*, 7–9; Gurr, *Playgoing in Shakespeare's London*, 147–50; Hertel, *Staging England in the Elizabethan History Play*, 211.

68. Bradbrook, *The Rise of the Common Player*, 68.

69. Gurr, *The Shakespearian Playing Companies*, 164–65.

70. Hattaway, *Elizabethan Popular Theatre*, 44.

71. Gurr, *The Shakespearian Playing Companies*, 55.

72. Manley and MacLean, *Lord Strange's Men and Their Plays*, 313, 315–16; Jowett, *The Tragedy of King Richard III*, 4; Honigmann, *Shakespeare: The "Lost Years,"* 63–64; Dutton, *Shakespeare's Theatre*, 60; Gurr, *The Shakespearian Playing Companies*, 258, 262.

73. Manley and MacLean, *Lord Strange's Men and Their Plays*, 317; Jowett, *The Tragedy of King Richard III*, 5–6; Andrew S. Cairncross, "Pembroke's Men and Some Shakespearean Piracies," *Shakespeare Quarterly* 9 (1960), 335–45.

74. Harrison, *Shakespeare at Work*, 53.

75. Holden, *William Shakespeare*, 119; Potter, *The Life of William Shakespeare*, 123; Gurr, *The Shakespearian Playing Companies*, 267–68.

76. Thomson, *Shakespeare's Professional Career*, 112.

77. Gurr, *The Shakespearean Stage*, 34.

78. Potter, *The Life of William Shakespeare*, 135; Schoenbaum, *William Shakespeare*, 137–38; Honan, *Shakespeare*, 199–200; Thomson, *Shakespeare's Professional Career*, 111–12; Holden, *William Shakespeare*, 134–35; Andrew Gurr, "Three Reluctant Patrons and Early Shakespeare," *Shakespeare Quarterly* 44.2 (summer 1993), 166; Dutton, *Shakespeare's Theatre*, 147–51; Keenan, *Acting Companies*, 19.

79. Holden, *William Shakespeare*, 135–36; Weis, *Shakespeare Revealed*, 114–15; Duncan-Jones, *Ungentle Shakespeare*, 95–96, 104–12; Bate, *Soul of the Age*, 160–61.

80. Honan, *Shakespeare*, 200.

81. Weis, *Shakespeare Revealed*, 150.

Chapter 8: "I Am Fire"

1. Charlton Hinman, *The Printing and Proof-Reading of the First Folio of Shakespeare* (Oxford Univ. Press, 1963), 2.521–24.

2. Chambers, *William Shakespeare*, 1.171–72; Stern, *Making Shakespeare*, 153; Chris

Laoutaris, *Shakespeare's Book: The Story Behind the First Folio and the Making of Shakespeare* (Pegasus, 2023), chap. 10.

3. Hinman, *The Printing and Proof-Reading of the First Folio*, 1.182–88.

4. Paul Edmondson, "His Editors John Heminges and Henry Condell," in Edmondson and Wells, *The Shakespeare Circle*, 322.

5. Douglas A. Brooks, *From Playhouse to Printing House: Drama and Authorship in Early Modern England* (Cambridge Univ. Press, 2000), 40–41.

6. Dutton, *Shakespeare, Court Dramatist*, 6, 203; Ioppolo, *Revising Shakespeare*, 128; Andrew Gurr, "Maximal and Minimal Texts: Shakespeare v. the Globe," *Shakespeare Survey* 52 (1999), 68–87.

7. McMillin, "Casting for Pembroke's Men," 152.

8. John E. Jordan, "The Reporter of *Henry VI, Part 2*," *PMLA* 64 (1949), 1095.

9. Barbara Kreps, "Bad Memories of Margaret? Memorial Reconstruction Versus Revision in *The First Part of the Contention* and *2 Henry VI*," *Shakespeare Quarterly* 51.2 (summer 2000), 163–71, 177. But see Hodgdon, *The End Crowns All*, 62–63.

10. Schoone-Jongen, *Shakespeare's Companies*, 121–22; A. W. Pollard, *Shakespeare Folios and Quartos: A Study in the Bibliography of Shakespeare's Plays, 1594–1685* (Methuen, 1909), 64–80; Peter Alexander, "*3 Henry VI* and *Richard, Duke of York*," *Times Literary Supplement* (November 13, 1924), 730; Peter Alexander, *Shakespeare's Henry VI and Richard III* (Cambridge Univ. Press, 1929), 63–65; Madeleine Doran, "*Henry VI, Parts II and III*: Their Relation to *The Contention* and *The True Tragedy*," *Univ. of Iowa Studies* 4 (1928), 81; D. L. Patrick, *The Textual History of Richard III* (Stanford Univ. Press, 1936); Steven Urkowitz, "Good News About 'Bad' Quartos," in Maurice Charney, ed., *"Bad" Shakespeare: Revaluations of the Shakespeare Canon* (Associated Univ. Presses, 1988), 189; Kathleen Irace, *Reforming the "Bad" Quartos: Performance and Provenance of Six Shakespearean First Editions* (Univ. of Delaware Press, 1994); Ioppolo, *Revising Shakespeare*, 128–30.

11. McMillin, "Casting for Pembroke's Men," 152.

12. Kreps, "Bad Memories of Margaret?" 178.

13. Miller, "Acting Up," 105–6.

14. Miller, "Acting Up," 106–12.

15. Leah Marcus, "Elizabeth," in Emma Smith, ed., *Shakespeare's Histories* (Blackwell, 2004), 165.

16. Gaw, *The Origin and Development of 1 Henry VI*, 29, 35.

17. Vincent, "Structuring and Revision in *1 Henry VI*," 379–80; Chernaik, "Shakespeare as Co-Author," 211.

18. Vincent, *When "harey" Met Shakespeare*, 173–76; Taylor and Egan, *The New Oxford Shakespeare: Authorship Companion*, 514–16; Chernaik, "Shakespeare as Co-Author," 211; Potter, *The Life of William Shakespeare*, 93; Gaw, *The Origin and Development of 1 Henry VI*, 32.

19. Emma Smith, *Shakespeare's First Folio: Four Centuries of an Iconic Book* (Oxford Univ. Press, 2016), 1, 4.

20. Stern, *Making Shakespeare*, 53; Ioppolo, *Revising Shakespeare*, 79–80.

21. Heidi Brayman Hackel, "'Rowme' of Its Own: Printed Drama in Early Libraries," in Cox and Kastan, *A New History of Early English Drama*, 113–19.

22. Akihiro Yamada, ed., *The First Folio of Shakespeare: A Transcript of Contemporary Marginalia in a Copy of the Kodama Memorial Library of Meisei University* (Yushodo, 1998), 155.

23. Smith, *Shakespeare's First Folio*, 136.

24. Marcus, *Puzzling Shakespeare*, 103–4. But see French, *Shakespeare's Division of Experience*, 17, 62–63.

25. Weis, *Shakespeare Revealed*, 275–76, 301.

26. Bevington, *Shakespeare and Biography*, 143; Janet Adelman, *Suffocating Mothers: Fantasies of Maternal Origin in Shakespeare's Plays*, Hamlet *to* The Tempest (Routledge, 1992), 199; Holden, *William Shakespeare*, 273.

27. Agnes Strickland, *Lives of the Queens of England* (Colburn, 1851), 5.189; Mary Eugenia Johnson, *Heroines of History* (T. M. Inchbold, 1859), 36.

28. Andrew Gurr, *The Shakespeare Company, 1594–1642* (Cambridge Univ. Press, 2004), 190–91, 201; Sophie Tomlinson, "She That Plays the King: Henrietta Maria and the Threat of the Actress in Caroline Culture," in Gordon McMullan and Jonathan Hope, eds., *The Politics of Tragicomedy: Shakespeare and After* (Routledge, 1992), 189–90; Karen Britland, *Drama at the Courts of Queen Henrietta Maria* (Cambridge Univ. Press, 2006), chap. 6; Quentin Bone, *Henrietta Maria: Queen of the Cavaliers* (Univ. of Illinois Press, 1972), 83; Sarah Poynting, ed., *The Shepherd's Paradise* (Malone Society, 1997), vii–xv; Martin Butler, *Theatre and Crisis, 1632–1642* (Cambridge Univ. Press, 1984), 1–3.

29. Bone, *Henrietta Maria*, 84; Britland, *Drama at the Courts of Queen Henrietta Maria*, 113; Michelle Anne White, *Henrietta Maria and the English Civil Wars* (Ashgate, 2006), 26–29.

30. Margot Heinemann, *Puritanism and Theatre: Thomas Middleton and Opposition Drama Under the Early Stuarts* (Cambridge Univ. Press, 1980), 31–32; Tomlinson, "She That Plays the King," 191–92.

31. N. W. Bawcutt, "Puritanism and the Closing of the Theaters in 1642," *Medieval and Renaissance Drama in England* 22 (2009), 184–85; Barbara Murray, *Restoration Shakespeare: Viewing the Voice* (Fairleigh Dickinson Univ. Press, 2001), 15.

32. Gary Taylor, *Reinventing Shakespeare: A Cultural History, from the Restoration to the Present* (Weidenfeld and Nicolson, 1989), 7–8; Gurr, *The Shakespeare Company*, 202.

33. Gurr, *The Shakespeare Company*, 203–5; Britland, *Drama at the Courts of Queen Henrietta Maria*, chap. 10; "Susanna Hall," *Shakespeare Birthplace Trust*.

34. Taylor, *Reinventing Shakespeare*, 9.

35. White, *Henrietta Maria and the English Civil Wars*, 193–94.

36. Taylor, *Reinventing Shakespeare*, 10–11; Gurr, *The Shakespeare Company*, 206. But see Emma Depledge, *Shakespeare's Rise to Cultural Prominence: Politics, Print and Alteration, 1642–1700* (Cambridge Univ. Press, 2018), 15.

37. Don-John Dugas, *Marketing the Bard: Shakespeare in Performance and Print, 1660–1740* (Univ. of Missouri Press, 2006), 1; Michael Dobson, *The Making of the National Poet: Shakespeare, Adaptation and Authorship, 1660–1769* (Oxford Univ. Press, 1992), chap. 1.

38. Stanley Wells, *Shakespeare: For All Time* (Oxford Univ. Press, 2003), 186. See also Taylor, *Reinventing Shakespeare*, 43.

39. Gurr, *The Shakespeare Company*, 206–8; Irwin Smith, *Shakespeare's Blackfriars Playhouse: Its History and Design* (Peter Owen, 1966), 503–4.

40. Taylor, *Reinventing Shakespeare*, 24–25; Dobson, *The Making of the National Poet*, 25–27.

41. Wells, *Shakespeare: For All Time*, 186–87; Dobson, *The Making of the National Poet*, 13; Depledge, *Shakespeare's Rise to Cultural Prominence*, 49–50.

42. Wells, *Shakespeare: For All Time*, 188–90.

43. Taylor, *Reinventing Shakespeare*, 20.

44. Depledge, *Shakespeare's Rise to Cultural Prominence*, 49–50; Taylor, *Reinventing Shakespeare*, 28–30.

45. Martin Wiggins, "Shakespeare Jesuited: The Plagiarisms of 'Pater Clarcus,'" *The Seventeenth Century* 20 (2005), 15; Smith, *Shakespeare's First Folio*, 243–45.

46. William Van Lennep, *The London Stage, 1660–1800: Part 1: 1660–1700* (Southern Illinois Univ. Press, 1960), 104; Wood, *The Stage History*, 61–69, 74–75.

47. On an apparent performance of *Richard III* in the 1680s or early 1690s that included a "Mrs. Knight" (evidently one of Charles II's mistresses) as Margaret, see James G. McManaway, "'Richard III' on the Stage," *Times Literary Supplement* (June 27, 1935), 416. See also Julie Hankey, ed., *Richard III* (Junction Books, 1981), 23.

48. Katherine West Scheil, "*Sauny the Scott*: or, *The Taming of the Shrew*: John Lacy and the Importance of Theatrical Context in the Restoration," *Restoration: Studies in English Literary Culture, 1660–1700* 21 (fall 1997), 66–72; Dugas, *Marketing the Bard*, 14, 42.

49. Taylor, *Reinventing Shakespeare*, 18; Gurr, *The Shakespeare Company*, 206–8; Howe, *The First English Actresses*, 21–23, 109. On this portrayal of Desdemona: Emmett L. Avery & Arthur H. Scouten, *The London Stage: 1660–1700* (Southern Illinois Univ. Press, 1968), 97; John Harold Wilson, *All the King's Ladies: Actresses of the Restoration* (Univ. of Chicago Press, 1974), 6–7; Elizabeth Howe, *The First English Actresses: Women and Drama, 1660–1700* (Cambridge Univ. Press, 1992), 19.

50. Taylor, *Reinventing Shakespeare*, 19.

51. Howe, *The First English Actresses*, 25.

52. Taylor, *Reinventing Shakespeare*, 18.

53. Howe, *The First English Actresses*, 34–36; Avery and Scouten, *The London Stage, 1660–1700*, 100; Wilson, *All the King's Ladies*, 14; Taylor, *Reinventing Shakespeare*, 19.

54. Susan Staves, *Players' Scepters: Fictions of Authority in the Restoration* (Univ. of Nebraska Press, 1979), 171–72; Howe, *The First English Actresses*, 37–39.

55. Harold M. Weber, *The Restoration Rake-Hero: Transformations in Sexual Understanding in Seventeenth-Century England* (Univ. of Wisconsin Press, 1986), 152.

56. Howe, *The First English Actresses*, 42–49, 56–57; Taylor, *Reinventing Shakespeare*, 19–20.

57. Wilson, *All the King's Ladies*, 20–21, 73, 78, 104, 159–61; Howe, *The First English Actresses*, 113–14.

58. Arthur Franklin White, *John Crowne: His Life and Dramatic Works* (Western Reserve Univ. Press, 1922), 25–31, 39, 52.

59. White, *John Crowne*, 39, 53–58, 107–8, 115; Matthew H. Wikander, "The Spitted Infant: Scenic Emblem and Exclusionist Politics in Restoration Adaptations of Shakespeare," *Shakespeare Quarterly* 37.3 (autumn 1986), 341–42; Joyce Green MacDonald, "'Hay for the Daughters!': Gender and Patriarchy in *The Miseries of Civil War* and *Henry VI*," *Comparative Drama* 24.3 (1990), 194–96.

60. Murray, *Restoration Shakespeare*, 250; Dugas, *Marketing the Bard*, 15; Depledge, *Shakespeare's Rise to Cultural Prominence*, 72; Van Lennep, *The London Stage*, 283.

61. Avery and Scouten, *The London Stage, 1660–1700*, 26.

62. Dugas, *Marketing the Bard*, 7 (citing Allan Richard Botica); Avery and Scouten, *The London Stage, 1660–1700*, 163–64; Emmett L. Avery, "The Restoration Audience," *Philological Quarterly* 45 (1966), 54–61.

63. Wilson, *All the King's Ladies*, 2.

64. Wilson, *All the King's Ladies*, 68–69.

65. John Crowne, "The Misery of Civil-War: A Tragedy, as It Is Acted at the Duke's Theatre, by His Royal Highnesses Servants," *Early English Books Online*, 9.

66. Crowne, "The Misery of Civil-War," 12.

67. Randall Martin, ed., *Henry VI, Part Three* (Oxford Univ. Press, 2001), 83.

68. Crowne, "The Misery of Civil-War," 37; Murray, *Restoration Shakespeare*, 141–43.

69. Crowne, "The Misery of Civil-War," 31.

70. Crowne, "The Misery of Civil-War," 26–27; Murray, *Restoration Shakespeare*, 141–42.

71. Crowne, "The Misery of Civil-War," 66–67.

72. Barbara Murray, "Lady Eleanor Butler and John Crowne's *The Misery of Civil-War* (1680)," *The Ricardian* 14 (2004), 55–57; White, *John Crowne*, 111–12.

73. Crowne, "The Misery of Civil-War," 37. See also MacDonald, "'Hay for the Daughters!,'" 197–98, 210–11.

74. Murray, "Lady Eleanor Butler," 54; Dobson, *The Making of the National Poet*, 63.

75. Van Lennep, *The London Stage*, 295; Dugas, *Marketing the Bard*, 16; Depledge, *Shakespeare's Rise to Cultural Prominence*, 72.

76. White, *John Crowne*, 117.

77. Depledge, *Shakespeare's Rise to Cultural Prominence*, 107; John Crowne, *Henry the Sixth, The First Part* (Cornmarket Press, 1969), 68.

78. Depledge, *Shakespeare's Rise to Cultural Prominence*, 108.

79. Murray, *Restoration Shakespeare*, 169; Dugas, *Marketing the Bard*, 50; White, *John Crowne*, 115.

80. Wikander, "The Spitted Infant," 348.

Chapter 9: "A Woman's Glory and the World Avow"

1. Ambrose Philips, *Humfrey, Duke of Gloucester. A Tragedy. As it is Acted at the Theatre-Royal in Drury-Lane, by His Majesty's Servants* (J. Roberts, 1723), 81–82.

2. Cf. Joseph Roach, *It* (Univ. of Michigan Press, 2007).

3. Joanne Lafter, *The Celebrated Mrs. Oldfield: The Life and Art of an Augustan Actress* (Southern Illinois Univ. Press, 1989), 1.

4. Emmett L. Avery, *The London Stage, 1700–1729: A Critical Introduction* (Southern Illinois Univ. Press, 1968), xxv; Robert Gore-Browne, *Gay Was the Pit: The Life and Times of Anne Oldfield, Actress, 1683–1730* (M. Reinhard, 1957), 34–44; Edward Robins, *Twelve Great Actresses* (Putnam's, 1900), 41–45; Sandra Richards, *The Rise of the English Actress* (St. Martin's, 1993), 24–34.

5. Robins, *Twelve Great Actresses*, 24.

6. Felicity Nussbaum, *Rival Queens: Actresses, Performance, and Eighteenth-Century British Theater* (Univ. of Pennsylvania Press, 2011), 6. See also Susan M. Martin, "Actresses on the London Stage, 1670–1755" (PhD diss., Pennsylvania State University, 2008), 127.

7. Kristine Johanson, *Shakespeare Adaptations from the Early Eighteenth Century: Five Plays* (Fairleigh Dickinson Univ. Press, 2013), 35–36.

8. Fiona Ritchie and Peter Sabor, introduction to *Shakespeare in the Eighteenth Century* (Cambridge Univ. Press, 2012), especially 7–8.

9. Avery, *The London Stage*, clx; Gore-Browne, *Gay Was the Pit*, 162.

10. Richard Hindry Barker, *Mr. Cibber of Drury Lane* (AMS, 1966), 35.

11. Richard R. N. Ashley, *Colley Cibber* (Twayne, 1965), 50.

12. Barker, *Mr. Cibber of Drury Lane*, 177–93; Susannah Maria Cibber, *An Account of the Life of That Celebrated Actress, Mrs. Susannah Maria Cibber, with Interesting and Amusing Anecdotes. Also the Two Remarkable and Romantic Trials Between Theophilus Cibber and William Sloper* (Reader, 1887), 25–47; Tiffany Stern, "Shakespeare in Drama," in Ritchie and Sabor, *Shakespeare in the Eighteenth Century,* 146; Fidelis Morgan, epilogue to Charlotte Charke, *The Well-Known Troublemaker: A Life of Charlotte Charke* (Faber and Faber, 1988), 192–213.

13. See B. R. S. Fone, introduction to Colley Cibber, *An Apology for the Life of Colley Cibber* (Univ. of Michigan Press, 1968), xxiii–xxv.

14. Ashley, *Colley Cibber*, 111.

15. Wood, *The Stage History*, chap. 4; Siemon, *Richard III*, 87.

16. Johanson, *Shakespeare Adaptations from the Early Eighteenth Century*, 40–42;

Helene Koon, *Colley Cibber: A Biography* (Univ. Press of Kentucky, 1986), 199; Avery, *The London Stage*, 729.

17. Theophilus Cibber, *An Historical Tragedy of the Civil Wars* [. . .] (J. Roberts, 1723), 55; Avery, *The London Stage*, 729.

18. Frans De Bruyn, "Reference Guide to Shakespeare in the Eighteenth Century," in Ritchie and Sabor, *Shakespeare in the Eighteenth Century*, 384–97.

19. Emmett L. Avery, "The Shakespeare Ladies Club," *Shakespeare Quarterly* 7.2, (spring 1956), 153–58; Stern, "Shakespeare in Drama," in Ritchie and Sabor, *Shakespeare in the Eighteenth Century*, 149.

20. Robert Shaughnessy, "Shakespeare and the London Stage," in Ritchie and Sabor, *Shakespeare in the Eighteenth Century*, 181–82; Avery, "The Shakespeare Ladies Club," 153–58; Dobson, *The Making of the National Poet*, 147–61; Fiona Ritchie, *Women and Shakespeare in the Eighteenth Century* (Cambridge Univ. Press, 2014), 142–56.

21. Avery, "The Shakespeare Ladies Club," 157.

22. Nicholas Rowe, *Some Account of the Life &c. of Mr. William Shakespear* (Pallas Athene, 1709, 2009 ed.), 61; Kevin Gilvary, "Who Wrote the First Shakespeare Biography? It was Not Nicholas Rowe in 1709!" *Brief Chronicles* 7 (2016), 2–7.

23. Jonathan Bate, *Shakespearean Constitutions* (Clarendon, 1989), 22–23; Emma Smith, "The Development of Criticism of Shakespeare's Histories," in Smith, *Shakespeare's Histories*, 4–14.

24. Jean I. Marsden, *The Reimaged Text: Shakespeare, Adaptation, and Eighteenth-Century Literary Theory* (Univ. Press of Kentucky, 1995), 76; Stern, "Shakespeare in Drama," in Ritchie and Sabor, *Shakespeare in the Eighteenth Century*, 144–45.

25. Dobson, *The Making of the National Poet*, 7.

26. Simon Williams, *Shakespeare on the German Stage, Volume 1, 1586–1914* (Cambridge Univ. Press, 1990), 221–22; George Leuca, "Wieland and the Introduction of Shakespeare into Germany," *German Quarterly* 28.4 (November 1955), 247–55.

27. Williams, *Shakespeare on the German Stage*; Roger Paulin, "Shakespeare and Germany," in Ritchie and Sabor, *Shakespeare in the Eighteenth Century*, 314–19.

28. Ernest J. Simmons, "Catherine the Great and Shakespeare," *PMLA* 47.3 (September 1932), 790–806; Wells, *Shakespeare for All Time*, 246.

29. Arnold Aronson, "Shakespeare in Virginia," in Philip C. Kolin, ed., *Shakespeare in the South: Essays on Performance* (Univ. Press of Mississippi, 1983), 24; Kevin J. Hayes, *Shakespeare and the Making of America* (Amberley, 2020), 96; Edwin Eliott Willoughby, "The Reading of Shakespeare in Colonial America," *Papers of the Bibliographical Society of America* 31.1 (1937), 48, 51–52; James G. McManaway, "Shakespeare in the United States," *PMLA* 7.5 (1964), 514.

30. Hayes, *Shakespeare and the Making of America*, 51–60, 128–30, 139–42, 160–62, 212–24; Kolin, *Shakespeare in the South*, chaps. 1–3; Hugh F. Rankin, *The Theater in Colonial America* (Univ. of North Carolina Press, 1960), chap. 3; Wells, *Shakespeare for All Time*, 246–47; James Shapiro, *Shakespeare in America* (Library of America, 2014), 17.

31. Thomas Francklin, *The Earl of Warwick, A Tragedy* (John Bell, 1792), 75–76.

32. But not the first work of art. Michael Drayton's poem, "The Miseries of Queene Margarite," predated Jerningham's play by more than a century.

33. Ben Ross Schneider Jr., *Index to the London Stage, 1660–1800* (Southern Illinois Univ. Press, 1979), 324, 458; Edward Jerningham, *Margaret of Anjou* (1777); Sarah Burdett, "'Weeping Mothers Shall Applaud': Sarah Yates as Margaret of Anjou on the London Stage, 1797," *Comparative Drama* 49.4 (2015), 420–21.

34. Roger Manvell, *Sarah Siddons: Portrait of an Actress* (Heinemann, 1970), 10–12; Laura Engel, "The Personating of Queens: Lady Macbeth, Sarah Siddons, and the Creation of Female Celebrity in the Late Eighteenth Century," in Nick Moschovakis, ed., *Macbeth: New Critical Essays* (Routledge, 2008), 240–45.

35. Robins, *Twelve Great Actresses*, 157.

36. James Boaden, *Mrs. Sarah Siddons* (Edinburgh Press, 1826), 2.75–77.

37. A Lady, *Observations on Mrs. Siddons* (P. Byrne, 1784), 24, held in the collection of the Huntington Library, San Marino, California.

38. Quoted in Thomas Campbell, *Life of Mrs. Siddons* (Edward Moxon, 1839), 158.

39. Boaden, *Mrs. Sarah Siddons*, 75.

40. George Taylor, *The French Revolution and the London Stage, 1789–1805* (Cambridge Univ. Press, 2000), 142.

41. Philip H. Highfill Jr., Kalman A. Burnim, and Edward A. Langhans, *A Biographical Dictionary of Actors, Actresses, Musicians, Dancers, Managers and Other Stage Personnel in London, 1660–1800* (Southern Illinois Univ. Press, 1993), 16.48–51.

42. Jeremy F. Bagster-Collins, *George Colman the Younger* (King's Crown Press, 1946), 45–48; Schneider, *Index to the London Stage, 1660–1800*, 179.

43. Elizabeth Inchbald, remarks in George Colman, *The Battle of Hexham* (Longman, Hurst, Rees, and Orme, 1808); Bagster-Collins, *George Colman the Younger*, 47; Taylor, *The French Revolution and the London Stage*, 49–50.

44. Dutton Cook, *Hours with the Players* (Chatto and Windus, 1883), 260–72; Harold Newcomb Hillebrand, *Edmund Kean* (AMS, 1966), 4–5, 28–29; John Travell, "The Horse with the Red Umbrella," *Hardy Society Journal* 10.2 (summer 2014), 88.

45. John Herman Merivale, *Richard, Duke of York; or, the Contention of York and Lancaster (as altered from Shakespeare's three parts of Henry VI)* (1817; Cornmarket Press, 1971); Raymund Fitzsimons, *Edmund Kean: Fire from Heaven* (Hamilton, 1976), 59, 61, 89; Gāmini Salgādo, *Eyewitnesses of Shakespeare: First Hand Accounts of Performance 1590–1890* (Harper and Row, 1975), 86–87; Susan Margaret Kay, "A Stage History of William Shakespeare's 'Henry VI' Trilogy" (master's thesis, University of Birmingham, 1980), 178; Hillebrand, *Edmund Kean*, 151–54; Giles Playfair, *The Flash of Lightning: A Portrait of Edmund Kean* (William Kimber, 1983), 47–53, 61; T. F. Grinsted, "Gallery of Theatrical Portraits," *Bentley's Miscellany* 41 (1857), 215; John Keats, "Mr. Kean," *Champion* (December 21, 1817).

46. Merivale, *Richard, Duke of York*, xv.

47. Merivale, *Richard, Duke of York*, 49.

48. John Joseph Knight, "Margaret Agnes Bunn," in Leslie Stephen, ed., *Dictionary of National Biography* (Macmillan, 1886), 7.269–70.

49. Hankey, *Richard III*, 54–57; Scott Colley, *Richard's Himself Again: A Stage History of Richard III* (Greenwood Press, 1992), 79–81; Siemon, *Richard III*, 95–97; W. C. Macready, *King Richard III* (Cornmarket Press, 1970, originally published 1821).

50. Macready, *King Richard III*, iv.

51. Rosa Baughan, *Shakespeare's Plays Abridged and Revised for the Use of Girls* (T. J. Allman, 1863), 1.86.

52. Anna Jameson, *Characteristics of Women: Moral, Poetical, and Historical*, 4th ed. (Saunders and Otley, 1846), 2.248–49. See also Amelia E. Barr, *The Young People of Shakespeare's Dramas: For Youthful Readers* (D. Appleton, 1882), 59–60, 63.

53. Quoted in Sprague, *Shakespeare's Histories*, 139.

54. Theatres Act 1843 (also known as the Theatre Regulation Act), 6 and 7 Vict. C. 68, Royal assent Aug. 22, 1843, repealed Sept. 26, 1968; Hankey, *Richard III*, 58; Colley, *Richard's Himself Again*, 92–93.

55. Siemon, *Richard III*, 97; Colley, *Richard's Himself Again*, 94–96; Shirley S. Allen, *Samuel Phelps and Sadler's Wells Theatre* (Wesleyan, 1971), 228–30.

56. "Music and the Drama," *The Athenaeum*, no. 1374 (February 25, 1854), 252.

57. *Times* review, February 24, 1845. Quoted in George C. D. Odell, *Shakespeare: From Betterton to Irving* (Scribner's, 1920), 2.269.

58. John Joseph Knight, "Mary Amelia Warner," in Sidney Lee, ed., *Dictionary of National Biography* (Elder, 1899), 59.397–98; W. May Phelps and John Forbes-Robertson, *The Life and Life-Work of Samuel Phelps* (Sampson Low, Marston, Searle, and Rivington, 1886), 25, 202; Sprague, *Shakespeare's Histories*, 129.

59. Frances Hays, *Women of the Day: A Biographical Dictionary of Notable Contemporaries* (J. B. Lippincott, 1885), 13; John Hanners, *"It Was Play or Starve": Acting in the Nineteenth-Century American Popular Theatre* (Bowling Green State Univ. Popular Press, 1993), 59–60.

60. Hays, *Women of the Day*, 13–14; Hanners, *"It Was Play or Starve,"* 60–67; Marlis Schweitzer, *Bloody Tyrants & Little Pickles: Stage Roles of Anglo-American Girls in the Nineteenth Century* (Univ. of Iowa Press, 2020), 130. See also Robert Samuel Badal, "Kate and Ellen Bateman: A Study in Precocity" (PhD diss., Northwestern University, 1971); Heather M. McMahon, "Profit, Purity, and Perversity: Nineteenth-Century Child Prodigies Kate and Ellen Bateman" (PhD diss., Indiana University, 2003).

61. *Richard III* program (1877), Lyceum Theatre, Old Vic (London) Archive, BTC30/2/1/41, University of Bristol Theatre Collection.

62. "Lyceum," *Lloyd's Weekly Newspaper* (May 6, 1877), 12; "Lyceum Theatre," *Daily Telegraph* (January 31, 1877), 3; "Lyceum Theatre," *Morning Post* (January 30, 1887), 6; "Shakespeare's Richard the Third," *The Times* (February 1, 1877), 6. See also Laurence Irving, *Henry Irving: The Actor and His World* (Macmillan, 1952),

281–84; Austin Brereton, *The Lyceum and Henry Irving* (Lawrence and Bullen, 1903), 202–05.

63. Michael Holroyd, *A Strange Eventful History: The Dramatic Lives of Ellen Terry, Henry Irving, and Their Remarkable Families* (Farrar, Straus and Giroux, 2008), 111–13; Jeffrey Richards, *Sir Henry Irving: A Victorian Actor and His World* (London: Hambledon, 2005), 4.

64. Isabel Bateman, *From Theatre to Convent: Memories of Mother Isabel Mary* (Society for Promoting Christian Knowledge, 1936).

65. Colley, *Richard's Himself Again*, 93.

66. Quoted in Ida Benecke, *Heine on Shakespeare: A Translation of His Notes on Shakespeare Heroines* (Archibald Constable, 1895), 86.

67. Quoted in Robert K. Sarlos, "Dingelstedt's Celebration of the Tercentenary: Shakespeare's Histories as a Cycle," *Theatre Studies* 5 (1964), 121 (translation original).

68. August Wilhelm Schlegel, *Lectures on Dramatic Art and Literature* (George Bell, 1902, originally published 1808), 419–20 (trans. John Black) (rev. A. J. W. Morrison).

69. The series excluded *King John* and *Henry VIII*, as they weren't part of the two tetralogies.

70. Sarlos, "Dingelstedt's Celebration of the Tercentenary," 117–22; Anita Michelle Hagerman, "Performing 'This England': Cycles of Shakespeare's Early Histories in the Postwar Era" (PhD diss., Washington University in St. Louis, 2009), 30–31; Ton Hoenselaars, "Introduction: Stage Adaptations of the Histories," in Ton Hoenselaars, ed., *Shakespeare's History Plays: Performance, Translation and Adaptation in Britain and Abroad* (Cambridge Univ. Press, 2004), 192.

71. Quoted in Sarlos, "Dingelstedt's Celebration of the Tercentenary," 121 (translation original).

72. Quoted in Sarlos, "Dingelstedt's Celebration of the Tercentenary," 124 (translation original).

73. "Louise Hettstedt, Nekrolog," *Shakespeare-Jahrbuch*, 29/30 (1894), 276–77; Genossenschaft Deutscher Bühnen-Angehöriger, ed., *Neuer Theater-Almanach* 5 (Jahrgang, 1894), 201–3.

74. Sarlos, "Dingelstedt's Celebration of the Tercentenary," 130; Cox and Rasmussen, *King Henry VI, Part 3*, 35.

Chapter 10: "I Rather Like Slightly Nasty Women"

1. W. B. Yeats, "At Stratford-On-Avon," in *Essays and Introductions* (Palgrave Macmillan, 1961), 96 (first published in *The Speaker*, 1901).

2. Levi Fox, *Historic Stratford-upon-Avon* (Jarrold, 1986), 12.

3. Colley, *Richard's Himself Again*, 145–6.

4. Yeats, "At Stratford-On-Avon," 96–97, 109.

5. Quoted in Pete Orford, "'Capable, but Uninspired': Evaluating Frank Benson's Hesitant/Heroic History Cycles," *Shakespeare Bulletin* 29.2 (2011), 133.

6. Hesketh Pearson, *The Last Actor-Managers* (White Lion, 1950), 34.

7. Sally Beauman, *The Royal Shakespeare Company: A History of Ten Decades* (Oxford Univ. Press, 1982), 8–25; Levi Fox, *In Honour of Shakespeare: The History and Collections of the Shakespeare Birthplace Trust* (Jarrold, 1972), 70.

8. Constance Benson, *Mainly Players: Bensonian Memories* (T. Butterworth, 1926), 202–3.

9. Orford, "Capable, but Uninspired," 160.

10. Kay, "A Stage History of William Shakespeare's 'Henry VI' Trilogy," 56.

11. Geneviève Ward, *Both Sides of the Curtain* (Cassell, 1918), 163.

12. Cf. Ward, *Both Sides of the Curtain*, 53–55.

13. Richard Findlater, *Lilian Baylis: The Lady of the Old Vic* (Allen Lane, 1976), 87–88.

14. Findlater, *Lilian Baylis*, 127–28; Elizabeth Schafer, *Lilian Baylis: A Biography* (Hertfordshire, 2006), 129–36.

15. Findlater, *Lilian Baylis*, 123.

16. Findlater, *Lilian Baylis*, 132.

17. Richards, *The Rise of the English Actress*, 174.

18. Elizabeth Sprigge, *Sybil Thorndike Casson* (Victor Gollancz, 1971), 114.

19. *Richard III* program (1918), Old Vic (London) Archive, OV/PG/21, University of Bristol Theatre Collection.

20. *Richard III* program (1944), Old Vic (London) Archive, OV/PG/446, University of Bristol Theatre Collection.

21. Quoted in Stanley Wells, *Great Shakespeare Actors: Burbage to Branagh* (Oxford Univ. Press, 2015), 149.

22. Sprigge, *Sybil Thorndike Casson*, 249.

23. Patricia J. Lennox, "Shakespeare's Movie Mothers: Maternal Representation in Films of 'A Midsummer Night's Dream,' 'Richard III,' 'Romeo and Juliet'" (PhD diss., City University of New York, 2002), 114, 133–38. See also Charles T. Wood, "Whatever Happened to Margaret of Anjou? On Olivier's Shakespeare and *Richard III*," *Iowa State Journal of Research* 53 (1979), 213–17.

24. Flyer promoting 1935 festival, folder 2, box 133, Pasadena Playhouse Records, the Huntington Library.

25. *Pasadena Playhouse News* (July 1, 1935), folder 2, box 133, Pasadena Playhouse Records, the Huntington Library.

26. Louise Wright George, "Shakespeare in La Ceiba," *Shakespeare Quarterly* 3 (1952), 359–61.

27. George, "Shakespeare in La Ceiba," 364–65.

28. George, "Shakespeare in La Ceiba," 362–63.

29. George, "Shakespeare in La Ceiba," 361.

30. Suyapa G. Portillo Villeda, *Roots of Resistance: A Story of Gender, Race, and Labor on the North Coast of Honduras* (Univ. of Texas Press, 2021).

31. Wilhelm Hortmann, *Shakespeare on the German Stage: The Twentieth Century* (Cambridge Univ. Press, 1998), 56–60.

32. Werner Habicht, "Shakespeare and Theatre Politics in the Third Reich," in

Hanna Scolnicov and Peter Holland, eds., *The Play Out of Context: Transferring Plays from Culture to Culture* (Cambridge Univ. Press, 1989), 110.

33. Habicht, "Shakespeare and Theatre Politics in the Third Reich," 111; Gerwin Strobl, "Shakespeare and the Nazis," *History Today* 47.5 (1997), 19.

34. Gerwin Strobl, "The Bard of Eugenics: Shakespeare and Racial Activism in the Third Reich," *Journal of Contemporary History* 34.3 (1999), 323; Hans F. K. Günther, "Shakespeares Mädchen und Frauen aus lebenskundlicher Sicht," *Jahrbuch der deutschen Shakespeare-Gesellschaft* 73, Neue Folge 14 (1937), 92, 97 (translation original).

35. Hortmann, *Shakespeare on the German Stage*, 113–19, 137–41; M. G. Aune, "The Uses of *Richard III*: From Robert Cecil to Richard Nixon," *Shakespeare Bulletin* 24.3 (2006), 33–36; Wilhelm Hortmann, "Berlin–Zürich–Düsseldorf: Aspects of German Theatre During the Nazi Period and After," in Edward J. Esche, ed., *Shakespeare and His Contemporaries in Performance* (Ashgate, 2000), 92; Ernst Leopold Stahl, *Shakespeare und das deutsche Theater* (W. Kohlhammer Verlag, 1947), 715–6; Hans-Thies Lehmann, "Richard der Dritte, 1937 – eine Skizze," in Gerhard Ahrens, ed., *Das Theater des deutschen Regisseurs Jürgen Fehling* (Quadriga, 1985), 172–83.

36. Claire Trask, "'Richard III' Adorns a Berlin Stage," *New York Times* (May 30, 1937). See also Alessandra Bassey, "Shakespeare on the Nazi Stage, 1933–1944: Performance as Negotiation" (PhD diss., King's College London, 2020), 68–88.

37. Amy Smith, *Hermine Körner* (Kranich-Verlag, 1970), 177.

38. Smith, *Hermine Körner*, 177.

39. Stahl, *Shakespeare und das deutsche Theater*, 660; Kay Weniger, *Zwischen Bühne und Baracke: Lexikon der verfolgten Theater-, Film- und Musikkünstler 1933 bis 1945* (Metropol, 2008), 9–10, 15.

40. Hortmann, *Shakespeare on the German Stage*, 140; Habicht, "Shakespeare and Theatre Politics in the Third Reich," 117; Strobl, "Shakespeare and the Nazis."

41. Sheila Mann, *Aelfrida Tillyard: Hints of a Perfect Splendour: A Novel Biography* (Wayment, 2013), 667, 673. See also Diya Gupta, "A Subterranean Mystery," *Cambridge Alumni Magazine* 60 (Easter 2010), 18–19.

42. Mann, *Aelfrida Tillyard*, 35, 49, 165, 255–56; Christopher N. L. Brooke, *A New History of the University of Cambridge: 1870–1990* (Cambridge Univ. Press, 1993), 4.506–7.

43. David Daniell, "Opening Up the Text: Shakespeare's *Henry VI* Plays in Performance," *Drama and Society: Themes in Drama* 1 (1979), 247.

44. Tillyard, *Shakespeare's History Plays*, 147, 160.

45. Tillyard, *Shakespeare's History Plays*, 23; Graham Holderness, "Agincourt 1944: Readings in the Shakespeare Myth," in Peter Humm, Paul Stigant, and Peter Widdowson, eds., *Popular Fictions: Essays in Literature and History* (Methuen, 1986), 176–94.

46. Grene, *Shakespeare's Serial History Plays*, 4; Robin Headlam Wells, "The Fortunes of Tillyard: Twentieth-Century Critical Debate on Shakespeare's History Plays," *English Studies* 66.5 (1985), 391–403; Paul N. Siegel, "Tillyard

Lives: Historicism and Shakespeare's History Plays," *Clio* 9.1 (1979), 5–23; David L. Frey, *The First Tetralogy: Shakespeare's Scrutiny of the Tudor Myth: A Dramatic Exploration of Divine Providence* (Mouton, 1976), 1–2.

47. Tillyard, *Shakespeare's History Plays*, 154.

48. Martin, *Henry VI, Part Three*, 84n1.

49. Mary Thomas Crane, "The Shakespearean Tetralogy," *Shakespeare Quarterly* 36.3 (autumn 1985), 286; Robert Adger Law, "Links Between Shakespeare's History Plays," *Studies in Philology* 50.2 (1953), 168–69.

50. Wilbur Sanders, *The Dramatist and the Received Idea* (Cambridge Univ. Press, 1968), 94, 100.

51. M. M. Reese, *The Cease of Majesty: A Study of Shakespeare's History Plays* (Edward Arnold, 1961), 175, 196.

52. J. P. Brockbank, "The Frame of Disorder: *Henry VI*," in Loughnane and Power, *Early Shakespeare*, 81.

53. Edward I. Berry, *Patterns of Decay: Shakespeare's Early Histories* (Univ. Press of Virginia, 1975), 70.

54. Riggs, *Shakespeare's Heroical Histories*, 133.

55. Subodh Chandra Sengupta, *Shakespeare's Historical Plays* (Oxford Univ. Press, 1964), 46.

56. John E. Jordan, "The Reporter of *Henry VI, Part 2*," *PMLA* 64 (1949), 1110.

57. Robert B. Pierce, *Shakespeare's History Plays: The Family and the State* (Ohio State Univ. Press, 1971), 60, 121–22.

58. Robert A. Ravich, "A Psychoanalytic Study of Shakespeare's Early Plays," *Psychanalytic Quarterly* 33.3 (1964), 395.

59. Stuart Hampton-Reeves, "*Henry VI* in Performance: History, Culture and Shakespeare Reproduced" (PhD diss., University of Warwick, 1997), 22.

60. Barry Jackson, "On Producing *Henry VI*," *Shakespeare Survey* 6 (1953), 49; Kay, "A Stage History of William Shakespeare's 'Henry VI' Trilogy," 60.

61. Hagerman, "Performing 'This England,'" 48–56, 68–69; Anita M. Hagerman, "Monumental Play: Commemoration, Post-war Britain, and History Cycles," *Critical Survey* 22.2 (2010), 110; Robert Shaughnessy, *Representing Shakespeare: England, History and the RSC* (Harvester Wheatsheaf, 1994), 39. But see Stuart Hampton-Reeves and Carol Chillington Rutter, *The* Henry VI *Plays* (Manchester Univ. Press, 2006), 52–53.

62. Quoted in Kay, "A Stage History of William Shakespeare's 'Henry VI' Trilogy," 81, 93.

63. Kay, "A Stage History of William Shakespeare's 'Henry VI' Trilogy," 60–62, 65, 78; Martin, *Henry VI, Part Three*, 83–86.

64. "Rep to Produce King Henry VI," *Birmingham Post* (May 25, 1953), 5.

65. E. M. W. Tillyard, "Shakespeare's Historical Cycle: Organism or Compilation?" *Studies in Philology* 51 (1954), 37, 39.

66. Jackson, "On Producing *Henry VI*," 50.

67. Dash, *Wooing, Wedding, and Power*, 159.

68. Martin, *Henry VI, Part Three*, 83.

69. Cf. Shaughnessy, *Representing Shakespeare*, 38.

70. Martin, *Henry VI, Part Three*, 87; Kay, "A Stage History of William Shakespeare's 'Henry VI' Trilogy," 96; Knowles, *King Henry VI Part 2*, 9; Kenneth Tynan, *Curtains: Selections from the Drama Criticism and Related Writings* (Longmans, 1961), 182–83; Philip Hope-Wallace, "Shakespeare's Problem Play: Old Vic 'Henry VI,'" *Manchester Guardian* (October 18, 1957), 9.

71. Milton Crane, "Shakespeare on Television," *Shakespeare Quarterly* 12 (1961), 324. See also Hampton-Reeves and Rutter, *The* Henry VI *Plays*, 111–12.

72. Stuart Hampton-Reeves, *Shakespeare in the Theatre: Peter Hall* (Arden, 2019), 58; Peter Hall, *Making an Exhibition of Myself* (Oberon Books, 2000), 182.

73. David Addenbrooke, *The Royal Shakespeare Company: The Peter Hall Years* (William Kimber, 1974), 24–25; Hampton-Reeves, *Shakespeare in the Theatre*, 1.

74. Peter Hall, *The Necessary Theatre* (TCG, 1999), 9; Hampton-Reeves and Rutter, *The* Henry VI *Plays*, 54.

75. Hampton-Reeves and Rutter, *The* Henry VI *Plays*, 56–57; Beauman, *The Royal Shakespeare Company*, 238–39; Hall, *Making an Exhibition of Myself*, 160; Alan Sinfield, "Royal Shakespeare: Theatre and the Making of Ideology," in Jonathan Dollimore and Alan Sinfield, eds., *Political Shakespeare: Essays in Cultural Materialism*, 2d ed. (Manchester Univ. Press, 1994), 183.

76. Hampton-Reeves, *Shakespeare in the Theatre*, 21; Michael Billington, *Peggy Ashcroft* (John Murray, 1988).

77. Hampton-Reeves and Rutter, *The* Henry VI *Plays*, 4, 56; Hampton-Reeves, "*Henry VI* in Performance," 40–47; Hagerman, "Performing 'This England,'" 72–73, 81.

78. Hall, *Making an Exhibition of Myself*, 82–83; Addenbrooke, *The Royal Shakespeare Company*, 43.

79. Hampton-Reeves, *Shakespeare in the Theatre*, 59; Hall, *Making an Exhibition of Myself*, 182–83; John Barton, "The Making of the Adaptation," John Barton and Peter Hall, *The Wars of the Roses* (BBC, 1970), xv.

80. Hampton-Reeves, "*Henry VI* in Performance," 10; Kay, "A Stage History of William Shakespeare's 'Henry VI' Trilogy," 103–4, 110, 174; Barton, "The Making of the Adaptation," xvi–xix; Gillian Day, *King Richard III* (London: Stratford, 2002), 21; Randall Martin, "Queen Margaret Thatcherized in Recent Productions of *3 Henry VI*," in Esche, *Shakespeare and His Contemporaries in Performance*, 324; Robert Potter, "The Rediscovery of Queen Margaret: 'The Wars of the Roses,' 1963," *New Theatre Quarterly* 4 (2009), 107–8.

81. Hall, *Making An Exhibition of Myself*, 182–83.

82. Kay, "A Stage History of William Shakespeare's 'Henry VI' Trilogy," 111.

83. Sinfield, "Royal Shakespeare," 184; Shaughnessy, *Representing Shakespeare*, 46; Peter Hall, introduction to Barton and Hall, *The Wars of the Roses*, x; Addenbrooke, *The Royal Shakespeare Company*, 192; Knowles, *King Henry VI Part 2*, 12.

84. Sinfield, "Royal Shakespeare," 185; Hall, *Making an Exhibition of Myself*, 184; Hampton-Reeves, *Shakespeare in the Theatre*, 62–63; Daniell, "Opening Up the Text," 251.

85. Jan Kott, *Shakespeare Our Contemporary* (Doubleday, 1964) (trans. Boleslaw Taborski), 3, 7–8, 14.

86. Hall, *Making an Exhibition of Myself*, 180–82, 185–86; Addenbrooke, *The Royal Shakespeare Company*, 34–35; Hampton-Reeves, *Shakespeare in the Theatre*, 58, 61; Beauman, *The Royal Shakespeare Company*, 267.

87. Kay, "A Stage History of William Shakespeare's 'Henry VI' Trilogy," 104; Hampton-Reeves and Rutter, *The* Henry VI *Plays*, 63–66; Hall, *Making an Exhibition of Myself*, 185; Addenbrooke, *The Royal Shakespeare Company*, 110, 212; Beauman, *The Royal Shakespeare Company*, 270.

88. Warren Chernaik, "*Henry VI* and the Critics: Stage History, 1963–2006," in *The Cambridge Introduction to Shakespeare's History Plays* (Cambridge Univ. Press, 2007), 25; Kay, "A Stage History of William Shakespeare's 'Henry VI' Trilogy," 115.

89. Hagerman, "Performing 'This England,'" 70; Knowles, *King Henry VI Part 2*, 12.

90. Hampton-Reeves, *Shakespeare in the Theatre*, 61–62; Kay, "A Stage History of William Shakespeare's 'Henry VI' Trilogy," 118; Addenbrooke, *The Royal Shakespeare Company*, 75.

91. Alice Griffin, "Shakespeare Through the Camera's Eye," *Shakespeare Quarterly* 17.4 (1966), 385; Kay, "A Stage History of William Shakespeare's 'Henry VI' Trilogy," 124.

92. Potter, "The Rediscovery of Queen Margaret," 112; Kat Hipkiss, "'My Body Shall Pay Recompense': The Embodiment of Margaret in Selected Staged and Televised Cycles of the First Tetralogy" (PhD diss., Bath Spa University, 2021), 40–41; James N. Loehlin, "Brecht and the Rediscovery of *Henry VI*," in Hoenselaars, *Shakespeare's History Plays*, 139; Kay, "A Stage History of William Shakespeare's 'Henry VI' Trilogy," 111.

93. T. C. Worsley, "2-Part 'Henry VI' Lasts 6½ Hours," *New York Times* (July 18, 1963), 14.

94. Hampton-Reeves, *Shakespeare in the Theatre*, 67; Hipkiss, "'My Body Shall Pay Recompense,'" 32, 35–36; Russ McDonald, "Peggy of Anjou," in Gordon McMullan, Lena Cowen Orlin, and Virginia Mason Vaughan, eds., *Women Making Shakespeare: Text, Reception and Performance* (Bloomsbury, 2014), 266; Kay, "A Stage History of William Shakespeare's 'Henry VI' Trilogy," 110–11.

95. Martin, *Henry VI, Part Three*, 87–89; Barton, "The Making of the Adaptation," xviii–xix. See also Potter, "The Rediscovery of Queen Margaret," 106.

96. Barton and Hall, *The Wars of the Roses*, 84.

97. Hampton-Reeves and Rutter, *The* Henry VI *Plays*, 78.

98. Hall, *Making an Exhibition of Myself*, 185.

99. Quoted in Addenbrooke, *The Royal Shakespeare Company*, 201.

100. Hampton-Reeves, "*Henry VI* in Performance," 8; Hortmann, *Shakespeare on the German Stage*, 227; Daniel Gallimore, "Shakespeare's History Plays in Japan," in Hoenselaars, *Shakespeare's History Plays*, 95; Herbert Whittaker, "Stratford's Henry VI Is More Successful Than Henry V," *Globe and Mail* (June 8, 1966),

14; Frank Occhiogrosso, "Shakespeare in New Jersey, 1983," *Shakespeare Quarterly* 34.4 (winter 1983), 476–78; Loehlin, "Brecht and the Rediscovery of *Henry VI*," 141–43.

101. Alan C. Dessen, "Oregon Shakespeare Festival," *Shakespeare Quarterly* 28 (1977), 245.

102. McDonald, "Peggy of Anjou," 266; Hagerman, "Performing 'This England,'" 41, 73.

103. Mel Gussow, "Theater: 'Richard III,'" *New York Times* (February 13, 1973), 28.

104. Carolyn G. Heibrun, "Meet Richard III, a Contemporary in All That's Evil," *New York Times* (August 12, 1990), H5.

105. Ray Loynd, "A Respectful, No-Frills 'Richard III' at Actors Alley," *Los Angeles Times* (February 10, 1989), 130.

Chapter 11: "One of the Greatest Parts Ever Written"

1. Hampton-Reeves and Rutter, *The* Henry VI *Plays*, 80–86, 94–95, 104 (noting Margaret's outfit, the spartan set, her "voluptuously" stabbing York and then "stretch[ing] her body as in orgasm"); Kay, "A Stage History of William Shakespeare's 'Henry VI' Trilogy," 129; Carol A. Chillington, "Theatre in Review: Henry VI, Parts I, II, III," *Educational Theatre Journal* 29.4 (December 1977), 567; Rutter, "Of Tygers' Hearts and Players' Hides," 186–88; Hipkiss, "'My Body Shall Pay Recompense,'" 57; Roger Warren, "Comedies and Histories at Two Stratfords, 1977," *Shakespeare Survey* 31 (1978), 149; Daniell, "Opening Up the Text," 274.

2. Nancy Weiss, *"Keep the Damned Women Out": The Struggle for Coeducation* (Princeton Univ. Press, 2017), 494, 507–8; Brooke, *A New History of the University of Cambridge*, 4.255, 4.527, 4.529; G. R. Evans, *The University of Cambridge: A New History* (I. B. Tauris, 2010), 49.

3. Carolyn Ruth Swift Lenz, Gayle Greene, and Carol Thomas Neely, preface to *The Woman's Part: Feminist Criticism of Shakespeare*, ix.

4. Lenz et al., *The Woman's Part*, ix.

5. Potter, "The Rediscovery of Queen Margaret," 113.

6. Fiedler, *The Stranger in Shakespeare*, 51.

7. Dusinberre, *Shakespeare and the Nature of Women*, 5. See also Carole McKewin, "Shakespeare Liberata: Shakespeare, the Nature of Women, and the New Feminist Criticism," *Mosaic* 10.3 (spring 1977), 157.

8. Jardine, *Still Harping on Daughters*, 1–3, 6; Rackin, *Stages of History*, xi; Levine, *Women's Matters*, 18.

9. Martin, "Queen Margaret Thatcherized," 321; Martin, *Henry VI, Part Three*, 90; Potter, "The Rediscovery of Queen Margaret," 113.

10. Fiedler, *The Stranger in Shakespeare*, 73–74; Patricia Silber, "The Unnatural Woman and the Disordered State in Shakespeare's Histories," *Proceedings of the PMR Conference* 2 (1979), 87–96; Dash, *Wooing, Wedding, and Power*, 174,

182–83; Lee, "Reflections of Power," 216; Linda Bamber, *Comic Women, Tragic Men: A Study of Gender and Genre in Shakespeare* (Stanford Univ. Press, 1982), 137; Martha A. Kurtz, "Rethinking Gender and Genre in the History Play," *Studies in English Literature, 1500–1900* 36 (spring 1996), 271. See also Potter, "The Rediscovery of Queen Margaret," 113.

11. Howard and Rackin, *Engendering a Nation*, 10, 82.

12. Hampton-Reeves, "*Henry VI* in Performance," 80, 197.

13. Day, *King Richard III*, 118–19, 127.

14. Quoted in Homer D. Swander, "The Rediscovery of *Henry VI*," *Shakespeare Quarterly* 29 (1978), 152–53.

15. Kay, "A Stage History of William Shakespeare's 'Henry VI' Trilogy," 148; Warren, "Comedies and Histories at Two Stratfords," 149.

16. Michael Billington, "Henry VI, Part 2," *Guardian* (UK) (July 14, 1977), 10; Michael Billington, "Shakespeare's Dance to the Broken Music of Time," *Guardian* (UK) (April 17, 1978), 8.

17. Daniell, "Opening Up the Text," 257–58. See also Martin, "Queen Margaret Thatcherized," 329.

18. Hipkiss, "'My Body Shall Pay Recompense,'" 63.

19. Hipkiss, "'My Body Shall Pay Recompense,'" 64.

20. Hampton-Reeves, "*Henry VI* in Performance," 173–74; Hodgdon, *The End Crowns All*, 90–91; Hampton-Reeves and Rutter, *The* Henry VI *Plays*, 141–42.

21. Rutter, "Of Tygers' Hearts and Players' Hides," 186–87; Penny Downie, "Queen Margaret in *Henry VI* and *Richard III*," in Russell Jackson, ed., *Players of Shakespeare 3* (Cambridge Univ. Press, 2000), 120.

22. Mel Gussow, "Denzel Washington Portrays Shakespeare's Top Schemer," *New York Times* (August 17, 1990), C1.

23. Colley, *Richard's Himself Again*, 213–14; Peter Holland, *English Shakespeares: Shakespeare on the English Stage in the 1990s* (Cambridge Univ. Press, 1997), 52; Martin, *Henry VI, Part Three*, 93–94.

24. Day, *King Richard III*, 155, 165–66, 169; Colley, *Richard's Himself Again*, 206, Michael Billington, "Richard III," *Guardian* (UK) (October 9, 1975), 8.

25. Colley, *Richard's Himself Again*, 231–32; Marie Tarsitano, "Sturua's Georgian *Richard III*," *Theatre History Studies* 9 (1989), 75n2.

26. Day, *King Richard III*, 14, 168–69, 173; Robert Smallwood, "Shakespeare at Stratford-upon-Avon, 1992," *Shakespeare Quarterly* 44 (1993), 361–62; Holland, *English Shakespeares*, 116–17.

27. Loehlin, "Brecht and the Rediscovery of *Henry VI*," 147.

28. Quoted in Shaughnessy, *Representing Shakespeare*, 82.

29. Downie, "Queen Margaret in *Henry VI* and *Richard III*," 139.

30. Hampton-Reeves, *Shakespeare in the Theatre*, 8–9.

31. Foster Hirsch, "The New York Shakespeare Festival—1970," *Shakespeare Quarterly* 21.4 (autumn 1970), 477; Clive Barnes, "Stage: 'The Wars of the Roses,' Part 2," *New York Times* (July 3, 1970), 15.

32. Michael Coveney, "Pam Brighton Obituary," *Guardian* (UK) (February 25, 2015).

33. Though Brighton is the first known woman to direct all the *Henry VI* plays, Valery Hovenden had directed just *Part 1* in 1959. In 1953, Margaret Webster directed *Richard III* in New York; José Ferrer played Richard and Florence Reed played Margaret.

34. Jacob Siskind, "Henry VI Gets the Heads Rolling," *Ottawa Journal* (August 15, 1980), 21.

35. Jamie Portman, "Stratford's Henry VI Is an Endurance Test," *Calgary Herald* (August 20, 1980), 14.

36. Portman, "Stratford's Henry VI Is an Endurance Test," 14; Siskind, "Henry VI Gets the Heads Rolling," 21; Gina Mallet, "Henry VI Proves Stratford Vitality," *Toronto Star* (August 14, 1980), 81.

37. Downie, "Queen Margaret in *Henry VI* and *Richard III*," 115–16.

38. Day, *King Richard III*, 81.

39. N. O. Holden, "Building the Engine Room: A Study of the Royal Court Young Peoples' Theatre and Its Development into the Young Writers' Programme" (PhD diss., University of Lincoln, 2018), 48–67.

40. Hardy M. Cook, "Jane Howell's BBC First Tetralogy: Theatrical and Televisual Manipulation," *Literature/Film Quarterly* 20.4 (1992), 326–31; Susan Willis, "Jane Howell's Approach," in *The BBC Shakespeare Plays: Making the Televised Canon* (Univ. of North Carolina Press, 1991), 165–86.

41. Lennox, "Shakespeare's Movie Mothers," 123–26.

42. Elizabeth Schafer, *Ms-Directing Shakespeare: Women Direct Shakespeare* (Women's Press, 1998), 171–73.

43. Hampton-Reeves, "*Henry VI* in Performance," 144.

44. Hipkiss, "'My Body Shall Pay Recompense,'" 12; Martin, "Queen Margaret Thatcherized," 330; MacDonald P. Jackson, "*The Wars of the Roses*: The English Stage Company on Tour," *Shakespeare Quarterly* 40 (1989), 208; Knowles, *King Henry VI Part 2*, 27; Chernaik, "*Henry VI* and the Critics," 26. See also Erin Rose Grant, "Playing the Queen Then and Now: An Interpretation of Shakespeare's Female Leaders" (master's thesis, McGill University, 2019), 63–75 (analyzing the 1991 film version).

45. Hampton-Reeves, "*Henry VI* in Performance," 181–82; Isobel Armstrong, "Thatcher's Shakespeare," *Textual Practice* 3 (1989), 9–10.

46. Michael Bogdanov and Michael Pennington, *The English Shakespeare Company: The Story of 'The Wars of the Roses,' 1986–1989* (Nick Hern, 1990), 214.

47. Bogdanov and Pennington, *The English Shakespeare Company*, 23–24; Hampton-Reeves and Rutter, *The* Henry VI *Plays*, 134. See also Hagerman, "Performing 'This England,'" 84–85.

48. Martin, "Queen Margaret Thatcherized," 325–26.

49. Hampton-Reeves and Rutter, *The* Henry VI *Plays*, 168–70, 177.

50. Barbara Hodgdon, "Making It New: Katie Mitchell Refashions

Shakespeare-History," in Marianne Novy, ed., *Transforming Shakespeare: Contemporary Women's Re-Visions in Literature and Performance* (St. Martin's, 1999), 16.

51. Sarra Belhia, "Adapting Shakespearean Tragedy into Arab Theatre: A Critical Comparative Edition of Sulayman Al Bassam's *An Arab Tragedy*" (PhD diss., University of Hertfordshire, 2022), 61.

52. Katherine Wilkinson, "A Brief Chronicle of the Time: Staging Shakespeare's English Histories, 2000–2010" (PhD diss., Sheffield Hallam University, 2010), 63–64.

53. Wilkinson, "A Brief Chronicle of the Time," 60–62.

54. Joseph Campana, "Review of *Richard III: An Arab Tragedy* (directed by Sulayman Al-Bassam for the Sabab/Sulayman Al-Bassam Theatre) at the Brooklyn Academy of Music, 9–12 June 2009," *Shakespeare* 5.4 (December 2009), 441.

55. Belhia, "Adapting Shakespearean Tragedy into Arab Theatre," 61.

56. Graham Holderness, "From Summit to Tragedy: Sulayman Al-Bassam's 'Richard III' and Political Theatre," *Critical Survey* 19.3 (2007), 125.

57. Wilkinson, "A Brief Chronicle of the Time," 65.

58. Holderness, "From Summit to Tragedy," 138.

59. Richard M. Devin, "Welcome to CSF's 44th Season—2001!," *Colorado Shakespeare Festival* (2001).

60. "Queen Margaret of England" folders, boxes 18–19, Robert A. Potter Plays, PA Mss 10, Special Research Collections, University of California, Santa Barbara.

61. Julia Cass, "A Pastiche of Shakespeare," *Courier-Post* (Camden, NJ) (February 26, 1977), 31; Philip F. Crosland, "Off-Broadway Memory Rekindled," *Wilmington News Journal* (March 13, 1977), 17; "UCSB Playwright Writes of Queen," *Goleta Today* (CA) (January 24, 1977), 10.

62. "Queen Margaret (2001, Colorado Shakespeare Festival)," *Internet Shakespeare* (2019).

63. On *Margaret: A Tyger's Heart* (Sexton): Finn, *The Last Plantagenet Consorts*, 145; Adam Hetrick, "Randy Harrison and Kate Forbes to Workshop *Margaret, Tyger's Heart* for Red Bull," *Playbill* (February 15, 2011). On *Queen Margaret* (Levy): Bruce Ingram, "Muse of Fire Keeps Busy with Shakespeare This Summer," *Chicago Tribune* (July 22, 2016); Max Maller, "Queen Margaret," *Chicago Reader* (August 11, 2016), 4; Hugh Iglarsh, "Every Rose Has Its Thorns," *New City Stage* (August 11, 2016). On *Margaret of Anjou* (Jansen-Parkes): "Margaret of Anjou," Those Women Productions (2016); Lily Janiak, "Those Women Say, #ImWithHerHighness," *SF Gate* (August 17, 2016); Natalie Orenstein, "Those Women Productions Find Feminism in the Classics," *Berkeleyside* (September 1, 2016). On *Margaret of Anjou* (Schafer/Kelly): "Introducing Margaret of Anjou," *Cal Shakes* (April 1, 2016); Rebecca McCutcheon, "Margaret of Anjou: A New Play by Shakespeare," *Rebecca McCutcheon* (personal website) (July 6, 2016); "Margaret of Anjou," *By Jove*

Theatre Company (2016). On *Queen Margaret* (O'Hare): Hailey Bachrach, "Shakespeare's Feminist History Plays: The Case of *Henry V* and *Queen Margaret*," *Shakespeare Bulletin* 37.4 (2020), 492–93, 499–500; Denise A. Walen, "Exiling Margaret in Shakespeare's *Richard III*," *Shakespeare Bulletin* 38.4 (2020), 635–36; Wright, *Shakespeare's Visionary Women*, 57–59; Hipkiss, "'My Body Shall Pay Recompense,'" 14; Michael Billington, "Frailty, Thy Name Isn't Woman: Fresh Feminist Takes on Shakespeare," *Guardian* (UK) (September 21, 2018). On *The Margriad* (Miller): "The Margriad," *Theatre: Washington* (2025); Kendall Mostafavi, "Avant Bard's 'The Margriad' Is an Exhilarating Shakespearean Remix," *DC Theater Arts* (March 13, 2025); Rachael F. Goldberg, "Review: The Margriad, Or, The Tragedy of Queen Margaret at Avant Bard Theatre," *Broadway World* (March 13, 2025); Trey Graham, "How to Mess with Shakespeare the Right Way," *Washington Post* (March 12, 2025).

64. Lois Potter, "Shakespeare Performed: English and American Richards, Edwards and Henries," *Shakespeare Quarterly* 54 (2004), 458–61.

65. Rutter, "Of Tygers' Hearts and Players' Hides," 196–97.

66. Kathryn Schwarz, *Tough Love: Amazon Encounters in the English Renaissance* (Duke Univ. Press, 2000), 2, 37.

67. On Martin's fandom: Jeffrey R. Wilson, *Shakespeare and* Game of Thrones (Routledge, 2021), 1–2.

68. Valerie Estelle Frankel, *Women in* Game of Thrones*: Power, Conformity and Resistance* (McFarland, 2014), 96; Kavita Mudan Finn, "Queen of Sad Mischance: Medievalism, 'Realism,' and the Case of Cersei Lannister," in Zita Eva Rohr and Lisa Benz, eds., *Queenship and the Women of Westeros: Female Agency and Advice in* Game of Thrones *and* A Song of Ice and Fire (Palgrave Macmillan, 2018), 35–37; Wilson, *Shakespeare and* Game of Thrones, 88–89, 110–13; J. L. Laynesmith, "Queens Consort of the Wars of the Roses," in Norrie et al., *Later Plantagenet and the Wars of the Roses Consorts*, 168.

69. "Bring Down the House: Educator Resource Guide," *Seattle Shakespeare* (2016), 8; Susannah Clapp, "Richard III Review—A Thoroughly Modern Game of Thrones," *Guardian* (UK) (February 19, 2017); Brangien Davis, "An All-Female 'Richard III' Crowns a Dame of Thrones," *Crosscut* (September 14, 2018); Tim Teeman, "'Richard III' Is a Tame Game of Thrones at Shakespeare in the Park," *Daily Beast* (July 11, 2022).

70. Hampton-Reeves and Rutter, *The* Henry VI *Plays*, 189–92; Hagerman, "Performing 'This England,'" 157; Wilkinson, "A Brief Chronicle of the Time," 98; David Oyelowo, *Henry VI, Part I* (Faber and Faber, 2003), 27–28.

71. Hagerman, "Performing 'This England,'" 219; Wilkinson, "A Brief Chronicle of the Time," 100.

72. Jennie M. Votava, "Through a Glass Darkly: Sophie Okonedo's Margaret as Racial Other in *The Hollow Crown: The Wars of the Roses*," *Shakespeare Survey* 73 (2020), 170–72. See also August Wilson, "The Ground on Which I Stand," *American Theatre* (July/August 2016).

73. LyaNisha R. Gonzalez, "True Lies: The Myth of Color-Blind Casting and the Silencing of the Black Playwright in American Theatre," *Theatre Symposium* 29 (2022), 150–62; Micha Frazer-Carroll, "'It's Dangerous Not to See Race': Is Colour-Blind Casting All It's Cracked Up to Be?" *Guardian* (UK) (August 11, 2020). See also Jocelyn A. Brown, "Assessing Color Blind Casting in American Theatre and Society" (PhD diss., University of Colorado, 2008).

74. Votava, "Through a Glass Darkly," 172, 181.

75. Francesca T. Royster, "The Chicago Shakespeare Theater's *Rose Rage*: Whiteness, Terror, and the Fleshwork of Theatre in a Post-Colorblind Age," in Ayanna Thompson, ed., *Colorblind Shakespeare: New Perspectives on Race and Performance* (Routledge, 2006), 233; Votava, "Through a Glass Darkly," 171.

76. "Margaret of Anjou," Those Women Productions; Janiak, "Those Women Say, #ImWithHerHighness"; Orenstein, "Those Women Productions Find Feminism in the Classics."

77. Barry David Horwitz, "Shakespeare and Ting Thrust into Present, Spectacularly," *Theatrius* (August 29, 2018).

78. On Globe (2003): Elizabeth Klett, *Cross-Gender Shakespeare and English National Identity: Wearing the Codpiece* (Palgrave Macmillan, 2009), 139–55; Potter, "Shakespeare Performed," 451. On Wales Millennium Centre (2015): Michael Kelligan, "Richard III, Omidaze Productions, WMC," *Art Scene in Wales* (February 13, 2015); Cathy Duncan, "All-Female Richard II Interview: Yvonne Murphy on Gender Equality in Theatre," *Cardiffian* (February 13, 2015); Gary Raymond, "Richard III, Wales Millennium Centre," *Arts Desk* (February 12, 2015). On Seattle Repertory Theater (2018): Davis, "An All-Female 'Richard III' Crowns a Dame of Thrones"; Misha Berson, "Bleak, Sleek and Fleet, 'Richard III' Gets a Blazing New Staging, with an All-Female Cast," *Seattle Times* (September 19, 2018). On New York Classical Theater (2023): Rhoda Feng, "Review: An All-Female 'Richard III' Makes for an Evening of Discontent," *New York Times* (June 27, 2023).

79. On the Welsh production (2016): P. B. Roberts, "Review of Shakespeare's *Henry VI* (directed by Yvonne Murphy for Omidaze Productions) at the Millennium Centre, Cardiff, 12 February 2016," *Shakespeare* 13.1 (2017), 91; Katharine Kavanagh, "'Henry VI,' by Omidaze," *Circus Diaries* (February 13, 2016). On the Seattle production (2017): "Bring Down the House," 8; Rich Smith, "*Bring Down the House*, a Diverse, All-Female *Henry VI*, Tests Shakespeare's Universality," *The Stranger* (February 6, 2017); Misha Berson, "Review: 'Bring Down the House' a Timely Look at Bloody Transition of Power," *Seattle Times* (February 9, 2017); Becs Richards, "An Excellent New All-Female Take on Shakespeare's 'Henry VI' Complicates the Gender Binary," *Seattle Weekly* (February 1, 2017).

80. Kate Chadwick, "Review Richard III Omidaze Productions," *Get the Chance* (February 18, 2015); Roberts, "Review of Shakespeare's *Henry VI*," 91.

81. Klett, *Cross-Gender Shakespeare*, 147, 149.

Epilogue: Her Future

1. Feng, "Review."

2. Klett, *Cross-Gender Shakespeare*, 27–28; Schweitzer, *Bloody Tyrants & Little Pickles*, chap. 1; Stephanie Tillotson, "From Gimmick Casting to Standard Practice: Re-gendering Shakespeare in Performance," in Cathy Leeney and J. Paul Halferty, eds., *Analysing Gender in Performance* (Palgrave Macmillan, 2022), 259.

3. Jason Zinoman, "One Reason Theatre Is in Crisis: The Slow Death of Criticism," *American Theatre* (December 18, 2023).

4. Sarah Lyons, "Shakespeare's Margaret of Anjou: 'Oure Queene Margarete to Signifie'" (master's thesis, Shakespeare Institute, University of Birmingham, 1990); Wifall, "Swords and Curses"; Gillian Heather Elton, "Gendered Lives: Patriarchy and the Men and Women in Shakespeare's Early History Plays" (master's thesis, Memorial University of Newfoundland, 1999); Sloan-Pace, "Articulating Agency"; Clay, "Performing Queenship in Premodern England"; Sarah E. Pagliaccio, "In Defense of Shakespeare's Queen Margaret of Anjou" (master's thesis, Harvard Extension School, 2016); Hipkiss, "'My Body Shall Pay Recompense'"; Miller, "Acting Up."

5. Isaac Butler, "American Theater Is Imploding Before Our Eyes," *New York Times* (July 19, 2023).

6. "Investing in Theatre," *UK Theatre* (July 1, 2024); David Maddox and Jabed Ahmed, "Hundreds of Theatres and Museums Face Closure as Crisis in Sectors Laid Bare," *Independent* (UK) (December 26, 2024).

7. Cara Joy David, "Unkindest Cuts," *American Theatre* (May 19, 2025).

8. Peggy Ashcroft, "Margaret of Anjou," *Jahrbuch / Deutsche Shakespeare-Gesellschaft West* (1973), 7; Judith Cook, *Women in Shakespeare* (Harrap, 1980), 73 (quoting Ashcroft); Downie, "Queen Margaret in *Henry VI* and *Richard III*," 139; Tina Packer, *Women of Will: Following the Feminine in Shakespeare's Plays* (Knopf, 2015), 23.

Image Credits

xii   Angus McBean photographs, 1936–1970, MS Thr 581, Harvard Theatre Collection (M_0624_0001 M 624). © Houghton Library, Harvard University.

11   From the British Library archive / Bridgeman Images.

17   John William Wright. *Queen Margaret* (mid-19th century). Image # 26215. Call # ART File S528k3c no. 52. Folger Shakespeare Library.

29   John de Witt. *The Swan Theatre in the time of Shakespeare, facsimile of a sketch made by Johannes de Witt, a learned Dutchman, during a visit to London in 1596.* Image # 8111. Call # ART Vol. d57 no. 45c. Folger Shakespeare Library.

45   Byam Shaw. *King Henry VI, part 2 (drawings)* (1901). Image # 35066. Call # ART Box S534 no. 13 part 2. Folger Shakespeare Library.

52   William Hamilton. *Second part of King Henry VI, act III, scene 2.* Image # 26885. Call # ART File S528k3b no. 18. Folger Shakespeare Library.

58   Byam Shaw. *King Henry VI, part 2 (drawings)* (1901). Image # 35070. Call # ART Box S534 no. 13 part 6. Folger Shakespeare Library.

74   Angus McBean photographs, 1936–1970, MS Thr 581, Harvard Theatre Collection (M_0624_0032 M 624) © Houghton Library, Harvard University.

89   Byam Shaw. *King Henry VI, part 3 (drawings)* (1901). Image # 35076. Call # ART Box S534 no. 14 part 5. Folger Shakespeare Library.

96   Alexandre Bida (1813–1895). *Henry VI 3me.* Image # 31323. Call # ART Box B584 no. 33. Folger Shakespeare Library.

97   Byam Shaw. *King Henry VI, part 3 (drawings)* (1901). Image # 35078. Call # ART Box S534 no. 14 part 7. Folger Shakespeare Library.

107   Byam Shaw. *King Henry VI, Part 1 (drawings)* (1901). Image # 35064. Call # ART Box S534 no. 12 part 7. Folger Shakespeare Library.

123   J. & L. Caswall. *Margaret of Anjou (Geneviève Ward)* (London: Virtue and Company, 1920–1921). Image # 29450. Call #: ART File W258.5 no. 13 PHOTO. Folger Shakespeare Library.

131   Jane Stuart. *Kean in the character of King Richard III* (19th century). Image # 36710. Call # ART Box S931 no. 1. Folger Shakespeare Library.

144   Samuel H. Kress Collection, National Gallery of Art.

153 *Mrs. Oldfield in the character of Rosamund* (London: J. Harrison, 1778). Image # 30551. Call # ART File O44.5 no. 3. Folger Shakespeare Library.

166 Courtesy of the Department of Special Collections, Stanford University Libraries. M2506, Theater and Film Collection, Box 15, folder 15.

167 Courtesy of the Garrick Club, London.

174 Hollis. *Miss Ellen Bateman as Richard 3rd, Miss Kate Bateman as Richmond, engraved by Hollis from a daguerreotype of Mayall* (London: London Printing and Publishing Company, 1843–1870). Image # 20982. Call # ART File B328.5 no. 1. Folger Shakespeare Library.

182 Ellis & Walery. *Mrs. Benson* (London: Rotary, 1880–1899). Image # 21027. Call # ART File B474.3 no. 2 PHOTO. Folger Shakespeare Library.

184 Lizzie Caswall Smith. *Mr. F. R. Benson.* (London: J. Beagles & Co., 1900–1920). image # 21031. Call # ART File B474.5 no. 2 part 3 PHOTO. Folger Shakespeare Library.

199 Thomas Holte © Shakespeare Birthplace Trust.

205 Joe Cocks Studio Collection © Shakespeare Birthplace Trust.

215 Photo by Ellie Kurttz © RSC.

219 © Carnival Film & Television Limited. All Rights Reserved.

220 Photo by Michael Brosilow, courtesy of Chicago Shakespeare Theater.

221 Photograph by Jay Yamada for California Shakespeare Theater.